Original Reviews for W9-ALV-133

THE SECULAR CITY

"Cox is introducing a new note into Protestant religious thought, is steadfastly relevant to the time in which he lives, and is rapidly becoming a culture hero to collegians."
—John Cogley, *The New York Times*

"The book is thought-provoking and is pervaded by a tone pleasant to encounter in that it indicates a trust in the future."
—*American City*

"Eagerly passed from hand to hand, quickly adopted by a variety of study groups, it has all the earmarks of a religious cause célèbre. It must, then, be meeting some deep need: the longing for a persuasive and unembarrassed theology of secularity."
—Daniel Callahan, *Commonweal*

"One of the nation's most radical and respected young Christian thinkers, Cox, 35, tries to go beyond existentialism and Bultmann-like 'demythologizing' in order to program theology for what he believes is a new era in man's history: the age of urban secularization."
—*Time*

"Here is a Christian acclamation of both the emergence of secular urban civilization and the breakdown of traditional religion. Secularization emancipates man from the domination of closed world views and the control of religious rituals and values. Rather than engaging in futile efforts to preserve these presecular modes of thought and practice, Dr. Cox invites us to heed the gospel call to become men of the new age and to join in partnership with God in the struggle to make life more human."
—George Bret Hall, *The Christian Century*

THE SECULAR CITY

THE SECULAR CITY

SECULARIZATION AND URBANIZATION

IN THEOLOGICAL PERSPECTIVE

By Harvey Cox

Twenty-fifth Anniversary Edition

COLLIER BOOKS
Macmillan Publishing Company
New York

Collier Macmillan Canada
Toronto

Maxwell Macmillan International
New York   Oxford   Singapore   Sydney

Collier Books
Macmillan Publishing Company
866 Third Avenue, New York, NY 10022

Collier Macmillan Canada, Inc.
1200 Eglinton Avenue East, Suite 200
Don Mills, Ontario M3C 3N1

Library of Congress Cataloging-in-Publication Data

Cox, Harvey Gallagher.
   The secular city: secularization and urbanization in theological perspective/by Harvey Cox.—25th Anniversary ed., 1st Collier ed.
      p. cm.
   Reprint, with new introduction. Previously published. Rev. ed. New York: Macmillan, 1966.
   ISBN 0-02-031155-9
   1. Church and the world. 2. Secularization (Theology) 3. City churches. 4. Cities and towns—United States. 5. Sociology, Urban. I. Title.
BR115.W6C65   1990   90-41932   CIP
261—dc20

Macmillan books are available at special discounts for bulk purchases for sales promotions, premiums, fund-raising, or educational use. For details, contact:

Special Sales Director
Macmillan Publishing Company
866 Third Avenue
New York, NY 10022

First Collier Books Edition 1990

10 9 8 7 6 5 4 3 2 1

Printed in the United States of America

ACKNOWLEDGMENTS

The author wishes to thank the editors of *The Commonweal* and of *Christianity and Crisis* for permission to use material already published in those magazines, and the Association Press for permission to use material that first appeared in their series of pamphlets *Revolution and Response*.

Grateful acknowledgment is hereby made for permission to quote from the following published works:

Allenson's, Naperville, Illinois, for permission to quote from *The Problem of History in Mark* by James Robinson.

George Braziller, Inc., for permission to quote from *Wait Without Idols* and *The Death of God* by Gabriel Vahanian.

T. & T. Clarke, Edinburgh, for permission to quote from *Church Dogmatics* by Karl Barth.

Doubleday & Company, Inc., for permission to quote from *The Ancient City* by Numa Denis Fustel de Coulanges.

Dover Publications, Inc., New York, for permission to quote from *Primitive Religion* by Paul Radin.

Harcourt, Brace & World, Inc., for permission to quote from *The City in History* by Lewis Mumford.

Harper & Row, Publishers, for permission to quote from "The Real Presence of the Hidden God," by Carl Michalson, in *Faith and Ethics*, ed. by Paul Ramsey, and from *The Later Heidegger and Theology*, Volume I, by James M. Robinson and John B. Cobb, Jr.

Harvard University Press, for permission to quote from *City Politics* by Edward G. Banfield and James Q. Wilson.

The Hogarth Press, Ltd., London, and Alfred A. Knopf, Inc., for permission to quote from *Moses and Monotheism* by Sigmund Freud.

Random House, Inc., for permission to quote from *The Death and Life of Great American Cities* by Jane Jacobs. © 1961 by Jane Jacobs.

Charles Scribner's Sons, for permission to quote from *The Protestant Ethic and the Spirit of Capitalism* by Max Weber.

Student Christian Movement Press, Ltd., London, for permission to quote from *The Biblical Doctrine of Work* by Alan Richardson.

The University of Chicago Press for permission to quote from *Meaning in History* by Karl Lowith.

World Student Christian Federation, for permission to quote from the following articles in *Student World:* Vol. LVI, 1st Quarter, 1963, No. 1 (Serial number 219), "The Mastery of Technological Civilization" by Harry Morton, pages 46 and 48; "Man and Reality—the History of Human Thought," by Cornelis A. van Peursen, pages 16, 17, 19, 20, and 21.

CONTENTS

The Secular City
Twenty-five Years Later

I wrote *The Secular City* after having lived for a year in Berlin, where I taught in a church-sponsored adult education program with branches on both sides of the barbed wire. The wall was constructed a few months before I arrived, so I had to commute back and forth through Checkpoint Charlie. Berlin was the home of Dietrich Bonhoeffer, the pastor and theologian killed by the Gestapo for his role in the plot to assassinate Hitler. So I read a lot of his work that year, especially the musings he set down during the last months of his life about the hiddenness of God and the coming of a "postreligious" age in human history. In the tense and tired Berlin of the early 1960s that made a lot of sense. In retrospect, of course, it is easy to see that human religiosity is a much more persistent quality than Bonhoeffer thought it was. Nearly everywhere we look in the world today we witness an unanticipated resurgence of traditional religion. The renaissance of Islamic culture and politics, the rebirth of Shinto in Japan, the appearance of powerful Jewish, Hindu, and Christian "fundamentalism" in Israel, India, and the United States—all raise important questions about the allegedly ineluctable process of secularization. But where does that leave us?

If anything, I believe these developments make the central thesis of *The Secular City* even more credible. I argued then that secularization—if it is not permitted to calcify into an ideology (which I called "secular*ism*")—is not everywhere and always an evil. It frees religious groups from their own theocratic pretensions and allows people to choose among a wider range of ethical and spiritual options. Today, in parallel fashion, it seems obvious that the resurgence of religion in the world is not everywhere and always a *good* thing. Do the long-suffering people of Iran believe that after the removal of their ruthless shah, the installation of a quasi-theocratic Islamic republic has turned out to be a wholly positive move? Do those Israelis and Palestinians who yearn for a peaceful settlement of the West Bank bloodletting believe that either the Jewish or the Muslim religious parties are helping? The truth is that both religious revival and secularization are morally ambigu-

xi

ous processes. We still desperately need what I tried to sketch out in 1965, a way of welcoming a pluralism of worldviews that does not deteriorate into nihilism, and a sober recognition that both religions and secular movements are morally ambiguous. Both can become either the bearers of emancipation or the avatars of misery, or some of each. Wouldn't a modest sprinkling of secularization, a dereligionizing of the issues come as a welcome relief in Ulster, and help resolve the murderous tensions in Kashmir and the Gaza Strip?

I can understand the people who are encouraged by the worldwide revival of religion today. The victims of atheistic and antireligious regimes are just as dead as those of clericalist terror. But the people who welcome the reemergence of the rites and values that give people a sense of dignity and continuity—a bar mitzvah in Warsaw, churches reopening in Smolensk, thousands of American college students thoughtfully exploring comparative religion— sometimes forget that a revival of religion is never an unmixed blessing. The same somber Russian icons that sustained millions of people through the winter of Stalinism and its aftermath also provide the current crop of Russian anti-Semites with their main symbols. How do we weigh the promising new interest in Judaism among so many young people in America against the fumings of Rabbi Meyer Kahane? Shinto is another case in point. The remarkable spirit of respect for the past and reverence for the land that enables the Japanese to adopt modern technologies without destroying their environment also feeds an ominous sense of special destiny and a revived emperor cult that democratically inclined Japanese are watching with extreme misgivings.

The thesis of *The Secular City* was that God is just as present in the secular as in the religious realms of life, and we unduly cramp the divine presence by confining it to some specially delineated spiritual or ecclesial realm. This idea has two implications. First, it suggests that people of faith need not flee from the allegedly godless contemporary world. But second, it also means that not all religion is good for the human spirit. The thesis was certainly not original with me. Indeed, the presence of the holy within the profane is suggested by the doctrine of the Incarnation, not a recent innovation. As for a suspicion of religion, both Jesus and the Hebrew prophets lashed out at some of the religion they saw around them. God *in* the secular: not an original idea but one that needs to be restated time and again. And today is surely no exception.

In rereading *The Secular City* after a quarter of a century I admit I smiled occasionally at its audacity, the way a father might

chuckle at the shenanigans of a rambunctious child. Its argument
is nothing if not sweeping. By page twelve of the introduction the
reader has been wafted through a dizzying tour of nothing less than
the whole of human history, from tribe to technopolis, from Sophocles to Lewis Mumford, from the Stone Age to Max Weber. And
all of this *before* chapter 1. Then comes a theological portrait of the
"coming" of the secular city in which Barth and Tillich and Camus
and John F. Kennedy jostle each other in what might have seemed
to all of them a somewhat unfamiliar proximity. The next part of
the book is devoted to what I called "revolutionary theology," a
phrase that, at least in those days, struck people as a world-class
oxymoron. It is followed by an attack on *Playboy* magazine (I
called it "anti-sexual") that drew me into a furious (at first) and
later tedious debate with that magazine's publisher. A lot of territory to cover in a 244-page book.

The final section is a polemic against the so-called "death of
God" theologians who were au courant at the time. I portrayed
them, correctly I think, as remaining obsessed—albeit negatively—
with the classical god of metaphysical theism, while I was talking
about Someone Else, the mysterious and elusive Other of the
prophets and Jesus who, like Jacques Brel, was very much alive and
well, although living in unexpected quarters. I have never been able
to understand why, after having unleashed this *guerre de plume*
against the death-of-godders, some trend-spotters persisted in including me among them. In any case, the death-of-god theology
had an unusually short half-life. On the other hand, the issues I,
in my youthful enthusiasm, tried to tackle—the significance, for
people of faith, of the ongoing battle between religion and secularization—rightly continue to stoke debate and analysis. To illustrate
the dilemma from my own Christian tradition, how many Mother
Teresas and Oscar Romeros does it take to balance a Jim and
Tammy Bakker? And how do we measure Pope John II's courageous vision of a Europe without borders against his worldwide
crusade against contraception? So much good and so much mis-
chief is done—as it always has been—in the name of God that the
suggestion with which I ended *The Secular City*, which sounded
radical to some readers then, still seems to be a good idea. It was
that we should learn something from the ancient Jewish tradition
of not pronouncing the name of the Holy One, live through a
period of reverent reticence in religious language, and wait for the
Spirit to make known a new language that is not so tarnished by
trivialization and misuse.

I actually said a little more than that, and the final paragraph
of the book may be worth recalling because it prepared the way for

the theological movement that was to pick up where *The Secular City* left off. On that last page I speculated on the significance of the puzzling fact that, according to the book of Exodus, when the Voice from the burning bush told Moses to lead the Israelite slaves from their Egyptian captivity, and Moses understandably asked for the name of the One who was mandating this immense task, God simply refused to give it. Moses was told to get about the business of liberating his people. "Tell them 'I will do what I will do' has sent you," the Voice said. That, apparently, was enough. The name would come, in God's good time. Reflecting in 1965 on this astonishing episode I wrote,

> The Exodus marked for the Jews a turning point of such elemental power that a new divine name was needed to replace the titles that had grown out of their previous experience. Our transition today . . . will be no less shaking. Rather than clinging stubbornly to antiquated appellations or anxiously synthesizing new ones, perhaps, like Moses, we must simply take up the work of liberating the captives, confident that we will be granted a new name by events of the future.

Although I was only dimly aware of it at the time, in this paragraph I was actually proposing an agenda for the next stage of theology, one which was taken up with a brilliance and daring far beyond my hopes, first by Latin American theologians and then by others throughout the world. For between these concluding lines, which crystallized the thrust of the entire book, can be detected what were to become the two basic premises of liberation theology.

The first premise is that for us, as it was for Moses, an act of engagement for justice in the world, not a pause for theological reflection, should be the first "moment" of an appropriate response to God. Get to work freeing the captives. The "name" will come later. Theology is important, but it comes after, not before, the commitment to doing, to what some still call "discipleship." This subverts the established Western assumption that right action must derive from correct ideas, that thought comes before life. This subversion is one of the most salutary contributions of liberation theology, which insists that thought-including theological thought—is embedded in the grittiness of real life. The second premise of liberation theology is that "accompanying" the poor and the captives in their pilgrimage not only is an ethical responsibility, but provides the most promising context for theological reflection. As the Catholic bishops of Latin America put it in their influential statement of 1968, one must think theologically from the perspective of a "preferential option for the poor." It is not hard to see now, although I was scarcely able to see it then, that the next logical step after *The Secular City* was liberation theology. But the link between the two was neither simple nor direct.

At first I was puzzled at how much attention the Spanish translation of my book, *La Ciudad Secular,* received from Latin American theologians. They critized it vociferously, but they also built on it. They invited me to Peru and Mexico and Brazil to debate it. But as I listened to their criticisms I became convinced that they understood it better than anyone else, maybe even better than I did myself. Still, they made use of it in a way I had not anticipated. Gustavo Gutierrez, whose controversial book *The Theology of Liberation* appeared a few years after mine, clarifies the connection best. In the economically developed capitalist countries, he explains, secularization tends to take a cultural form. It challenges the hegemony of traditional religious worldviews, calls human beings to assume their rightful role in shaping history and opens the door to a pluralism of symbolic universes. In the poor countries, however, secularization assumes quite a different expression. It challenges the misuse of religion by ruling elites to sacralize their privileges, and it enlists the powerful symbols of faith into the conflict with despotism. In the Third World, as Gutierrez puts it in one of his best known formulations, the theologian's conversation partner is not the "the nonbeliever" but rather "the nonperson." This means that among the tarpaper shantytowns of Lima and São Paulo the interlocutor of theology is not some skeptical "modern man" who thinks religion stifles thought; rather it is the hungry and the homeless whose hope wanes because tyrannies grounded in some religious or nonreligious mythology strangle them into an early death. The distinction Gutierrez makes shows that he is applying the same praxis-oriented approach to theology I advocated in a different religious and political environment. Liberation theology is the legitimate, though unanticipated, heir of *The Secular City.*

Heirs, of course, go their own way, and there is one part in my book that I wish had played a larger role in the subsequent development of Third World liberation theologies. In one section I argued that in the Soviet-dominated countries of Eastern Europe it was not religion but communism that needed "secularizing." Here I wrote from direct observation. I had personally seen the bizarre attempts of communist regimes to set up ersatz confirmation, wedding, and burial services. I had noticed that in Poland, smothered under an imposed sovietized culture, it was the Catholic intellectuals who were the most outspoken advocates of "cultural pluralism." I can still remember the young Czech pastor who told me in 1964, four years before the Prague spring, that he opposed communism "not because it is rationalist but because it is not rational enough . . . too metaphysical." By entering into an honest dialogue with the Marxists who ran their countries at the time, Christians, he said, were trying to force the communists "to be what they said they were, socialist and scientific, and to get them to stop trying to create a new holy orthodoxy." It was these courageous Christians, I believe, who eventually saw the fruit of their patience blossom in 1989. Unlike some other believers, they refused either to flee to the West or to knuckle under to the regimes or to retreat into "inner immigration." They opted to stay, to participate, to criticize, and to be ready when dialogue became possible. They were also practicing a form of liberation theology, staying in a difficult situation and accompanying an oppressed people in the long quest for freedom. When an interviewer asked the pastor of one of the churches in Leipzig that had provided the space, the inspiration, and the preparation for the East German revolution of November 1989 what the theological basis for his contribution was, he answered that it was "Dietrich Bonhoeffer and Latin American liberation theology."

There is much continuity. But there are also many important contemporary theological currents for which I can find little foreshadowing in *The Secular City.* For starters, in reading the book again in 1990 I winced every time I saw the word "man" blatantly wielded to refer to anybody and everybody. The first page of the introduction: "The world has become man's task and man's responsibility. Contemporary man has become the cosmopolitan." And so on. I would feel better if I could claim that it was, after all, only a matter of blunderbuss pronouns; that today my language would be gender-inclusive. But I know it cuts deeper than that. The truth is that *The Secular City* was written without the benefit of the two decades of feminist theological scholarship that was to begin shortly after it was published. What difference would it have made?

A lot. In fact, knowing what I know now, I would have had to recast virtually every chapter. How could I rely so heavily on the themes of disenchantment and desacralization, as I did in the opening section, without coping with the obvious fact that these historical processes—which I saw in a positive light—suggest a certain patriarchal domination of the natural world with which women have been so closely identified in Hebrew and Christian religious symbolization? Further, in the chapter called "Work and Play in the Secular City," my discussion seems oblivious to the presence—even then—of millions of women in the workplace.

Since 1965 I have learned, often from my own students, that we can no longer read the Bible without recognizing that it comes to us already severely tampered with, expurgated, and perhaps even edited with an eye to perpetuating the authority of men. I have learned that many of the classical sources I was taught to rely on so heavily, from Augustine to Tillich, sound very different when they are read with women's questions in mind. And my last chapter, "To Speak in a Secular Fashion of God," would have to take into consideration that employing exclusively male language for the deity has contributed to the marginalization of half the people of the world.

Can I say anything in my defense? Perhaps my one hope is to point to the chapter in *The Secular City* that, to my amazement, became the most widely discussed and quoted. Entitled "Sex and Secularization," it contains the aforementioned onslaught against *Playboy* which exposes the pseudosex of the airbrushed centerfold, the ideal woman pimply adolescent boys prefer because she makes no demands whatever. They can safely fold her up whenever they want to, which is not possible with the genuine article. It also lampoons the Miss America festival as a repristination of the old fertility goddess cults, reworked in the interests of male fantasies and commodity marketing. I like to think that in both of these I reveal myself as at least a protofeminist. Not on a par with current feminist cultural criticism, but not too bad for twenty-five years ago, and for a man.

There is another important theological current that at first seems strangely missing from *The Secular City* but whose absence, in retrospect, one can understand if not forgive. The American city is the principal locus of African-American theology. It was not until a few years after the publication of my book, however, that black theologians began making that fact evident to the wider theological community. It is all the more surprising that I overlooked African-American religion in 1965 since I was actively caught up in the civil rights movement personally. I had first met Martin Luther King, Jr., in 1956, during the summer of the Montgomery bus boycott. At the time I was chaplain at Oberlin College in Ohio and I invited him to come speak. He flew in a few months later and we started a friendship that was to last until his death in 1968. As a member of his Southern Christian Leadership Conference I marched and demonstrated in both the north and the south. I responded to the call to come to Selma, was arrested and jailed briefly in Williamstown, North Carolina, and took some of the responsibility in organizing the SCLC's effort to desegregate St. Augustine, Florida. All through

these years my family and I lived in Roxbury, the predominantly
African-American section of Boston.

Still, it was only later, with the advent of the Black Power
movement and the coming of black theology, that I began to take
seriously what the modern American city meant to African
Americans. Again, if I had thought about this very carefully at
the time I could have foreseen some of the reservations black
theologians had about *The Secular City*. My controlling meta-
phors of "the man at the giant switchboard" and "the man in the
cloverleaf," which were meant to symbolize the communication
grid and the mobility network of the modern metropolis, seemed
implausible to people who had been denied both mobility and
communication, and for whom the city was often not a place of
expanded freedom but the site of more sophisticated humilia-
tions. It was only as the years passed that it became clear to me
that the perspective from which I had written *The Secular City*
was that of a relatively privileged urbanite. The city, secular or
otherwise, feels quite different to those for whom its promise
turns out to be a cruel deception.

In the years that have passed since *The Secular City* was published much has happened to the cities of the world, including
American cities, and most of it has not been good. Instead of
contributing to the liberative process, many cities have become
sprawling concentrations of human misery, wracked with racial,
religious, and class animosity. Even the names Beirut, Calcutta,
South Bronx, and Belfast conjure images of violence, neglect, and
death. Ironically the cities of the world have often become the
victims of their own self-promotion and of the failure of the rural
environs to sustain life. Millions of people, both hopeful and desperate, stream into them to escape the unbearable existence they
must endure in the devastated countryside.

If Mexico City spells the future of the city, then the future looks
grim. Lewis Mumford, who began his life as a celebrant of the
possibility of truly urbane life, became disillusioned before his
death in 1990. He once wrote that when the city becomes the whole
world the city no longer exists. That prediction now seems increasingly possible. By the year 2000 Mexico City will have nearly 32
million residents, of whom 15 million will eke out a marginal
existence in its slums and shantytowns. Calcutta, Rio de Janeiro,
Jakarta, Manila, and Lima will not be far behind, all with populations between 10 and 20 million, with half the people in each city
locked into ghettos of poverty. Indeed, in some African cities such
as Addis Ababa and Ibadan, somewhere between 75 and 90 percent
of the population will live in the squalor of slums.

In the cities of the United States we have not fared much better. Real estate values gyrate, making millions for a select few, while homeless people, now including increased numbers of women with children, crowd into church basements and temporary shelters. The already marvelous cultural mix of our cities, spiced by the recent arrival of increasing numbers of Asians and Latin Americans, could enable us to prove to the world that ethnic diversity is a plus instead of a minus. Instead, in some cities at least, we seem to be on the edge of a technicolor *war of all against all:* white against black against yellow against brown. And the whole picture is worsened by the diminution of the middle class and the increasing chasm between those who have too much and those with too little. One is sometimes tempted simply to give up on the city.

We should not. One of my main purposes in writing *The Secular City* was to challenge the antiurban bias that infects American religion (at least white church life). How many times did I hear, as child, that "God made the country, but man made the city"? My argument in 1965 was, and is now, that this is a gravely deficient doctrine of God. We need a spirituality that can discern the presence of God, not just "In the Garden" as the old Protestant hymn puts it, but also as a better hymn says,

> Where cross the crowded ways of life,
> Where sound the cries of race and clan . . . .

The Bible portrays a God who is present in the jagged reality of conflict and dislocation, calling the faithful *into* the vortex of pain and new birth, not away from it. Nothing is further removed from this biblical God than the inward-oriented serenity cults and get-rich-now salvation schemes that inundate the airwaves and pollute the religious atmosphere. Here Bonhoeffer had it exactly right. From his prison cell he wrote that we are summoned as human beings to "share the suffering of God in the world." If the divine mystery is present in a special way among the poorest and most misused of His or Her children, as the biblical images and stories—from the slaves in Egypt to Jesus' official lynching—constantly remind us, then allegedly religious people who insulate themselves from the city are putting themselves at considerable risk. By removing ourselves from the despised and the outcast we are at the same time insulating ourselves from God, and it is in the cities that these, "the least of them," are to be found.

I have no intention of rewriting *The Secular City* with benefit of nearly three decades of hindsight. Besides, even if I wanted to it would be pointless. After it was published I learned through personal experience what I had read in articles by literary critics, that any work of art—a poem, a painting, even a book of theology—quickly escapes its creator's hand and takes on a life of its own. Within a few months of its modest first printing (10,000 copies), and even though it was scarcely noticed by reviewers, the book began to sell so briskly the publisher moved to multiple reprintings. Soon it appeared on the bestseller lists, unheard of at the time for a book on theology. It was translated into German, Dutch (also becoming a bestseller in Holland), French, Spanish, Swedish, Italian, Portuguese, Japanese, Korean, and even into Catalan, the language spoken in the region around Barcelona. Sales moved into the hundreds of thousands. The publisher was astonished, as was I.

I cannot pretend not to have enjoyed those initial years of unsought notoriety. I was attacked, celebrated, commended, analyzed, refuted. A publishing house that had refused the manuscript when I first submitted it thoughtfully telephoned to ask if I was planning to write a sequel. The book seems to have become a special favorite with Roman Catholics, perhaps since it came out just as the Second Vatican Council was ending, and they were eager to test the new atmosphere of free inquiry. Even the late Pope Paul VI read it and, in an audience I had with him later, told me that although he did not agree with what I wrote he had read it "with great interest." Professors began requiring it in classes. Church study groups took it up. Within a couple of years the book's sales, in all editions and translations, were approaching a million.

What did I learn from all this? For one thing, that most theologians and most publishers had severely underestimated the number of people who were willing to spend good money on serious books about religion. *The Secular City* may well have marked the end of the unchallenged reign of clerical and academic elitism in theology. Lay people were obviously ready to get into the discussion. In fact they were demanding to be part of it and were unwilling to allow theologians to continue to write books just for each other. Whatever one may think about the ideas in *The Secular City,* they are neither simple nor obvious. The book cannot be read with the television on. I do not take credit for having called forth the vociferous and critical laity we now seem to have in every church, and perhaps especially the Catholic church, who make so much marvelous trouble for ecclesiastical leaders. But I like to think that *The Secular City* helped create the climate that forced clerical and theological professionals to come down from their balconies and out of their studies and talk seriously with the ordinary people who constitute 99 percent of the churches and other religious bodies in the world.

Of course there are things I would do differently today, not only in how I would write *The Secular City,* but in virtually every other area of my life. "We get too soon old," as the Pennsylvania Dutch aphorism puts it, "and too late smart." Knowing what I do now about the Jewish religious tradition, I would not counterpose Law and Gospel as captivity to the past versus openness to the future, as Rudolf Bultmann and a whole tradition of German theologians taught me to do. The Law too, I have come to see, is a gift of grace. I would also no doubt try not to base my theological reading of current world history so narrowly in my own tradition, but would try to draw on the insights of the others, as we must all increasingly do at a time when the world religions elbow each other in unprecedented closeness. After all, Muslims and Buddhists and Hindus had already created cosmopolitan world cities when Western Christendom still consisted of backwater villages. We may have something to learn from them about transforming our urban battlefields into communities that nurture life instead of throttling it. We need all the help we can get if Mumford's dystopian nightmare—a planet transformed into a vast urban noncity—is to be avoided.

Some have suggested that *The Secular City* was a harbinger of postmodernism. The word itself did not exist then, and I am not sure I know what it means today. But if it suggests a willingness to live with a certain pragmatism and provisionality, a suspicion of all-encompassing schemes, a readiness to risk a little more disorder instead of a little too much *Ordnung*, then I think it qualifies. Nearly ten years after *The Secular City* Jonathan Raban published a book entitled *Soft City: The Art of Cosmopolitan Living.* It is sometimes cited today as the first clearly postmodernist text. If it is, it may be significant that when I read it, a few years after its publication, I immediately felt I had found a compatriot:

> The city and the book are opposed forms: to force the city's spread, contingency, and aimless motion into the tight progression of a narrative is to risk a total falsehood. There is no single point of view from which we can grasp the city as a whole. That indeed is the distinction between the city and the small town ... A good working definition of metropolitan life would center on its intrinsic illegibility. (p. 219)

This "illegibility" also characterizes the new, secular world city we are called to live in today, bereft of the inclusive images and all-embracing world-pictures that sustained our ancestors. We need images, and we always will. But today we know they are broken, and therefore we must learn to appreciate them in a new way. We need our religious traditions, but only when we can understand that no one of them, and not even all of them together, can provide a point of view by which the totality can be grasped. In short, living in the city should be the school of living in the postmodern, "illegible" world. It should be a continuous lesson in "citizenship," in how to live in the world city. But we still have not learned. As Raban says,

> We live in cities badly; we have built them up in culpable innocence and now fret helplessly in a synthetic wilderness of our own construction. We need . . . to comprehend the nature of citizenship, to make a serious, imaginative assessment of that special relationship between the self and the city; its unique plasticity, its privacy and its freedom. (p. 226)

It's true: "we live in cities badly." But we *must* learn to live in cities or we will not survive. We are missing our big chance, an opportunity that God or destiny has provided us and which, if we muff it, may never come up again.

Tucked away on page 145 of the revised edition of *The Secular City* comes a little-noticed paragraph that perhaps I should have used as an epigraph for this essay, or maybe it should be put in italics; anything to underscore how important I think it is. Secularization, I wrote, *"is not the Messiah. But neither is it anti-Christ. It is rather a dangerous liberation."* It *"raises the stakes,"* vastly increasing the range both of human freedom and of human responsibility. It poses risks *"of a larger order than those it displaces. But the promise exceeds the peril, or at least makes it worth taking the risk."*

All I could add today is that we really have no choice about whether we take the risk. We already live in the world city. We live there badly, but there is no way back. To say that this will require faith in God may sound odd, but I believe it will. It is a quality not of faith but of unfaith to have to flee from the complexity and disruption changes bring, or to scurry around constantly trying to relate every segment of experience to some comforting inclusive whole, as though the universe might implode unless we can hold it together with our own conceptualizations. We must learn to approach life in the illegible city without feeling the need for a Big Key, but this does not mean we have become nihilists. Far from it. Several years ago a friend told me he thought the implicit concept underlying *The Secular City* is the good old Calvinist doctrine of Providence. At first I balked, but I have come to believe he is right. We live today without the map or timetables in which our ancestors invested such confidence. To live well instead of badly we need a certain strange confidence that, despite our fragmented and discontinuous experience, somehow it all eventually makes sense. But *we* don't need to know the *how.* There is Someone Else, even in the Secular City, who sees to that.

Preface to the Revised Edition

If anyone had suggested to me while I was writing *The Secular City* that a revised edition would one day be necessary I would have found the idea ludicrous. I wrote the book for a specific and limited purpose. It was to serve as a study resource for a series of conferences planned for 1965 by the National Student Christian Federation. I constantly wrote with this audience of young, intelligent, mainly Protestant lay people in mind. I was hoping to persuade them that in the light of Biblical faith, secularization and urbanization do not represent sinister curses to be escaped, but epochal opportunities to be embraced. I had no wider audience and no larger questions in mind.

It quickly became evident, however, that the book had reached a much wider circle of readers, and this fact has brought me a mixture of joy and regret. I am gratified that an affirmative vision of the urban world as man's responsibility speaks to so many people today: I regret, however, that I did not produce a more carefully reasoned and precise statement. When American and foreign theologians began arguing over the book, when sociologists and city planners took to discussing it, and when it reached an unexpectedly large Catholic audience and then went into multiple printings, I began to wish I had written the kind of refined and scholarly work for which any theologian secretly wishes to be remembered by posterity.

But in my calmer moments I recognized that a tome of greater academic respectability, even if I were able to write one, would not have reached such an audience—and I would probably wish that I had written *The Secular City*. Certainly in a mixed intellectual economy there is ample room for both kinds of books, and if it takes a certain incautious directness or selective focus to get essential issues discussed today, I do not regret that *The Secular City* has served this function. Indeed, the fact that it has been read by both theologians and laymen may have helped enlarge the ambience of the theological conversation, which is certainly all to the good. Consequently, even in this second edition, *The Secular City* remains a tract. It makes no claim to scholarly balance or universal thoroughness. Tracts never do. But a second edition does enable me to correct some of the more egregious overstatements, tone down an occasional vivid passage, and respond at points to the helpful criticisms the book has elicited.

I have, for example, softened some of the passages about the "end of religion" because I have learned that Bonhoeffer's call for a "nonreligious interpretation of the Gospel" can sometimes be misleading in America where religion has played a somewhat different role than it has in Germany. Likewise, in discussing "metaphysics" I have tried to make clear that metaphysical *questions* cannot be muted by the secular age, but that metaphysical *systems* will neither again integrate whole societies nor still men's persistent questions as once they did.

I have made some larger changes in the chapter on work and play and in the chapter on the university. In the first I have retreated from the apocalyptic economics of the Triple Revolution thinkers to a view that technological change should be seen in a more thoroughly political context. My main thesis in that section, however, that cybernation requires of us an unprecedented exercise in social maturity, remains completely unaltered. In the chapter on the university I have reworded my line of thinking to make clear that it is not the organized church as such that is unwelcome in the university, but its institution-centered and imperialist attitude. In other chapters I have made small alterations in order to clarify my basic argument, not to change it. In short, I still stand by the major theses of *The Secular City* without reservation.

I am grateful to my friend Ann Orlov of Harvard University Press for her many sensible suggestions about the revision of this book. I also want to thank Daniel Callahan of *Commonweal* and Wayne Cowan of *Christianity and Crisis* for the crucial part played by the discussions in their journals in helping me rethink my arguments. Finally, I wish to acknowledge the countless letters and questions from students and readers; skeptics and nuns; missionaries and ministers; atheists, Catholics, Protestants, and Jews; slum dwellers and suburbanites. Without them, this past year would have been much duller. Many of them will find echoes of their ideas in this new edition.

Harvey Cox

Roxbury, Massachusetts
February 20, 1966

The Epoch of the Secular City

The rise of urban civilization and the collapse of traditional religion are the two main hallmarks of our era and are closely related movements. Urbanization constitutes a massive change in the way men live together, and became possible in its contemporary form only with the scientific and technological advances which sprang from the wreckage of traditional world views. Secularization, an equally epochal movement, marks a change in the way men grasp and understand their life together, and it occurred only when the cosmopolitan confrontations of city living exposed the relativity of the myths men once thought were unquestionable. The way men live their common life affects mightily the way they understand the meaning of that life, and vice versa. Villages and cities are laid out to reflect the pattern of the heavenly city, the abode of the gods. But once laid out, the pattern of the polis influences the way that succeeding generations experience life and visualize the gods. Societies and the symbols they live by influence each other. In our day the secular metropolis stands as both the pattern of our life together and the symbol of our view of the world. If the Greeks perceived the cosmos as an immensely expanded polis, and medieval man saw it as the feudal manor enlarged to infinity, we experience the universe as the city of man. It is a field of human exploration and endeavor from which the gods have fled. The world has become man's task and man's responsibility. Contemporary man has become the cosmopolitan. The world has become his city and his city has reached out to include the world. The name for the process by which this has come about is *secularization*.

What is secularization? The Dutch theologian C. A. van Peursen says it is the deliverance of man "first from religious and then from metaphysical control over his reason and his language."[1] It is the loosing of the world from religious and quasi-religious understandings of itself, the dispelling of all closed worldviews, the breaking of all supernatural myths and

I

sacred symbols. It represents "defatalization of history," the discovery by man that he has been left with the world on his hands, that he can no longer blame fortune or the furies for what he does with it. Secularization occurs when man turns his attention away from worlds beyond and toward this world and this time (*saeculum* = "this present age"). It is what Dietrich Bonhoeffer in 1944 called "man's coming of age."[2]

To some, Bonhoeffer's words still sound shocking, but they really should not. He was merely venturing a tardy theological interpretation of what had already been noticed by poets and novelists, sociologists and philosophers for decades. The era of the secular city is not one of anticlericalism or feverish antireligious fanaticism. The anti-Christian zealot is something of an anachronism today, a fact which explains why Bertrand Russell's books often seem quaint rather than daring and why the antireligious propaganda of the Communists sometimes appears intent on dispelling belief in a "God out there" who has long since been laid to rest.

The forces of secularization have no serious interest in persecuting religion. Secularization simply bypasses and undercuts religion and goes on to other things. It has relativized religious world views and thus rendered them innocuous. Religion has been privatized. It has been accepted as the peculiar prerogative and point of view of a particular person or group. Secularization has accomplished what fire and chain could not: It has convinced the believer that he *could* be wrong, and persuaded the devotee that there are more important things than dying for the faith. The gods of traditional religions live on as private fetishes or the patrons of congenial groups, but they play no significant role in the public life of the secular metropolis.

Of course there are events and movements which momentarily raise questions about whether secularization is really succeeding in unseating the gods of traditional religion. The self-immolation of a Buddhist monk, the rise of fanatic sects such as Soka Gakkai in Japan, the appearance of the Black Muslims in America, even the new vigor of Roman Catholicism—all seem to suggest that the published obituaries of religion have been premature. But a more careful look will reveal that these phenomena cannot be understood apart from certain swift flowing secular currents in the modern world. These currents either express themselves in quasi-religious form or else elicit adjustments in religious systems which alter them so radically that they pose no real threat to the secularization process. Thus the revival of ancient Oriental religions gives voice to the nationalistic political aspirations of peoples who preserve antiquated symbols but use them for utterly novel purposes. Pluralism and tolerance are the children of secularization. They represent a society's unwillingness to enforce any particular world view on its citizens. Movements within the Roman Catholic Church culminating in the Second Vatican Council indicate Catholicism's growing readiness to be open to truth from all sides. Pluralism is asserting itself where once a closed system stood.

This is the age of the secular city. Through supersonic travel and instantaneous communications its ethos is spreading into every corner of the globe. The world looks less and less to religious rules and rituals for its morality or its meanings. For some, religion provides a hobby, for others a mark of national or ethnic identification, for still others an esthetic delight. For fewer and fewer does it provide an inclusive and commanding system of personal and cosmic values and explanations. True, there are some people who claim that our modern age has its secular religions, its political saints, and its profane temples. They are right in a manner of speaking; but to call, for example, Nazism or communism "religions" overlooks a very significant difference between them and traditional religions. It obscures the fact that Nazism was a throwback to a lost tribalism and that every day communism becomes more "secularized" and hence less "religious."

The effort to force secular and political movements of our time to be "religious" so that we can feel justified in clinging to *our* religion is, in the end, a losing battle. Secularization rolls on, and if we are to understand and communicate with our present age we must learn to love it in its unremitting secularity. We must learn, as Bonhoeffer said, to speak of God in a secular fashion and find a nonreligious interpretation of biblical concepts. It will do no good to cling to our religious and metaphysical versions of Christianity in the idle hope that one day religion or metaphysics will once again regain their centrality. They will become even more peripheral and that means we can now let go and immerse ourselves in the new world of the secular city. The first step in such an immersion is learning something about its peculiar characteristics. But before we do we must ask more precisely about the other key term we have used in describing the ethos of our time, *urbanization*.

If secularization designates the content of man's coming of

age, urbanization describes the context in which it is occurring. It is the "shape" of the new society which supports its peculiar cultural style. In trying to define the term *urbanization*, however, we are confronted with the fact that social scientists themselves are not entirely agreed about what it means. It is clear, however, that urbanization is not just a quantitative term. It does not refer to population size or density, to geographic extent or to a particular form of government. Admittedly some of the character of modern urban life would not be possible without giant populations concentrated on enormous contiguous land masses. But urbanization is not something that refers only to the city. As Vidich and Bensman have shown in *Small Town in Mass Society*,[3] high mobility, economic concentration, and mass communications have drawn even rural villages into the web of urbanization.

Urbanization means a structure of common life in which the diversity and the disintegration of tradition are paramount. It means an impersonality in which functional relationships multiply. It means that a degree of tolerance and anonymity replace traditional moral sanctions and long-term acquaintanceships. The urban center is the place of human control, of rational planning, of bureaucratic organization—and the urban center is not just in Washington, London, New York, and Peking. It is everywhere. The technological metropolis provides the indispensable social setting for a world where the grip of traditional religion is loosened, for what we have called a secular style.

The age of the secular, technological city, like all preceding ages, does have its own characteristic *style*—its peculiar way of understanding and expressing itself, its distinctive character, coloring all aspects of its life. Just as the poets and architects, the theologians and the lovers of the thirteenth century all partook of a common cultural substance, so in our time we all share a fund of unspoken perspectives. Just as the straight aisles and evenly clipped hedges of the eighteenth-century formal garden exhibited a style found also in deist theology and in neoclassic verse, so our secular urban culture makes itself felt in all our intellectual projects, artistic visions, and technical accomplishments.

The French philosopher Maurice Merleau-Ponty (1908–1961) means the same thing when he speaks of a particular *"manière d'être."* He says:

If indeed philosophy and the film agree, if reflection and techniques of work participate in a common meaning, it is because the philosopher and the film maker have in common a certain manner of being (*manière d'être*), a certain view of the world which is that of a generation.[4]

For purposes of convenience we shall divide the *manière d'être* of the secular city into its *shape* (the social component) and its *style* (the cultural aspect) and shall deal with these ideas in Chapters 2 and 3, respectively.

We must now describe more fully what we mean by the *secular epoch,* and in order to do so it may be helpful to contrast it with two other cultural epochs which expressed different patterns of human community. For purposes of comparison we shall make use of a somewhat contrived word, *technopolis.* It will be used here to signify the fusion of technological and political components into the base on which a new cultural style has appeared. Although the term is an artificial one, it reminds us that the contemporary secular metropolis was not possible before modern technology. Modern Rome and modern London are *more than* larger versions of their Augustinian or Chaucerian forebears. There comes a point at which quantitative development releases qualitative change, and that point was reached in urban development only after the modern Western scientific revolution. Manhattan is inconceivable without structural steel and the electric elevator. Technopolis represents a new species of human community. The fact that it is a neologism will remind us that it is not yet fully realized.

By way of contrast to technopolis, let us arbitrarily designate the preceding epochal styles, according to their characteristic social forms, the *tribe* and the *town.*

The styles or periods of the tribe, the town, and the technopolis are in no sense merely successive. Nor are they mutually exclusive. If modern Paris is not simply a larger version of medieval Paris, neither should its discontinuity be exaggerated. As Lewis Mumford has shown, the roots of the modern city reach back into the Stone Age.[5] Our modern metropolis became possible only after technical advances had solved some of the problems which had heretofore placed iron limits on the size of cities; but the technical metropolis in a sense simply actualized in steel and glass, in pace and personality, what had already been present embryonically in Athens and Alexandria. Nor is tribalism merely a historical category. Even today we can find people in Africa and the South Pacific who still live a tribal existence, and we find residents of New York City with a tribal mentality. Town culture, representing a kind of transition from tribe to technopolis, still persists within and around the urban centers; its residue influences the viewpoint of everyone whose youth was marked by small town and rural values—and whose was not?

We are all tribal, town, and technopolitan to some degree, but technopolitan culture is the wave of the future. With this caution let us look at the characteristics of these three epochal styles.

When man appears in history he is already a social animal living in a collective group. Whatever purposes were served by the various social-contract theories of Rousseau or Locke in advancing personal rights, they can now be seen as sheer fiction, as social myths with little grounding whatever in history. The tribe is the setting where man becomes man. It represents an extension of blood and kinship ties, and tribal man celebrates this familial solidarity by singing songs of the common ancestors of all his people. Thus among African pygmies, Australian bushmen, American Indians, wherever remnants of tribal structure have been preserved, the venerable ancestors who are often semidivine beings are ritually conjured in wine, dance, and ballad.

Tribal societies and primitive peoples have supplied one of the recurrent fascinations of modern man. It began perhaps with curiosity about the beginnings of human societies, especially among the French philosophers who wanted to develop a rational rather than a theological version of man's origins. This interest was fed by the discovery and investigation of the allegedly less civilized peoples of North America and the South Pacific. The romantic myth of the Noble Savage marks one enthusiastic stage of this fascination. More recently it has evolved into the science of cultural anthropology.

By *tribal society* we have in mind a stage in human social development which has been described variously as totemic, preliterate, primitive, and even savage or prelogical. The variousness of the terms illustrates the problem, since they include descriptive and pejorative labels as well as terms designed to illuminate different aspects in the lives of peoples who seem increasingly remote from us in the modern technopolis. No one word, not even *tribal*, describes them accurately. One thinks, for instance, of Clyde Kluckhohn's Navaho,[6] of W. Lloyd Warner's black Australian Murngin,[7] of Bronislaw Malinowski's Trobriand Islanders.[8] These peoples, all in some sense "primitive," differ widely from one another.

In addition, it has become increasingly clear since the early studies of Frazer, Taylor, and Durkheim not only that primitive societies vary widely from each other, but that even within these societies one can discover greater disparities among personalities than scholars had originally supposed. Paul Radin has reminded a later generation that in any society, for example, one can find some people who take its religion more seriously than others. As he says, there is always the simple pragmatist who wants his religion to "work," as well as the "priest-thinker" who systematizes and orders beliefs.[9]

But one consensus has clearly emerged from modern anthropological studies. It is that the religion and culture of a society cannot be studied apart from its economic and social context. Religion is embedded in behavior and institutions before it is consciously codified, and the alteration of social and economic patterns always entails religious change. As Paul Radin puts it, "No correlation is more definite or more constant than that between a given economic level of society and the nature of the supernatural beings postulated by the tribe at large or by the religious individual in particular."[10] When man changes his tools and his techniques, his ways of producing and distributing the goods of life, he also changes his gods. Tribal, town, and technopolitan existence represent first of all different forms of social, economic, and political community. As such they symbolize different religions or belief systems.

For this reason, tribal societies, despite their idiosyncrasies, do exhibit certain common features.

Tribal life grows out of kinship ties. It is really an expanded family, a group in which tradition prescribes the proper relationship with any person one is likely to meet during a normal lifetime. Tribal societies are compact and enclosed. Prolonged contact with the outside world is bound to be disruptive, but such disruption catches up with every tribe sooner or later. There are no hiding places left on our shrunken globe for the Noble Savage. Oil wells dot our Indian reservations and industrialism is on the march in Africa. Ours may be the last generation to be able to study primitive peoples directly.

So tribal life has to be studied as a process, not as a static category. The tribe represents that stage during which man moves from a belief in ghosts and demons to a belief in gods, from spells and incantations to prayers, from shamans and sorcerers to priests and teachers, from myth and magic to religion and theology. All of this happens only when the economic structure of the society allows for a group of self-conscious religious specialists to emerge. There is no time for codification if everyone's energy is spent in simply keeping alive. There is no need for a definition of the relationships between the mythical heroes and divinities until questions are raised or other tribes with other divinities are encountered. As the tribe moves toward a more settled life, the camp, the village, and the town begin to appear.

The transition from tribe to town represents one of the decisive breakthroughs of human history. It is best epitomized by the emergence of the Greek *polis*. The polis appeared when bellicose clans and rival houses met here and there to form a new type of community, loyalty to whose laws and gods replaced the more elemental kinship ties which had previously held force. The gods of the tribes were demoted and a new religion arose, often centering on a common divine ancestor. As the nineteenth-century French scholar Fustel de Coulanges asserts in his classic study *The Ancient City*,[11] the founding of the polis was a religious act. A new cultus was formed whose gods were higher than those of the constituting clans. To be a citizen of the city was to be a member of the new cultus, often centered around a semidivine founder such as Aeneas.

But the conflict of loyalties between family custom and the law of the town, between blood ties and the more impersonal justice of the polis, deeply disturbed the soul of the ancient Greek. Sophocles' tragedy *Antigone* projects this conflict onto the stage. In *Antigone* we watch a struggle between the needs of the arising polis for order and equality, symbolized by King Creon, and the deeper bonds of blood, represented by Antigone. Antigone feels she must bury her brother, Polynices, who has fallen in a revolt against the polis. Creon has decreed that as a traitor Polynices must lie unburied, to be devoured by the dogs and the birds. Caught in the fatal contradiction between family and polis, Antigone and Creon collide, with catastrophic effects for both. Though the play is often interpreted and directed as a portrait of religion and the laws of God (Antigone) versus the tyranny and the laws of men (Creon), the Athenians who first witnessed it knew better. They realized that they were watching a reproduction of the anguished struggle going on within their own breasts, a struggle in which gods and values were ranged on both sides.

Antigone signals the painful transition of a culture from tribe to town, a metamorphosis whose fearful scope and psyche-threatening uncertainty can be matched only by the present transition from town to technopolis.

The tribe was a family writ large. Its roots reached back to a common mythological past and its members were locked together in lines of consanguinity. It bestowed on all its members an unquestioned place and a secure identity. It answered most of the great questions of human existence—marriage, occupation, life goals—almost before they were raised. Tribal tradition gave the answers. Tradition, whether danced, chanted, or carved into masks or figurines, provided a rich, complex, and utterly complete catalog of images, identities, and values.

Tribal man is hardly a personal "self" in our modern sense of the word. He does not so much live in a tribe; the tribe lives in him. He is the tribe's subjective expression. He grasps himself within a closed system of compact meanings in which there is no room for any transcendent point of view or critical detachment.[12] Man and nature, the animals and the gods, all form one continuous life process whose meaning courses through it just below the surface and can erupt anywhere in a transparent moment of magical or religious power.

The appearance of currency and the development of the alphabet supply two essential ingredients in the shattering step from tribe to town. Both devices tend to free individuals from traditionally prescribed relationships and to expand enormously the possible occasions for human contact. A man with a sheep to barter for bread must find a person who both has bread and wants wool or lamb stew. The range of possibilities is small and will tend to be directed by tradition. Sheep raising and bread baking will be passed on from father to son. Economic contacts and familial patterns will not be distinguishable. But the man who can sell a sheep and buy bread with the money is at once a more mobile and a more independent operator. The jingle of coins tolls the end of tribal existence and signals the beginning of a more impersonal, more rationalized way of living together.

In the same way, as writing develops, man's dependence on the person of the shaman or the oracle is undercut. Now he can begin to examine documents himself. Books and parchments can circulate and be perused outside the dim circle of the sacred fire where one had to cling to the storyteller's every

syllable and defer to his traditional role in order to find out
about the world. Writing depersonalizes man's access to information.

Once again the economic framework is crucial. Writing
began as a tool of commerce, but quickly became a way to
acquire knowledge and therefore power. Thus it had political
and religious consequences. Contact with the "outside," with
ideas and possibilities not accessible within the tribe, provided
one key to the development of town culture. It was difficult,
but not impossible, for strangers to become a part of the
town. As Lewis Mumford has correctly seen, one became part
of the tribe solely by accident of birth or blood, whereas the
town provides a place where strangers can become fellow
citizens.[13]

This transformation of "strangers and outsiders" into "fellow citizens and members of one another" recalls, of course,
an expression close to the heart of the New Testament message (see Ephesians 2). It suggests one good reason why the
early church, from its outset a detribalizing movement in
which there was "no longer Jew nor Greek," spread most
quickly in the towns and cities. We shall return to this later
on, but here it does raise the interesting question of why even
the storied Greek polis never realized in full the ideals of town
life. It never became fully open or fully universal. It always
remained partly a tribe. Athens and Rome felt it necessary to
preserve the fiction that all their citizens had sprung from the
loins of a common ancestor. Both failed to see that universal
citizenship could not be reconciled with slavery and imperial-
ism. There are in fact two reasons why Athens never became
a city or a metropolis in the modern sense of the word, why it
never achieved the population size, the complexity, the
anonymity, or the uncanny vastness of the modern urban
area. The first is that these elements were just not possible
until modern scientific technology had set the stage. But the
second is that the universality and radical openness of Christianity were not yet present to dispel the remnants of tribalism. Fustel de Coulanges believes that what was missing from
the Greek and Roman "cities" was the universal God of
Christianity. The ancients, he says, "never represented God to
themselves as a unique being exercising his action upon the
universe. . . . Religion was entirely local . . . special to each
city."[14] It was the lack of that totally inclusive claim of the
Gospel that kept the ancients' towns to some extent tribal.
Only after the beginning of the Christian era was the *idea* of

an inclusive metropolis conceivable, and even then it took
nearly two millennia to realize it. "Christianity," Fustel de
Coulanges goes on, ". . . was not the domestic religion of any
family, the national religion of any city or of a race. It belonged neither to a caste nor to a corporation. From its first
appearance it called to itself the whole human race."[15]

Antigone is the tragic figure who symbolizes the painful
transition from tribe to town, from kinship to civic loyalties.
In a sense Socrates represents a comparable tragedy in the
transition from polis to cosmo-polis, from the gods of the city
to the universal community of mankind. He did not reject the
"gods of the city" as his accusers claimed he did. Rather he
simply refused to take them with unqualified seriousness. He
saw that they have a place, but only a limited and provisional
place. His execution marks Athens' refusal to develop from a
provincial polis into a universal metropolis.[16]

Perhaps what we have called the "town" will eventually be
recognized as itself merely a transitional stage between the
tribe and the technopolis, between two forms of communal-
collective existence, between the preliterate man of the cave
painting and the postliterate man of the electronic image.
There are indeed striking analogies between tribal and technopolitan life. In fact, for Marxist theory, the "bourgeois"
period (which actually means "the age of the town dweller")
constitutes nothing more than a long, conflict-ridden transition
from primitive communism to Socialist communism.

But for most of us town culture cannot be dismissed as
merely transition. It is a part of us. The age of the towns gave
us printing and books, rational theology, the scientific revolution, investment capitalism, and bureaucracy. It gave us many
other things as well, but these are the ones which relate
closely to what Max Weber, in characterizing the age, has
called "rationalization."[17] Especially in the Calvinist Puri-
tanism which was in many ways the prototypical religion of
the period, Weber saw a classical instance of what he termed
the "routinization of charisma." These are also the aspects
which provide the most evident contrast with both tribe and
technopolis. The shaman is the symbol of tribal man. He
dances and chants his religion. The Puritan or maybe even the
Yankee is his town-culture counterpart. Town man meditates
on the word and hears it preached. Tribal man merges with
his daemon and his group. Town man is a discreet individual
who reads *Robinson Crusoe*. Tribal man's gods whirl with
him in the night of sensual ecstasy. Town man's God calls

him from an infinite distance to work soberly in the daylight of self-discipline. This comparison may make town man sound spare and astringent, but we should not deal with him too harshly, first because he rarely lived up to the image we have painted of him, and secondly because he was preparing the way for technopolitan civilization. Without him it could never have begun.

NOTES TO INTRODUCTION

1. Professor C. A. van Peursen's remark is quoted from a mimeographed report assembled by Professor Charles West on a conference held at the Ecumenical Institute of Bossey, Switzerland, September 1959; it is included in Section I of the Appendices. For more on van Peursen's work, see Chap. 3.

2. Dietrich Bonhoeffer's statements will be found in his *Ethics* (New York: Macmillan, 1959) and his *Letters and Papers from Prison* (New York: Macmillan, 1962; London: SCM Press, 1953).

3. Arthur J. Vidich and Joseph Bensman, *Small Town in Mass Society* (Garden City, N.Y.: Anchor Books, 1958).

4. Maurice Merleau-Ponty, *Sens et non-sens* (Paris: Nagel, 1948), p. 309. My translation.

5. Lewis Mumford, *The City in History* (New York: Harcourt, Brace, & World, 1961; London: Secker & Warburg), see especially Chaps. 1–3.

6. Clyde Kluckhohn has written a number of books and articles on Navaho culture; see his *The Navaho*, with Dorothea Leighton (Harvard University Press, 1946).

7. W. Lloyd Warner, *A Black Civilization* (New York: Harper & Row, 1958).

8. Bronislaw Malinowski, *Magic, Science and Religion and Other Essays* (Garden City, N.Y.: Doubleday, 1954).

9. Paul Radin (ed.), *Primitive Religion* (New York: Dover, 1957).

10. *Ibid.*, p. 192.

11. Numa Denis Fustel de Coulanges, *The Ancient City* (Garden City, N.Y.: Doubleday, 1956; London: Mayflower Books), Book Three, Chaps. 3–5.

12. For a discussion of the contrast between "compact" and "differentiated" symbol system, see Eric Voegelin, *Order and History*, Vol. I: "Israel and Revelation" (Baton Rouge: Louisiana State University Press, 1956), pp. 1–11.

13. Lewis Mumford, *op. cit.*

14. Fustel de Coulanges, *op. cit.*, p. 151.

15. *Ibid.*, p. 391.

16. Maurice Merleau-Ponty, *Eloge de la Philosophie* (Paris: Gallimard, 1953), pp. 48–57.

17. Max Weber, *The Protestant Ethic and the Spirit of Capitalism* (New York: Scribner, 1958; London: Allen & Unwin).

PART ONE

THE COMING OF THE SECULAR CITY

CHAPTER I

The Biblical Sources of Secularization

Secularization is the liberation of man from religious and metaphysical tutelage, the turning of his attention away from other worlds and toward this one. But how did this emancipation begin? What are its sources?

Secularization, as the German theologian Friedrich Gogarten once remarked, is the legitimate consequence of the impact of biblical faith on history.[1] This is why it is no mere accident that secularization arose first within the culture of the so-called Christian West, in the history within which the biblical religions have made their most telling impact. The rise of natural science, of democratic political institutions, and of cultural pluralism—all developments we normally associate with Western culture—can scarcely be understood without the original impetus of the Bible. Even though the conscious connection has long since been lost sight of, the relationships are still there. Cultural impulses continue to work long after their sources have been forgotten.

In this chapter the biblical sources of secularization will be covered once more. Our purpose is not to elicit either gratitude or rebuke for the Bible, depending on one's attitude toward secularization, but rather to strengthen our capacity to deal with secularization by describing its origins.

There are three pivotal elements in biblical faith which have each given rise to one aspect of secularization. Thus, the *disenchantment of nature* beings with the Creation, the *desacralization of politics* with the Exodus, and the *deconsecration of values* with the Sinai Covenant, especially with its prohibition of idols. Far from being something Christians should be against, secularization represents an authentic consequence of biblical faith. Rather than oppose it, the task of Christians should be to support and nourish it. But before we deal with these matters let us look briefly at the word *secularization* itself.

Secularization versus Secularism

The English word *secular* derives from the Latin word *saeculum,* meaning "this present age." The history of this word's career in Western thought is itself a parable of the degree to which the biblical message has been misunderstood and misappropriated over the years. Basically *saeculum* is one of the two Latin words denoting "world" (the other is *mundus*). The very existence of two different Latin words for "world" foreshadowed serious theological problems since it betrayed a certain dualism very foreign to the Bible. The relationship between the two words is a complex one. *Saeculum* is a time word, used frequently to translate the Greek word *aeon,* which also means age or epoch. *Mundus,* on the other hand, is a space word, used most frequently to translate the Greek word *cosmos,* meaning the universe or the created order. The ambiguity in the Latin reveals a deeper theological problem. It traces back to the crucial difference between the Greek spatial view of reality and the Hebrew time view. For the Greeks, the world was a place, a location. Happenings of interest could occur *within* the world, but nothing significant ever happened *to* the world. There was no such thing as world history. For the Hebrews, on the other hand, the world was *essentially* history, a series of events beginning with Creation and heading toward a consummation. Thus the Greeks perceived existence spatially; the Hebrews perceived it temporally. The tension between the two has plagued Christian theology since its outset.

The impact of Hebrew faith on the Hellenistic world, mediated through the early Christians, was to "temporalize" the dominant perception of reality. The world *became* history. *Cosmos* became *aeon; mundus* became *saeculum.* But the victory was not complete. The whole history of Christian theology from the apologists of the second century onward can be understood in part as a continuing attempt to resist and dilute the radical Hebrew impulse, to absorb historical into spatial categories. There have always been counterpressures and countertendencies. But only in our own time, thanks largely to the massive rediscovery of the Hebrew contribution through renewed Old Testament studies, have theologians begun to notice the basic mistake they have been making. Only recently has the task of restoring the historical and temporal tenor to theology begun in earnest. The word *secular* was an early victim of the Greek unwillingness to accept the full brunt of Hebrew historicity.

From the very beginning of its usage, secular denoted something vaguely inferior. It meant "this world" of change as opposed to the eternal "religious world." This usage already signifies an ominous departure from biblical categories. It implies that the true religious world is timeless, changeless, and thus superior to the "secular" world which is passing and transient. Thus the vocation of a "secular priest," one who served in the "world," though technically on the same level, was actually thought of as somehow less blessed than that of the "religious" priest who lived his life in the cloister, contemplating the changeless order of holy truth.

The medieval synthesis resolved the tension between Greek and Hebrew by making the spatial world the higher or religious one and the changing world of history the lower or "secular" one. The biblical assertion that under God all of life is drawn into history, that the cosmos is secularized, was temporarily lost sight of. In its first widespread usage, our word *secularization* had a very narrow and specialized meaning. It designated the process by which a "religious" priest was transferred to a parish responsibility. He was secularized. Gradually the meaning of the term was widened. When the separation of pope and emperor became a fact of life in Christendom, the division between the spiritual and the secular assumed institutional embodiment. Soon, the passing of certain responsibilities from ecclesiastical to political authorities was designated "secularization." This usage continued through the period of the Enlightenment and the French Revolution and obtains even today in countries with a Catholic cultural heritage. Consequently, for example, when a school or hospital passes from ecclesiastical to public administration, the procedure is called secularization.

More recently, secularization has been used to describe a process on the cultural level which is parallel to the political one. It denotes the disappearance of religious determination of the symbols of cultural integration. Cultural secularization is an inevitable concomitant of a political and social secularization. Sometimes the one precedes the other, depending on the historical circumstances, but a wide imbalance between social and cultural secularization will not persist very long. In the United States there has been a considerable degree of political secularization for many years. The public schools are officially secular in the sense of being free from church control. At the same time, the cultural secularization of America has come about more slowly. The Supreme Court decisions in the early 1960s outlawing required prayers pointed up a disparity which had continued for some years. In Eastern Europe, on the other hand, the historical process has been just the opposite. A radically secular culture has been imposed very quickly in Czechoslovakia and Poland, but religious practices Americans would find strikingly unconstitutional still obtain. In Czechoslovakia, for example, all priests and ministers are paid by the state. In Poland, in some instances religious instruction is still permitted in public schools. These discontinuities are due in part to the disparate pace with which social and cultural secularizaton occur, a subject discussed in Chapter 4.

In any case, secularization as a descriptive term has a wide and inclusive significance. It appears in many different guises, depending on the religious and political history of the area concerned. But wherever it appears, it should be carefully distinguished from secular*ism*. Secularization implies a historical process, almost certainly irreversible, in which society and culture are delivered from tutelage to religious control and closed metaphysical world views. We have argued that it is basically a liberating development. Secularism, on the other hand, is the name for an ideology, a new closed world view which functions very much like a new religion. While secularization finds its roots in the biblical faith itself and is to some extent an authentic outcome of the impact of biblical faith on Western history, this is not the case with secularism. It is a closed ism. It menaces the openness and freedom secularization has produced; it must therefore be watched carefully to prevent its becoming the ideology of a new establishment. It must be especially checked where it pretends not to be a world view but nonetheless seeks to impose its ideology through the organs of the state.

Secularization arises in large measure from the formative influence of biblical faith on the world, an influence mediated first by the Christian church and later by movements deriving partly from it. What, then, are the elemental components of secularization and how did they originate?

Dimensions of Secularization

CREATION AS THE DISENCHANTMENT OF NATURE

Presecular man lives in an enchanted forest. Its glens and groves swarm with spirits. Its rocks and streams are alive with friendly or fiendish demons. Reality is charged with a magical power that erupts here and there to threaten or benefit man. Properly managed and utilized, this invisible energy can be supplicated, warded off, or channeled. If real skill and esoteric knowledge are called into play, the energies of the unseen world can be used against a family foe or an enemy of the tribe.

Anthropologists now concede that magic is not simply one aspect of primitive life. It is a world view. "Everything is alive," reported a Pit Indian to his scholarly interrogator; "that's what we Indians believe. White people think everything is dead." Magic constitutes the style of presecular, tribal man. Furthermore, the bushes and beasts are his brothers. He perceives the world as an inclusive cosmological system in which his own kinship groups extend out to encompass every phenomenon in one way or another. Totemism, as the great anthropologist A. F. Radcliffe-Brown (1881–1955) understood it, is a vast network of kinship ties by which the creatures of the natural world are incorporated into the basically familial organization of the tribe.[2]

Many historians of religion believe that this magical world view, although developed and organized in a very sophisticated way, was never really broken through until the advent of biblical faith. The Sumerian, Egyptian, and Babylonian religious systems, despite their fantastically complicated theologies and their enormously refined symbol systems, remained a form of high magic, relying for their cohesion on the integral relation between man and the cosmos. Thus the annual flooding of the Nile, the predictable revolution of the stars, and the commanding presence of the sun and moon provided the framework by which the society was held together. Sun-gods, river goddesses, and astral deities abounded. History was subsumed under cosmology, society under nature, time under space. Both god and man were part of nature.

The Hebrew view of Creation signals a marked departure from this closed circle. It separates nature from God and distinguishes man from nature. This is the beginning of the disenchantment process. True, the Hebrews freely borrowed the material of the Creation story from their mythologically oriented neighbors of the ancient Near East. The themes and motifs are in no sense original. But what the Hebrews did with these myths, how they modified them, is the important thing to notice. Whereas in the Babylonian accounts, the sun, moon, and stars are semidivine beings, partaking of the divinity of the gods themselves, their religious status is totally rejected by the Hebrews. In Genesis, the sun and moon became creations of Yahweh, hung in the sky to light the world for man; they are neither gods nor semidivine beings. The stars have no control over man's life. They too are made by Yahweh. None of the heavenly bodies can claim any right to religious awe or worship.

The Genesis account of Creation is really a form of "atheistic propaganda." It is designed to teach the Hebrews that the magical vision, by which nature is seen as a semidivine force, has no basis in fact. Yahweh, the Creator, whose being is centered outside the natural process, who calls it into existence and names its parts, allows man to perceive nature itself in a matter-of-fact way. It is true, as some modern writers have pointed out, that modern man's attitude toward disenchanted nature has sometimes shown elements of vindictiveness. Like a child suddenly released from parental constraints, he takes savage pride in smashing nature and brutalizing it. This is perhaps a kind of revenge pressed by a former prisoner against his captor, but it is essentially childish and is unquestionably a passing phase. The mature secular man neither reverences nor ravages nature. His task is to tend it and make use of it, to assume the responsibility assigned to The Man, Adam.

Nor is man tied to nature by kinship ties. The lines of kinship in the Bible are temporal, not spatial. Instead of reaching out to encompass kangaroos and totem shrubs, they reach back to the sagas of the fathers and forward to the fortunes of the children's children. The structure of Hebrew kinship is linear; it is historical, not cosmological. The Bible, with one or two quaint exceptions (Eve's serpent and Balaam's ass), is devoid of the animal fables which abound in the legends and myths of magical peoples. Just after his creation man is given the crucial responsibility of naming the animals. He is their master and commander. It is his task to subdue the earth. Nature is neither his brother nor his god. As such it offers him no salvation. When he looks up to the hills,

Hebrew man turns from them and asks where he can gain strength. The answer is, Not from the hills, but from Yahweh, who *made* heaven and earth. For the Bible, neither man nor God is defined by his relationship to nature. This not only frees both of them for history, it also makes nature itself available for man's use.

Max Weber has called this freeing of nature from its religious overtones "disenchantment." The word is intended to connote not disillusionment but matter-of-factness. Man becomes in effect a subject facing nature. He can still enjoy it and delight in it, perhaps even more so since its terrors have been reduced for him. But man is not a mere expression of nature, and nature is not a divine entity.

This disenchantment of the natural world provides an absolute precondition for the development of natural science. Since today's technical city would not have been possible without modern science, disenchantment is also an essential precondition for modern urbanization. Science is basically a point of view. However highly developed a culture's powers of observation, however refined its equipment for measuring, no real scientific breakthrough is possible until man can face the natural world unafraid. Wherever nature is perceived as an extension of himself or his group, or as the embodiment of the divine, science as we know it is precluded. This is evident in Assyrian culture, where an uncanny accuracy in astronomical observation developed, but in which the heavenly bodies were still experienced as the determinants of human destiny; hence no real scientific astronomy emerged.

It remains true in so-called underdeveloped cultures today that the mere introduction of modern technological devices and procedures will never suffice to produce a scientific culture. Somehow nature must be disenchanted, which results in the undermining of many traditional religions. This undermining took place in the past century mainly under the auspices of Christian missions. More recently it has resulted from the spread of Communist ideology. In this instance, Christianity and communism, despite their differences, played nearly identical roles in the removal of traditional religious restraints to scientific and technological change. Both are historically oriented ways of perceiving natural reality. Both exorcise the magical demons and open nature for science. More recently still, less precise socialistic ideologies of a vague planned welfare state have had the same influence. The disenchantment of nature is one of the essential components of secularization.

THE EXODUS AS THE DESACRALIZATION OF POLITICS

No one rules by divine right in secular society. In presecular society, everyone does. Just as nature is perceived by tribal man both as a part of his family and as the locus of religious energy, so the political power structure is accepted as an extension of familial authority and as the unequivocal will of the gods. The identification of the political with the religious order, whether in a primitive tribe where the chief is also the sorcerer, or in the Roman Empire where the emperor is both political ruler and *pontifex maximus,* betrays the same sacral legitimation of political power.

A "pure" sacral-political identification is difficult to find. All societies begin early to differentiate roles and responsibilities; whether this separation of powers can be carried through to a successful conclusion depends entirely on whether the basic symbol system of the culture allows for such differentiation.

Significant political and social change is almost impossible in societies in which the ruling regime is directly legitimated by religious symbols, in which the ruler is believed to be divine or a direct expression of the divine intention. Political change depends on a previous desacralization of politics. The process is closely related to the disenchantment of nature. Nature with its tides and seasons always repeats itself. History never does. Thus the emergence of history rather than nature as the locus of God's action opens a whole new world of possibilities for political and social change.

In tracing the desacralization of politics to its biblical roots, the Exodus must be the focal point of study. For the Hebrews Yahweh spoke decisively not in a natural phenomenon, such as a thunderclap or an earthquake, but through a historical event, the deliverance from Egypt. It is particularly significant that this was an event of social change, a massive act of what we might today call "civil disobedience." It was an act of insurrection against a duly constituted monarch, a pharaoh whose relationship to the sun-god Re constituted his claim to political sovereignty. There had no doubt been similar escapes before, but the Exodus of the Hebrews became more than a minor event which happened to an unimportant people. It became the central event around which the Hebrews organized their whole perception of reality. As such, it symbolized the deliverance of man out of a sacral-political order and into history and social change, out of religiously legitimated monarchs and into a world where political leadership would be based on power gained by the capacity to accomplish specific social objectives.

The Exodus delivered the Hebrews from Egypt, yet there was a persistent temptation to return to sacral politics, especially during the period of the monarchy. But the prophetic bands always stood in the way, preventing such a relapse. Since the prophets always had a source of authority separate from the royal favor, the priest-king was never really possible again. The Exodus made it forever impossible to accept without reservation the sanctions of any monarch. Yahweh could always stage a new Exodus, or work through history to bring down a monarch with delusions of grandeur. No royal house was ever afterward unquestionably secure on its throne.

The contest between pope and emperor in the Middle Ages is a parable of the futility of any attempt to return to simple sacral politics once the secularization process has begun. The emperor would have liked to be the religious as well as the political sovereign of the West—wistful longings for a "Holy Roman Empire" headed by a monarch with sacral functions indicate this desire. Similarly, many of the popes would have liked to wield the sword of empire as well as the Keys of Saint Peter—theological efforts to subsume the temporal under the spiritual realm testify to this incessant hankering. Neither side won. The pope finally lost his temporal power along with the Papal States and the emperor lost everything when the Empire itself dissolved. Since then, however, the spiritual and moral authority of the pope has increased. At the same time, political leaders in the West have by and large accepted the fact that they can make only provisional and limited demands on their citizens. When a political leader makes religious or totalitarian claims, when a Hitler or a Stalin tries once again to assert himself as the pure expression of the *Zeitgeist* or the dialectic, free men recognize this as an affront to their deepest convictions about politics. Our political consciences have all been secularized.

The tension between Judaeo-Christian religion and political absolutism has been a recognized element in the tradition of Western political philosophy since Augustine. In fact, conflict between church and state is really possible only on ground prepared by the biblical faiths. There is no conflict if a faith is antipolitical, as were the mystery cults, or if it merges imperceptibly with the political system, as did the imperial religion of Rome. The mystery cults turned their backs on "this world" and thus gave the political regime an open field to fashion whatever tyrannies it chose. The imperial cult simply identified the establishment with the will of the gods. Only with the Christian church did a real tension become possible, a tension for which Saint Augustine spelled out the basis. Augustine said that the state has its own good, but that this good is not the highest or truest good. The state is an order, but is good order only insofar as man is a sinner. It has no contribution to make to the salvation of man. To grant the state a *provisional* worth strikes a harder blow at tyranny than a total devaluation of the state, which allows the church to withdraw into an enclave.[3]

The early years of the Christian church present a particularly good example of how this desacralization of politics worked out in practice. It was accomplished not by a wholesale rejection of political authority but by a conditional acceptance. The first Christians were willing to pray for the emperor but not to burn incense on his altar. The difference between these two acts is crucial. To pray for the emperor is to grant him the right to exercise authority in a particular, restricted realm, a realm defined not by him but by the one who is praying. To refuse to put incense on his altar is to deny him any sacral-religious authority. The early Christians thus made a telling contribution to the desacralization of politics and were in this sense relentless and consistent secularizers.

In Dietrich Bonhoeffer's term, the early Christians exhibited a kind of "holy worldliness." They rejected the cults of Cybele, Isis, and Mithra because these mystery religions were escapist and the Christians did not wish to abandon a world God had made and to which their Lord, they believed, would soon return in visible triumph. But they also rejected the cult of the emperor because, although worldly, it was not holy enough. It did not cohere with the sharp chasm between the Holy One and the political system which they confessed when they called Jesus the only true *Kyrios*. It did not conform to the desacralized politics which had begun with the Exodus and continued to call into question all sacral-political systems. Holding the tension between holiness and worldliness, the Christians thus constituted a threat to the Roman imperial tyranny. This produced a series of cruel persecutions but ended with the toppling of the empire itself.

The conversion of Constantine presented the early Christians with a new test. Some theologians tried to rewrite Christianity into an imperial ideology—and almost succeeded for a time. But their attempt to resacralize politics never eliminated the tension between God and the regime which the biblical faith had planted in the consciousness of man. From now on, no political system could ever safely claim a direct and undisputed sacral legitimation, and no sovereign could infringe on that aspect of his subjects' lives which pointed them to an authority beyond him. Indeed, the tension between Christian faith and political authority was so pointed that it has continued to bother Western political thinkers in every generation. Niccolò Machiavelli (1469–1529), the Renaissance philosopher and statesman, argued that it was impossible to build a strong state among Christians since the Christian religion elicited universalistic feelings that subverted the required nationalism.[4] Marsilius of Padua (died *c.* 1342) contended in his *Defensor Pacis* that it was extremely difficult even to have a state where the church puts forward its cutomary claims. How can a state defend its citizens, he wanted to know, when there is one group within its borders which claims a kind of supranational loyalty and will grant only conditional allegiance to the earthly monarch? This line of thought came to lucid expression in the French philosopher Pierre Bayle (1647–1706), who moved even further in seeking to deal with the same tension. He believed not only that a state of atheists was possible, but also that it was probably even desirable, since an atheistic state would not be tempted to force one particular world view or metaphysic on any of its citizens. Bayle failed to foresee the rise of a fanatical political atheism just around the corner, a secularistic religion which would prove just as oppressive as the theistic religions of the past. It is worth noting here that Ludwig Feuerbach (1804–1872), whose work greatly influenced Karl Marx, dedicated his first book to Bayle. Marx himself resolved the tension by suggesting that eventually both religion and the state would disappear. His prediction is not likely to be fulfilled, but it does illustrate the fact that no political thinker can avoid dealing in some way with the inherent limitation of politics that is built into Western culture through the desecralization of political power.

Of course remnants and residues of sacral politics do remain in our modern world. The Archbishop of Canterbury crowns the sovereign of England *Defensor Fidei,* defender of the faith, intoning all the while that he or she is monarch *gratia dei,* by the grace of God. These vestiges of a sacral society amuse Britons vastly and remind them of the history and dignity of the monarchy. But no one takes them the least bit seriously. Sacral politics in Britain has become purely decorative. In fact, even the British Communist party has solemnly promised that if it ever wins power it will not abolish the monarchy.

In America, the President is installed with an oath spoken while his hand rests on a Bible. Priests, rabbis, and ministers intone prayers in a kind of ritual investiture. But here too the matter is all effect with no substance. Significantly, the Chief Justice of the Supreme Court, who holds the Bible, presides over a body which has ruled that its reading cannot be required in public schools.

Sacral politics have not been completely abolished. Secularization is a process, not a state of affairs. In Spain a quasisacral state still obtains, as it does in such small Asian countries as Nepal. Furthermore, the danger of a relapse into a neosacral politics is always present. National socialism in Germany and fascism in Italy represented relapses of catastrophic proportions; the Stalinist cult of personality was another. There are indications that the regime of Kwame Nkrumah in Ghana may have represented a kind of neotribal politics. But the secularizing counterforces are nearly omnipresent today and will eventually strengthen the tendency toward the desacralization of politics. Communist social theory, as already mentioned, since it teaches that the state apparatus merely expresses the will of the ruling elite, envisages the eventual withering away of the state in the classless society. However improbable this may appear in reality, it does deprive a regime of the kind of ultimate legitimation available in sacral societies. It strengthens the recent Marxist contention that the cult of Stalin, rather than being an expression of the essence of communism, in reality marked a grave departure from it. In any case, the presence today of the desacralizing currents of the biblical faith and of the movements deriving from it suggests that in the urbanized technological world of tomorrow no significant reversal of the trend toward secularization can be expected.

THE SINAI COVENANT AS THE DECONSECRATION OF VALUES

Both tribal man and secular man see the world from a particular, socially and historically conditioned point of view. But modern secular man knows it, and tribal man did not;

therein lies the crucial difference. The awareness that his own point of view is relative and conditioned has become for secular man an inescapable component of that point of view. His consciousness has been relativized. He knows that not only his language, his customs, and his clothing style, but also his science, his values, and his very way of perceiving reality are conditioned by his personal biography and the history of his group. In our time the Copernican revolution has reached out to incorporate everything into its sweep. All things are relative. Everything "depends on how you look at it."

Paul Tillich once called this age, marked as it is by the disappearance of securely grounded values, the "land of broken symbols"—an apt image. Secular man's values have been deconsecrated, shorn of any claim to ultimate or final significance. Like nature and politics, they are no longer the direct expression of the divine will. They have become what certain people at a particular time and place hold to be good. They have ceased to be values and have become valuations. Secular man knows that the symbols by which he perceives the world and the values by which he makes his decisions are the products of a particular history. As such they are limited and partial. The man who has moved beyond tribal culture and its town or bourgeois afterglow knows that he must bear a burden the people of those eras never bore. He must live with the realization that the rules which guide his ethical life will seem just as outmoded to his descendants as some of his ancestors' practices now appear to him. No previous generation has had to live in the glaring light of this realization. Simple ethical certainty, of the sort once available to man, will never be possible again.

How, in such a situation, is it possible to avoid a dizzy descent into pure anarchic relativism? How can secularization, if it results in the deconsecration and consequent relativization of values. lead in the end to anything but nihilism?

The answer is that there is a crucial difference between a willingness to concede that one's own attitudes and standpoints are relative, and a sweeping denial of any reality toward which one's attitudes and values are directed. The two are not the same. The relativization of values does not have to lead to either individual or group solipsism. It can have a much more constructive result, the recognition that since everyone's perspective is limited and conditioned, no one has the right to inflict his values on anyone else. In political terms, a certain degree of healthy relativism provides the philosophical basis for a pluralist society.

The relativization of all human values, one of the integral dimensions of secularization, stems in part from the biblical opposition to idolatry. Beginning with the prohibition against "graven images" which is part of the Sinai Covenant, the Old Testament is characterized by an uncompromising refusal to allow any replication of the deity. The enormous relevance of this prohibition is frequently misunderstood by modern readers. Since, for the ancients, gods and value systems were the same thing, this interdiction against idols means that the Hebrews were forbidden to worship (that is, to take with any real moral seriousness) anything which could be fashioned by man himself. It was not that the Hebrews feared that by making an idol religious worship might be cheapened or misled. Rather, it was believed that Yahweh, the Holy One of Israel, was by his very nature impossible of replication by human effort. The commandment against idolatry is a clue to Yahweh's essence. Any deity which could be expressed in the form of an idol was *ipso facto* not Yahweh. The gods were thereby demoted. The Bible does not deny the reality of the gods and their values; it merely relativizes them. It accepts them as human projections, as "the work of man's hand," and in this sense is very close to the modern social sciences. It was because they believed in Yahweh that, for the Hebrews, all human values and their representations were relativized.

The same observation holds for the continuing tradition of iconoclasm in Christian history. Iconoclasm is a form of deconsecration. It represents the extension of the commandment against idols. Biblical iconoclasm, as Gabriel Vahanian puts it, is

> . . . a deflation of man's natural inclination to deify himself, or his society, or the State, or his culture . . . a relentless exposing of the manifold, constant proclivity to elevate the finite to the level of the infinite, to give the transitory the status of permanent, and to attribute to man qualities that will deceive him into denying his finitude.[5]

The persistent protest against idols and icons which runs through the history of biblical faith provides the basis for a constructive relativism. It makes possible a stance by which the national, racial, and cultural idolatries of the age can be put in their place. It allows secular man to note the transience and relativity of all cultural creations and of every value system without sinking into an abyss of nihilism. He can confess the subjectivity of his perception while insisting that the object of that perception is nonetheless real. As Richard Niebuhr once wrote,

> Relativism does not imply subjectivism or skepticism. It is not evident that the man who is forced to confess that his view of things is conditioned by the standpoint he occupies must doubt the reality of what he sees. It is not apparent that one who knows that his concepts are not universal must also doubt that they are concepts of the universal.[6]

Historical relativism is the end product of secularization. It is the nonreligious expression of what Jews have expressed in their consistent opposition to idols, and Christians in their sporadic attacks on icons. Idols of all kinds are expressions of what Émile Durkheim, the great sociologist of religion, once called the *"representation collective."* They are the symbols and values of a tribe, a clan, a nation, projected into the heavens and given the status of divine beings. Durkheim's Jewish forebears might well have been proud of his scientific extension of the ruthless exposure of human sources of religious images which is so close to the heart of Israelite faith. Iconoclasm—and therefore a kind of relativism—is the necessary and logical consequence of faith in the Creator. We noted a few pages back that Marxist atheism, despite fundamental differences from Christianity, performs an analagous cultural function by disenchanting nature, while its theory of politics also desacralizes ruling regimes. The same is true in the deconsecration of values. Marx taught that all values were merely the projection of the economic power interests of a class. This bears a close resemblance to the biblical exposure of idols.

A question might legitimately arise at this point about those myriad modern men who feel the full weight of relativism but have no faith. Must it not be conceded that, for them, Ivan Karamazov is right when he says that if God is dead, then anything is possible?

There is a real danger that a relativization of values can lead to ethical anarchism and metaphysical nihilism. But this need not be the case. Nihilism itself is an ism. It is a value system with its own idols and icons, even if they appear as gargoyles. Nihilism represents the adolescent phase of the relativization of values. It swings back and forth from a giddy celebration of the freedom man has when the gods are dead to a wistful longing for the return of a world of secure and dependable meanings and norms. In psychoanalytic terms, the nihilist displays a deep ambivalence toward the authority figure represented by God and traditional values. Having rejected the father, he still cannot achieve maturity and self-actualization. Nihilism therefore sometimes becomes a kind of diabolism. The nihilist uses his newfound freedom from the tyranny of God not to become a true man but to revel in all the things the dead God once forbade. Nihilism has in effect a new god, the nihil, the negative shadow of the dead God.

Nihilism is the equivalent in the ethical realm of the vengeful onslaught against nature which may follow its disenchantment. Both are essentially adolescent reactions to liberation from previous restraints. In both cases, the mature mastery of this newly won freedom lies in a very different direction.

The relativization of values does cut the ground out from under many people. It melts the paste of traditional social cohesion and things begin to fall apart. Since all societies require an element of value consensus, it poses the problem of a new form of social cohesion. But despite claims to the contrary, the relativization of values does *not* make impossible human society with its prerequisite of some degree of social consensus. What it *does* do is force man to reconstitute that consensus on a wholly new basis, quite a different matter. How is this to be done?

First of all it requires real maturity. It demands that all men be drawn into the secularization process so that no one clings to the dangerous precritical illusion that his values are ultimate. All idols and icons must be exposed for the relative, conditional things they are. Tribal naïveté must be laid to rest everywhere, and everyone must be made a citizen of the land of broken symbols. In this way the process which has destroyed the old basis for social solidity now provides the basis for a new one. Paradoxically, the mutual discovery by all parties concerned that their various value systems are in fact relative puts them all into the same boat. It supplies a common experience and outlook which can become the basis for a new social consensus. We may even find that the consensus achieved is wider and more significant. Thus it is now possible for the United Nations to develop a Declaration of Human Rights based on a consensus of all the nation-states involved. It does not, like the American founding documents, rest on affirmations concerning the inalienable right with which men are "endowed by their Creator. . . ." Nor is it based on some theory of natural law. It is the expression of a consensus which draws together several cultural and religious traditions including those which believe neither in a Creator nor in any form of natural law.

Man once believed that the state was a changeless expression of divine will. Now he knows it to be a creation of man. Conservatives (for example Edmund Burke) argued that such a desacralization of politics would be disastrous. They feared that once sacral legitimation had disappeared, no respect for law or political authority would remain. Burke was wrong. Man now works within political institutions he knows to be human artifices. The same can be true for ethics. There is no reason that man must believe the ethical standards he lives by came down from heaven inscribed on golden tablets. He can accept the fact that value systems, like states and civilizations, come and go. They are conditioned by their history and claim no finality. Like models for scientific inquiry and the traditional institutions for exercising political power, they can be altered and modified. But insofar as they represent a consensus and provide a fabric of corporate life, they should not be tampered with frivolously or capriciously. Secularization places the responsibility for the forging of human values, like the fashioning of political systems, in man's own hands. And this demands a maturity neither the nihilist nor the anarchist wishes to assume.

We have described the three central threads of the secularization process and traced them back to sources in the biblical faith itself. Where does that leave us today? Clearly, those whose present orientation to reality is shaped by the biblical faith can hardly in good faith enter the lists as opponents of secularization. Our task should be to nourish the secularization process, to prevent it from hardening into a rigid world view, and to clarify as often as necessary its roots in the Bible. Furthermore, we should be constantly on the lookout for movements which attempt to thwart and reverse the liberating irritant of secularization.

This means we should oppose the romantic restoration of the sprites to the forest. It may seem pleasant at first to reinstate the tribal spirits, but—as Hitler made all too clear—once the Valkyries return, they will seek a bloodthirsty revenge on those who banished them. We should also be wary of any attempt to resacralize politics. Political leaders and movements should never be granted any sacred significance, and all efforts to use the public authority to support traditional religious beliefs or the quasi-religious beliefs of ideological secularists must be resisted.

Perhaps it is in the realm of values and ethics that the nurture of secularization becomes most ambiguous and problematical. Yet even here the broad lines of action are clear. Of course no group can be prevented from claiming that its values are ultimate. But it can be prevented from employing state power or cultural coercion to validate its case. No one can deny a Mississippi café proprietor his right to believe that Negroes suffer the curse of Ham. But he can be prevented from utilizing the property the state protects and regulates for him to humiliate Negroes because of his farfetched religious opinion. A highly disparate conglomerate of value systems can coexist in a society so long as they all repudiate the privilege of winning the others over by rack and thumbscrew. But even this repudiation demands a huge step for those still ensnarled in mythical and metaphysical sureties. Releasing them to maturity is the work of the God of Creation, Exodus, and Sinai. Calling them to maturity is the task of the community of faith.

NOTES TO CHAPTER I

1. Friedrich Gogarten, *Verhängnis und Hoffnung der Neuezeit* (Stuttgart: Friedrich Vorwerk Verlag, 1953); *Der Mensch zwischen Gott und Welt* (Stuttgart: Friedrich Vorwerk Verlag, 1956).
2. A. F. Radcliffe-Brown, *Structure and Function in Primitive Society* (New York: The Free Press, 1952; London: Cohen & West). For my discussion of the magical world view I am indebted to the lucid discussion by Rosalie H. and Murray Wax, "The Magical Worldview" in *Journal for the Scientific Study of Religion*, 1, 2 (Spring 1962), pp. 179–188.
3. Saint Augustine, *The City of God*, XV/1, XVI/10.
4. Niccolò Machiavelli, *Discourses*, II/2, III/1.
5. Gabriel Vahanian, *Wait Until Idols* (New York: Braziller, 1964), p. 24.
6. Richard Niebuhr, *The Meaning of Revelation* (New York: Macmillan, 1960), p. 18.

CHAPTER 2

The Shape of the Secular City

What comes to mind when we think of the *shape* of technopolis? We visualize contours. We envisage networks of radial and circumferential thoroughfares, grids of disparate but interlocking land-use regions, a profile carved out by the city's natural topography—a mountain range, a lakefront, a river. We also see buildings, short and squat, tall and erect. Terminals, stations, offices, residences jostle each other for space. These are the physical shapes of the city.

But what about the social shape of the secular metropolis, its human silhouette, the institutional basis for its culture? The shape of the secular city, along with its style, comprises its *manière d'être*. Its shape is its social system as distinguished from its cultural system. The distinction is of course merely analytic. In reality shape and style merge, but for purposes of discussion, in this chapter we shall focus on the shape of the secular city and on its style in the following one.

Let two images drawn from the physical setting of technopolis suggest the elements of its social shape on which we wish to concentrate. The first is the *switchboard,* the key to communication in the city, linking human beings to one another through modern electronic magic. The next is the highway *cloverleaf,* the image of simultaneous mobility in many different directions. These symbols suggest both possibility and problems. They illustrate two characteristic components of the social shape of the modern metropolis: *anonymity* and *mobility*. But why focus on them?

Not only are anonymity and mobility central. They are also the two features of the urban social system most frequently singled out for attack by both religious and nonreligious critics. How often has one heard that urban man's existence has been depleted and despoiled by the cruel anonymity and ceaseless mobility of the city? How frequently is urban man depicted by his detractors as faceless and depersonalized,

33

rushing to and fro with no time to cultivate deeper relationships or lasting values? Anonymity and mobility can of course become damaging. But since they have been made into antiurban epithets it is even more important to examine their positive side. Anonymity and mobility contribute to the sustenance of human life in the city. They are indispensable modes of existence in the urban setting. Seen from a theological perspective, anonymity and mobility may even produce a certain congruity with biblical faith that is never noticed by the religious rebukers of urbanization.

Anonymity

Every college sophomore knows that modern man is a faceless cipher. The stock in trade of too many humanities courses and religious-emphasis weeks is the featureless "mass man," reduced to a number or a series of holes in an IBM card, wandering through T. S. Eliot's "waste land" starved for a name. "Loss of identity" and "disappearance of selfhood" have come to play an ever larger role in the popular pastime of flagellating urban culture. Where does this fear of anonymity originate?

Regardless of how cheapened and trite such criticisms have become in our time, they do stem from an impressive intellectual ancestry. Søren Kierkegaard fulminated brilliantly against certain elements of mass society and urban life in *The Present Age* (1846). José Ortega y Gasset, the Spanish philosopher, exemplifies the aristocratic repugnance for the erasing of class lines and the anonymous character of modern society in his *Revolt of the Masses* (1932). Rainer Maria Rilke's book *Notebooks of Malte Lauridi Brigge* (English translation, 1930) displays a metaphysical horror for the impersonality of life and for the loss of the mystery of things which he found in the city. Above all, the refusal of Franz Kafka to endow the main characters of two of his later novels with any name has sometimes been interpreted as a protest against urban and bureaucratic anonymity.

Must the modern writer be antiurban?

The truth is that, for a genuine literary artist, the city is the setting but not the real target of his onslaught. Many nineteenth- and early twentieth-century writers did not see that urban anonymity has its distinct benefits as well as its horrors.

A writer who becomes *essentially* antiurban forfeits his claim to greatness, for what is often left unsaid by the morbid critics of anonymity is, first, that without it, life in a modern city could not be human, and second, that anonymity represents for many people a liberating even more than a threatening phenomenon. It serves for large numbers of people as the possibility of freedom in contrast to the bondage of the law and convention. The anonymity of city living helps preserve the privacy essential to human life. Furthermore, anonymity can be understood theologically as Gospel versus Law.

THE MAN AT THE GIANT SWITCHBOARD

Technopolitan man sits at a vast and immensely complicated switchboard. He is *homo symbolicus,* man the communicator, and the metropolis is a massive network of communications. A whole world of possibilities for communication lies within his reach. The contemporary urban region represents an ingenious device for vastly enlarging the range of human communication and widening the scope of individual choice. Urbanization thus contributes to the freedom of man. This is perfectly evident when we think, for example, of cinema theaters and restaurants. Residents of a city of ten thousand may be limited to one or two theaters, while people who live in a city of a million can choose among perhaps fifty films on a given night. The same principle holds for restaurants, schools, and even in some measure for job opportunities or prospective marriage partners. Urban man is free to choose from a wider range of alternatives. Thus his manhood as *homo symbolicus* is enhanced.

But freedom always demands discipline. The mere availability of such a wide spectrum of possibilities requires an adjustment of urban man's behavior. He must exercise choice more frequently, and choice always means exclusion. He doesn't just "go to the movies" on a free evening, as his more rural counterpart might; he must choose one from among the fifty films now showing. This means a conscious decision *not* to see the other forty-nine.

In the area of personal relationships this selectivity becomes more demanding. Urban man has a wider variety of "contacts" than his rural counterpart; he can choose only a limited number for friends. He must have more or less impersonal relationships with most of the people with whom he comes in contact precisely in order to nourish and cultivate certain friendships. This selectivity can best be symbolized perhaps by the unplugged telephone or the unlisted number. A person does not request an unlisted number to cut down on the depth of his relationships. Quite the opposite; he does so to guard and deepen the worthwhile relationships he has against being dissolved in the deluge of messages that would come if one were open on principle and on an equal basis to anyone who tried to get through, including the increasing army of telephone salesmen who violate one's privacy so arrogantly. Those we want to know have our number; others do not. We are free to use the switchboard without being victimized by its infinite possibilities.

Urban man must distinguish carefully between his private life and his public relationships. Since he depends on such a complex net of services to maintain himself in existence in a modern city, the majority of his transactions will have to be public and will be what sociologists call functional or secondary. In most of his relationships he will be dealing with people he cannot afford to be interested in as individuals but must deal with in terms of the services they render to him and he to them. This is essential in urban life. Supermarket checkers or gas-meter readers who became enmeshed in the lives of the people they were serving would be a menace. They would soon cause a total breakdown in the essential systems of which they are integral parts. Urban life demands that we treat most of the people we meet as persons—not as things, but not as intimates either. This in turn produces the kind of "immunization" against personal encounters which Louis Wirth explains this way:

> Characteristically, urbanites meet one another in highly segmental roles. They are, to be sure, dependent upon more people for the satisfactions of their life-needs than are rural people and thus are associated with a greater number of organized groups, but they are less dependent upon particular persons, and their dependence upon others is confined to a highly fractionalized aspect of the other's round of activity. This is essentially what is meant by saying that the city is characterized by secondary rather than primary contacts. The contacts of the city may indeed be face to face, but they are nevertheless impersonal, superficial, transitory, and segmental. The reserve, the indifference, and the blasé outlook which urbanites manifest in their relationships may thus be regarded as devices for immunizing themselves against the personal claims and expectations of others.[1]

This immunization results in a way of life which often appears cold and even heartless to those unfamiliar with the dynamics of urban living. Here both writers and sociologists have missed the point. Cultural romantics such as Rilke and Ortega recoiled in distaste at what they took to be the cruelty of the city. In sociology a similar criticism was also voiced. Relationships in the city, it was complained, tended to be divested of their really human substance and made mechanical and lifeless.

One of the most influential sociological critics of the shape of urban life was the German scholar Ferdinand Tönnies (1855–1936), whose work has continued to exert a considerable influence on modern sociology and cultural analysis. In 1887 Tönnies published a book in which he contrasted the coherent, organic togetherness of *Gemeinschaft* (community) with the more rational, planned, and partial nexus of the *Gesellschaft* (society). Kaspar Naegele summarizes Tönnies' distinction:

> Relations of the *Gemeinschaft* type are more inclusive; persons confront each other as ends, they cohere more durably. . . . In *Gesellschaft* their mutual regard is circumscribed by a sense of specific, if not formal obligations. . . . A transaction can occur without any other encounters, leaving both parties virtually anonymous.[2]

Tönnies is talking about what some sociologists describe as "primary" versus "secondary" relationships, or "organic" versus "functional" relationships. Having lived both as a villager and as an urbanite I know just what these terms mean. During my boyhood, my parents never referred to "the milkman," "the insurance agent," "the junk collector." These people were, respectively, Paul Weaver, Joe Villanova, and Roxy Barazano. All of our family's market transactions took place within a web of wider and more inclusive friendship and kinship ties with the same people. They were never anonymous. In fact, the occasional salesman or repairman whom we did not know was always viewed with dark suspicion until we could make sure where he came from, who his parents were, and whether his family was "any good." Trips to the grocery store, gasoline station, or post office were inevitably social visits, never merely functional contacts.

Now, as an urbanite, my transactions are of a very different sort. If I need to have the transmission on my car repaired, buy a television antenna, or cash a check, I find myself in functional relationships with mechanics, salesmen, and bank clerks whom I never see in any other capacity. These "contacts" are in no sense "mean, nasty, or brutish," though they do tend to be short, at least not any longer than the time required to make the transaction and to exchange a brief pleasantry. Some of these human contacts occur with considerable frequency, so that I come to know the mannerisms and maybe even the names of some of the people. But the relationships are unifaceted and "segmental." I meet these people in no other context. To me they remain essentially just as anonymous as I do to them. Indeed, in the case of the transmission repairman, I hope I never see him again—not because he is in any way unpleasant, but because my only possible reason for seeing him again would be a new and costly breakdown in my car's gearbox. The important point here is that my relationships with bank clerks and garagemen are no less human or authentic merely because we both prefer to keep them anonymous. Here is where much theological analysis of urbanization has gone hopelessly astray.

Theologians have spent themselves in well-intentioned forays against the "depersonalization of urban life," often fed by a misunderstanding of Martin Buber's philosophy of "I and Thou" relationships. In contrast to those who utilize his categories in a different manner, Buber himself never claimed that *all* our relationships should be of the deep, interpersonal I–Thou variety. He knew this experience was a rich and rare one. But Buber did open the door for misunderstanding by neglecting to study with sufficient thoroughness the place of types of relationships which actually constitute most of our lives, a point to which we shall return shortly.

A recent survey by some Protestant ministers in a new urban high-rise apartment area where they intended to establish house church groups illustrates the misplaced emphasis on I–Thou relationships that has marked modern Christian theology. In conducting their study, the pastors were shocked to discover that the recently arrived apartment dwellers, whom they expected to be lonely and desperate for relationships, did not want to meet their neighbors socially and had no interest whatever in church or community groups. At first the ministers deplored what they called a "social pathology" and a "hedgehog" psychology. Later, however, they found that what they had encountered was a sheer survival technique. Resistance against efforts to subject them to neighborliness and socialization is a skill apartment dwellers must de-

velop if they are to maintain any human relationships at all. It
is an essential element in the shape of the secular city.

In condemning urban anonymity, the ministers had made
the mistake of confusing a preurban ethos with the Christian
concept of *koinonia*. The two are not the same. The ministers
had wanted to develop a kind of village togetherness among
people, one of whose main reasons for moving to high-rise
apartments is to escape the relationships enforced on them by
the lack of anonymity of the village. Apartment dwellers, like
most urbanites, live a life in which relationships are founded
on free selection and common interest, usually devoid of
spatial proximity. Studies have shown that even friendship
patterns within a large apartment complex follow age, family
size, and personal interest lines. They do not ordinarily spring
from the mere proximity of apartments. Thus, to complain
that apartment people often live for years just down the hall
from another family but do not "really get to know them"
overlooks the fact that many specifically choose *not* to
"know" their spatial neighbors in any intimate sense. This
allows them more time and energy to cultivate the friends
they themselves select. This does not mean the apartment
dweller cannot love his next-door neighbor. He can and often
does so, certainly no less frequently than the small-town resi-
dent. But he does so by being a dependable fellow tenant, by
bearing his share of the common responsibility they both have
in that segment of their lives shaped by residence. This does
not require their becoming cronies.

All this means that the urban secular man is summoned to
a different *kind* of neighborliness than his town-dwelling predecessor practiced. Much like the Samaritan described by Jesus
in the story he told in response to the question "Who is my
neighbor?," his main responsibility is to do competently what
needs to be done to assure his neighbor's health and well-
being. The man who fell among thieves was not the next-door
neighbor of the Samaritan, but he helped him in an efficient,
unsentimental way. He did not form an I–Thou relationship
with him but bandaged his wounds and made sure the inn-
keeper had enough cash to cover his expenses.

Urban anonymity need not be heartless. Village sociability
can mask murderous hostility. Loneliness is undoubtedly a
serious problem in the city, but it cannot be met by dragoon-
ing urban people into relationships which sabotage their privacy and reduce their capacity to live responsibly with increasing numbers of neighbors. The church investigators who

shook their heads over the evasiveness of the apartment dwellers had forgotten this. They had come to the city with a village theology and had stumbled upon an essential protective device, the polite refusal to be chummy without which urban existence could not be human. They had overlooked the fact that technopolitan man *must* cultivate and guard his privacy. He must restrict the number of people who have his number or know his name.

The small-town dweller, on the other hand, lives within a restricted web of relationships and senses a larger world he may be missing. Since the people he knows also know one another, he gossips more and yearns to hear gossip. His private life is public and vice versa. While urban man is unplugging his telephone, town man (or his wife) may be listening in on the party line or its modern equivalent, gossiping at the kaffee-klatsch.

Urban man, in contrast, wants to maintain a clear distinction between private and public. Otherwise public life would overwhelm and dehumanize him. His life represents a point touched by dozens of systems and hundreds of people. His capacity to know some of them better necessitates his minimizing the depth of his relationships to many others. Listening to the postman gossip becomes for urban man an act of sheer graciousness, since he probably has no interest in the people the postman wants to talk about. Unlike my parents, who suspected all strangers, he tends to be wary not of the functionaries he doesn't know but of those he does.

ANONYMITY AS DELIVERANCE FROM THE LAW

How can urban anonymity be understood theologically? Here the traditional distinction between Law and Gospel comes to mind. In using these terms we refer not to religious rules or to fiery preaching, but to the tension between bondage to the past and freedom for the future. In this sense Law means anything that binds us uncritically to inherited conventions, and Gospel is that which frees us to decide for ourselves.

As the contemporary German theologian Rudolf Bultmann once wrote, Law means the "standards of this world."[3] It is what Riesman calls the power of "other-direction" driving us toward conformity to the expectations and customs of the culture, enforced in a thousand small, nearly unnoticeable ways by the people who make our choices for us. When Law rather than Gospel becomes the basis for our lives, it militates against choice and freedom. It decides for us, thus sapping our powers of responsibility. Similarly, Gospel in a broader sense means a summons to choice and answerability. It designates not merely the verbal message of the church, but also the call which comes to any man when he is confronted with the privilege and necessity of making a free and responsible decision, not determined by cultural background or social convention. Our use of the Law–Gospel dialectic here suggests that it has a broader relevance than is ordinarily accorded it in theology. It suggests that in the historical process itself man meets the One who calls him into being as a free deciding self, and knows that neither his past history nor his environment determines what he does. In the anonymity of urban culture, far from the fishbowl of town life, modern man experiences both the terror and the delight of human freedom more acutely. The biblical God is present for man today in the world of social reality, and Law and Gospel provide us an angle of vision by which to understand secular events, including urbanization. The God of the Gospel is the One who wills freedom and responsibility, who points toward the future in hope. The Law, on the other hand, includes any cultural phenomenon which holds men in immaturity, in captivity to convention and tradition. The Law is enforced by the weight of human opinion; the Gospel is the activity of God creating new possibilities in history. Law signifies the fact that man does live in society; Gospel points to the equally important fact that he is more than the intersection of social forces. He feels himself summoned to choose, to actualize a potential selfhood which is more than the sum of genes plus glands plus class. Man cannot live without Law, but when Law becomes wholly determinative, he is no longer really man.

From this perspective, urbanization can be seen as a liberation from some of the cloying bondages of preurban society. It is the chance to be free. Urban man's deliverance from enforced conventions requires that he choose for himself. His being anonymous to most people permits him to have a face and a name for others.

This is not an easy thing to accomplish. The challenge of living responsibly within segmental relationships is formidable, especially for those who have been reared in small-town or traditional cultures. Often a nagging sense of guilt plagues the urban man with rural roots because he cannot possibly

cultivate an I–Thou relationship with everyone. Unfortunately
the church, largely bound to a preurban ethos, often ex-
acerbates his difficulty by seeking to promote small-town intimacy among urban people and by preaching the necessity of
I–Thou relationships as the only ones that are really human.
But this represents a misreading of the Gospel and a disservice
to urban man. Relationships among urbanites do not have to
be lifeless or callous just because they are impersonal. Jane
Jacobs in her *Death and Life of Great American Cities* has
caught the flavor of urban neighborliness exceptionally well.
It necessitates learning how to enjoy public relationships
without allowing them to become private:

> Nobody can keep open house in a great city. Nobody
> wants to. And yet if interesting, useful and significant
> contacts among the people of cities are confined to ac-
> quaintanceships suitable for private life, the city becòmes
> stultified. Cities are full of people with whom, from your
> viewpoint, or mine, or any other individual's, a certain
> degree of contact is useful or enjoyable; but you do not
> want them in your hair. And they do not want you in
> theirs either.[4]

Theologians would do well to appreciate this characteristically
urban "togetherness" so aptly described by Jane Jacobs and to
see in its impersonal, even anonymous, interrelatedness an
authentic form of corporate human existence in the urban
epoch.

We need to develop a viable theology of anonymity. In
doing so, it might be useful to add another type of human
relationship to Buber's famous pair. Besides I–It relationships,
in which the other person is reduced to the status of an object,
and in addition to the profound, personally formative I–Thou
encounter, why could we not evolve a theology of the I–*You*
relationship? Buber's philosophy suffers from an unnecessary
dichotomy. Perhaps between the poles of the two types of
human relationship he has elaborated we could designate a
third. It would include all those public relationships we so
enjoy in the city but which we do not allow to develop into
private ones. These contacts can be decidedly human even
though they remain somewhat distant. We like and enjoy
these people, but as Jane Jacobs says, we "don't want them in
our hair, and they don't want us in theirs either."

The danger with an I–Thou typology is that all relationships which are not deeply personal and significant tend to be
swept or shoved into the I–It category. But they need not be.

The development of an I–*You* theology would greatly clarify the human possibilities of urban life, and would help stall attempts to lure urban people back into preurban conviviality under the color of saving their souls.

The development of such a theology would help expose the *real* dangers inherent in urban anonymity, as opposed to the pseudodangers. Technopolitan possibilities *can* harden into rigid new conventions. Freedom can always be used for anti-human purposes. The Gospel can ossify into a new legalism. But none of these hazards can be exposed if we continue to insist on judging urban life by preurban norms. Despite its pitfalls, the anonymous shape of urban life helps free man from the Law. For many people it is a glorious liberation, a deliverance from the saddling traditions and burdensome expectations of town life and an entry into the exciting new possibilities of choice which pervade the secular metropolis.

Mobility

Every tendency in modern society points to accelerated mobility. Technology closes the saddlemaker's shop and opens electronic labs. Industrialization not only lures people off the farms and into the cities; it also invades the farms, transforming them into food factories and steadily diminishing the number of hands required to do the work. The modern city is a mass movement. It has been described by one writer as a kind of staging area where people pause in their complex movements from one place to another. Not only do we migrate between cities in search of improvement, but we migrate within cities to find more convenient or congenial surroundings. Commutation represents a small daily migration. We commute not only to work but also to play, to shop, to socialize. Everybody is going places, but what is happening to us as a people along the way?

Many view the high mobility of modern life in the most negative possible light. A whole literature of protest has grown up, much of it religious in nature, which bewails the alleged shallowness and lostness of modern urban man. Countless sermons deplore the "rush-rush of modern living" and the diminution of spiritual values supposed to accompany the loss of more sedentary cultural patterns. On a more serious level, themes of rootlessness and alienation constantly appear in contemporary literature. Indeed, the greatest novelists of our century have chosen to create heroes who wander far from home in the midst of strangers and foreigners. Thomas Mann's *Joseph in Egypt,* James Joyce's *Ulysses,* and Franz Kafka's *The Castle* come to mind immediately. Albert Camus and André Gide dealt with similar themes. Time and again there returns the image of man as a harried and homeless wanderer, frequently with absorbing artistic power. The question is, however: Must man necessarily be impoverished by mobility? Can he travel without getting lost? Can he move without meandering?

Before turning to these questions, it is worth pointing out that American men of letters have seldom taken such a cheerless view of mobility. Indeed, telling the stories of people on the go has been almost a speciality of American writers. Though *Moby Dick* has to do with more than whaling, it is impossible to read it, or Melville's other novels such as *Typee* or *Billy Budd,* without sensing his real fondness for ships and travel. In *Huckleberry Finn* Mark Twain tells of the complicated relationship between a white boy and a black man, but it is noteworthy that the characters find themselves riding a raft down the Mississippi. Ernest Hemingway is the prototype of the American traveler-writer, and Thomas Wolfe nourished a lifelong passion for railroads. Henry James is nearly as famous for his travel diaries as he is for his novels and essays. John Steinbeck and John Dos Passos have both written with gusto about people on the move. Perhaps the fascination for automobiles one finds in John Updike and Jack Kerouac represents the newest phase of the American writer's traditional intoxication with going places.

America has produced a series of writers who tend to celebrate rather than denigrate mobility. But Americans have always been a mobile people. They had to be, even to come here. With one important exception, the Negroes, Americans all stem from people who voluntarily left home to come to a new land. Sociologists know that people who have already moved once are more likely to move again than are people who have never moved. They know also that mobile people are generally tolerant of new ideas and possibilities. Having entertained and acted on one big change already, they are never reticent to entertain the possibility of others.

THE MAN IN THE CLOVERLEAF

Technopolitan man is on the go. In addition to the gaint switchboard, he can be pictured as a driver in a cloverleaf intersection. Other images of the city include the airport control tower, high-speed elevators, and perpetually moving escalators in department stores and offices. The modern metropolis is a system of roads—thruways, subways, airways—linking the city to others and parts of the city to each other. It is also a system of vertical facilitators, snatching people from the street to the penthouse, from the janitor's basement to the executive suite and back again. Urban man is certainly in motion, and we can expect the pace and scope of mobility to increase as time goes on.

Analysts sometimes distinguish between two types of mobility—geographic and occupational. Sometimes status mobility, class mobility, and other forms of "social" mobility are added. But since these are so closely related to job and residence mobility, we shall restrict ourselves here to discussing the problems and possibilities of movement to new jobs and homes.

There are many critics of residential and occupational mobility. They use different rhetoric but quite frequently paint verbal landscapes of home and vocation which are laden with religious sentiments. For many people these images have a real appeal. To be born and reared in the same clapboard house where one may even grow old and die does have a certain cozy attractiveness. To work at the same job in the same place through all one's adult years might also provide elements of comfort. But those who bewail the passing of the era in which this stable, idyllic condition was supposed to have obtained forget one important fact: only a tiny minority of people ever really enjoyed such pastoral permanence. The majority of people in premobile societies lived and worked in ways we would not want to return to. Most of us today would vigorously object to living in the house or doing the job our great-grandfathers did. The fact is that most people's great-grandparents were dirt poor and lived in hovels. Most of us are much better off today because our forebears *were* mobile. Mobility is always the weapon of the underdog. The desire to combat mobility, to encourage residential and occupational *im*mobility, is a romantic distortion which springs from a reactionary mentality.

Mobility is closely linked to social change; so guardians of the status quo have always opposed mobility. They are perfectly consistent is doing so. They sense that changes in one area of life—job or residence—will lead to other kinds of change; and they are against change. The conservatives in the polis of Athens were right in their fierce opposition to constructing a port at Piraeus. They knew that mixed with the exotic products of foreign shores there would come strange people with exotic ideas which would shake their security. Virulent opposition to the building of railroads was voiced by the lords of the English establishment in the early nineteenth century, not just because railroads were loud or dirty, but because even lowly villagers would now travel to other towns. There they could not be kept from coming under strange influences since they would wander about without the normal social controls. Worst of all, it was argued, they would meet people who had never heard of their local squires. They would see their own towns in perspective and might lose all respect for traditional authority.

The World War I song "How Ya Gonna' Keep 'Em Down on the Farm Now that They've Seen Paree?" illustrates the relationship between mobility, urbanization, and social change. Those who have been drawn into the tradition-demolishing orbit of urban life are never quite the same again. They will always know that things *could* be different; they will never again accept the farm as given; and this is the seedbed of revolution.

In our own country the emergence of the Negro Freedom Movement provides a particularly good example of the link between mobility and social change. Many observers believe that the movement of large numbers of Negroes out of rural areas in the South and into urban industrial centers, plus the experience of thousands of young Negroes in the military service, supplied the indispensable social exposure which has resulted in the civil rights revolution. Negroes discovered that things did not have to be the way they were. Those who acted against oppression were young, and they were geographically and occupationally mobile. Their battles, unlike those of the Civil War which took place at heretofore unknown villages —Bull Run and Gettysburg—now took place in urban centers such as Birmingham, and spread to the provinces. Mobility had unlocked the cage.

Geographic mobility always points to social or occupational mobility. Even in the storybooks, the son leaves the family homestead "to seek his fortune." Mobility in one area signifies mobility in another. People on the move spatially are usually on the move intellectually, financially, or psychologically. All of this naturally threatens those who already occupy the positions of power and influence in the society. It is the people on the bottom who have everything to gain and nothing to lose from a mobile society. Consequently it is not difficult to discover class prejudice behind religious objections to mobility. Since romanticism and reaction often stroll hand in hand, it is equally easy to spot an aristocratic or conservative ideology in those pleas for occupational stability and home-sweet-home inertness that are often fused with religious appeals.

An advanced industrial society strangles without mobility. People must be ready to move. New jobs appear in different places. Technology renders skilled operators obsolescent; even if they are retrained, their newly acquired skill may become equally obsolescent before they know it. Promotion in most firms and increasingly in educational institutions involves moving from place to place. Travel and vacationing expose people to numberless new vistas of experience. Those tendencies in our society which tend to retard or discourage mobility almost always arise from people who are trying to prevent other people from enlarging their share of the power or the rewards of the society. But impairing mobility inevitably damages the whole society. Thus housing and employment patterns which reduce the mobility of Negroes, for example, function like sand in the gear box of the economy, and the whole society suffers. But what about the destructive effects of mobility?

YAHWEH AND THE BAALIM

Let us admit at once that high mobility does play havoc with traditional religion. It separates people from the holy places. It mixes them with neighbors whose gods have different names and who worship them in different ways. But since we have already noted the important connection between urbanization and secularization, we need not pause to lament this process. What we do wish to say is that, from biblical perspective, mobility can also be viewed positively. Without ignoring the dangers it can bring or the problems it creates, still, mobility offers positive possibilities for individuals.

When we seek to understand the phenomenon of mobility from a theological perspective, it is well to remember that the whole Hebrew view of God arose in the social context of a nomadic, essentially homeless people. Only for relatively brief periods in their history did the Hebrews have a "home of their own," and these periods are usually viewed as the least creative periods in their career as a people. The experience of the escape from Egypt, the wandering in the wilderness, and the battles in Canaan supplied the axial events on which the Israelite faith was based. The greatest prophets, Jeremiah and Second Isaiah, did their work either as the security of the homeland was being crushed or in political exile. Israel's level of prophetic insight after they returned to their former homes under Ezra and Nehemiah dropped to an all-time low. Indeed, the universalism which broke through during the exile was almost lost sight of during the regressive period of the return. In short, when they were wandering and homeless the Hebrews seem to have been closest to fulfilling their calling.

The key characteristics of Yahweh, the Old Testament God, are linked to his mobility. He is the Lord of history and time. He is not spatially placed. It was because Yahweh, like the Hebrews, was a nomad, that the period of settlement in Canaan sparked the titanic battle between Yahweh and the Baalim. The struggle arose because the Baalim were the recognized deities of Canaan, and when the nomadic children of Israel finally settled there, they had to face the question of what to do with these local gods. The word *baal* itself means "possessor" or "inhabitant." The Baalim of Canaan were the proprietors of certain activities or more frequently of particular towns and places. They were *immobile* gods. A particular Baal expected deference from people only so long as they were within its territorial jurisdiction. The Baalim were the gods of a sedentary people who were suspicious of any sort of change.

Yahweh, on the other hand, was not a place god. True, He had appeared at particular places such as Sinai or in the burning bush, but He was certainly not restricted to these places. He not only moved with His people, but "went before them." Although the view of Yahweh as a nomadic, nonspatial God was constantly threatened by syncretism with the Canaanite Baalim, it finally withstood the test. With the Second Isaiah, it became clearly established that not even the rock of Zion in Jerusalem had any claim to Yahweh, that He ruled over all peoples and moved wherever He wanted to. This was a crucial victory for the Yahwist faith, since the historical character of Israel's vision of life depends on Yahweh's stalwart refusal to be a hearth god of some home sweet home.

One of the clearest evidences of Yahweh's mobility is the Ark of the Covenant, about which biblical archeologists have speculated. It is described at several places in the Old Testament. Some believe the Ark was a chest in which sacred stones were carried by the Hebrews into battle. Others believe it was a throne on which the invisible Yahweh rode with His people. Regardless of what it actually looked like, it is clear that the Ark was mobile. Unlike the Inca temples, the Egyptian sphinxes, or the Baylonian ziggurats, it could be picked up and carried wherever the people went. Unlike the Baalim, it was not stationary. Most important, however, when the Ark was finally captured by the Philistines, the Hebrews began to realize that Yahweh was not localized even in it. The seizure of the Ark prepared them for the eventual destruction of the Temple and the loss of their homeland. This whole historical movement by which Yahweh was divested of spatiality has enormous theological significance. It meant that Yahweh could not be localized at any given geographic spot. He traveled with His people and elsewhere.

The despatialization of the deity moves in tandem with the appearance of a God active in historical events.

The nomadic life of the early Israelites provided the necessary social setting for the emergence of a view of God that was startlingly at variance with those of Israel's neighbors. Yahweh was a God of history, not of nature. He disclosed Himself in political and military events, including defeats. He spoke through events of social change. For this reason, during the settlement in Canaan and the confrontation with the fertility gods of that culture, it was the farmers and the ruling elites who flirted with abandoning Yahweh and turning to the Baalim. The farmers did so because they were the most sedentary group, the rulers because they were the most conservative. The rural "high places" and the sad saga of Queen Jezebel provide the clearest examples. Yahweh won the contest with the agricultural deities not by becoming one but by absorbing many of the harvest and procreation festivals into what still remained an essentially nonspatial, historical faith.[5] The rise of a monarchy with its requisite ideology put an even more fearful strain on the Yahwist faith. But still Yahwism survived. Diluted during the monarchy, it was renewed in military defeat, captivity, and exile. Thus the faith was strengthened and revived precisely by a new period of homelessness and mobility.[6]

Jesus picked up the tradition of opposing sacred places and holy homelands. Thus he rejected the promptings of the Zealots, chiefly Judas Iscariot, to save the sacred homeland from the pagan Romans; he refused to allow his disciples, in the story of the Transfiguration, to build permanent monuments to him; he repeatedly promised to destroy the Temple of Jerusalem, the existence of which was always on the verge of respatializing God. His identifying the new temple with the risen body must be seen as his way of carrying the despatialization motif to its ultimate conclusion. The early church's belief in the Ascension can be read as its refusal to allow its Lord to be localized or spatially restricted. The Ascension in its simplest terms means that Jesus is mobile. He is not a Baal, but the Lord of all history.

Motifs of mobility and homelessness, of wandering and of pilgrimages informed the self-understanding of the earliest Christian community. They knew that here they had "no lasting city." In fact, the earliest designation given them was not "Christian" but "The People of the Way." They were essentially travelers. This understanding of the Christian life as a journey appears time and again in Christian history, from Saint John of the Cross to Dante's *Divine Comedy* to Bunyan's *Pilgrim's Progress* to Kierkegaard. Unfortunately it has often been individualized, whereas the earliest vision was of a people moving together; nonetheless the basic image remained.

After Constantine's conversion the church's newly acquired social position led to a de-emphasis on the stranger-and-pilgrims motif. The church soon made itself at home in the culture and a period analogous to the period of the monarchy in Israel's history began. The temptation to fashion a sacral civilization to transmute the Christian Gospel into a Baal cultus was not successfully resisted in the medieval period. The whole concept of Christendom was the result. It represents a fatal respatialization of Christianity. The Christian faith became the "religion of Western Europe," with only vestigial remnants of its universal scope remaining. Saint Francis did try to win the Sultan, but people thought he was crazy.

Contrary to most Protestant opinion, the historical, universal, and nonspatial genius of the Christian faith was not rediscovered at the Reformation. Luther and Calvin were mainly concerned with a religious reshuffling within Christendom. Only with the missionary movement of the nineteenth century and the ecumenical movement of the twentieth did the mistaken notion of Christendom begin to disappear. The death of Christendom has been hurried also by the rapid secularization of so-called Christian countries and by the appearance of self-conscious "non-Western" churches in both Afro-Asia and Eastern Europe.

Mobility is not the menace religious romantics paint it. It has its pitfalls. Endless movement from place to place can betray the same kind of unwillingness to take responsibility for decisions which can be seen in switching wives. But by and large the mobile man is less tempted than the immobile man to demote Yahweh into a Baal. He will usually not idolatrize any town or nation. He will not be as likely to see the present economic and political structure as the unambiguous expression of how things always have been and always should be. He will be more open to change, movement, newness. There is no reason why Christians should deplore the accelerating mobility of the modern metropolis. The Bible does not call man to renounce mobility, but to "go to a place that I will show unto you." Perhaps the mobile man can even hear with less static a Message about a Man who was born during a journey, spent his first years in exile, was expelled from his own home town, and declared that he had no place to lay his head. High mobility is no assurance of salvation, but neither is it an obstacle to faith.

NOTES TO CHAPTER 2

1. Louis Wirth, "Urbanism as a Way of Life" in Paul K. Hatt and Albert J. Reiss, Jr. (eds.), *Cities and Society* (New York: The Free Press, 1957), p. 54.
2. Kaspar D. Naegele, "The Institutionalization of Action," in Talcott Parsons, *et al.* (eds.), *Theories of Society* (New York: The Free Press, 1961), p. 184.
3. Bultmann's discussion of the Law can be found in his *Theology of the New Testament* (New York: Scribner, 1951; London: SCM Press), Section 27, pp. 259–269. The best discussion of the broader significance of the Law is found in Friedrich Gogarten's *Mensch zwischen Gott und Welt* (Stuttgart: Friedrich Vorwerk Verlag, 1956), especially Section I and the first part of Section II.
4. Jane Jacobs, *The Death and Life of Great American Cities* (New York: Vintage, 1963; London: Cape), pp. 55–56.
5. An absorbing account of the sociological aspects of Israel's conflict with the religious and cultural forces of Canaan will be found in Max Weber's *Ancient Judaism* (New York: The Free Press, 1952; London: Allen & Unwin).
6. For a masterful discussion of the clash between Yahwist faith and the ideology of kingship, see Eric Voegelin, *Order and History*, Vol. I: "Israel and Revelation" (Baton Rouge: Louisiana State University Press, 1956), Part III, pp. 185ff.

CHAPTER 3

The Style of the Secular City

Technopolis, like the civilization it displaces, has its own characteristic style. The word *style* here refers to the way a society projects its own self-image, how it organizes the values and meanings by which it lives. The secular-urban style springs in part from the societal shape provided by the anonymity and mobility we have just discussed. But it is not merely a product of these factors. The style has a life of its own which in turn influences and alters the shape on which it is based. Style and shape affect each other. Both comprise that configurational whole which we have called the *manière d'être* of the secular city.

Two motifs in particular characterize the style of the secular city. We call them *pragmatism* and *profanity*. We use these words at some risk of confusion, since for many people pragmatism refers to a particular movement in American philosophy and profanity simply means obscene language. Both these usages are derivative, however, and our intention here is to call to mind their original meanings.

By *pragmatism* we mean secular man's concern with the question "Will it work?" Secular man does not occupy himself much with mysteries. He is little interested in anything that seems resistant to the application of human energy and intelligence. He judges ideas, as the dictionary suggests in its definition of pragmatism, by the "results they will achieve in practice." The world is viewed not as a unified metaphysical system but as a series of problems and projects.

By *profanity* we refer to secular man's wholly terrestrial horizon, the disappearance of any supramundane reality defining his life. *Pro-fane* means literally "outside the temple"— thus "having to do with this world." By calling him profane, we do not suggest that secular man is sacrilegious, but that he is unreligious. He views the world not in terms of some other world but in terms of itself. He feels that any meaning he finds must be found in this world itself. Profane man is simply *this*-worldly.

To make even clearer what we mean by pragmatism and profanity, two characteristically twentieth-century men will be introduced as personifications of these elements of the secular style. The late American President John F. Kennedy embodies the spirit of the pragmatic; Albert Camus, the late French novelist and playwright, illustrates what we mean by this-worldly profanity.

In the preceding chapter, we rejected some of the condemnations of anonymity and mobility that are often made by religious people. We insisted that these elements give shape to urban life and that without them it would be less than human. We showed also that if one evaluates such things in the light of the Bible rather than from the perspective of preurban society, a real appreciation for both is possible. The shape of the secular city does not necessarily contradict the framework of biblical faith.

But what about its style? That is a more difficult matter. Certainly the contrast, even the contradiction, between the style of the secular city and our traditional faith appears at first glance to be serious. Indeed, if we do accept man as pragmatic and profane, we seem to sabotage the cornerstone of the whole theological edifice. If secular man is no longer interested in the ultimate mystery of life but in the "pragmatic" solution of particular problems, how can anyone talk to him meaningfully about God? If he discards suprahistorical meanings and looks in his "profanity" to human history itself as the source of purpose and value, how can he comprehend any religious claim at all? Should not theologians first divest modern man of his pragmatism and his profanity, teach him once again to ask and to wonder, and then come to him with the Truth from Beyond?

No. Any effort to desecularize and deurbanize modern man, to rid him of his pragmatism and his profanity, is seriously mistaken. It wrongly presupposes that a man must first become "religious" before he can hear the Gospel. It was Dietrich Bonhoeffer who firmly rejected this erroneous assumption and pointed out that it bore a striking parallel to the long-discarded idea that one had to be circumcised a Jew before becoming a Christian. Bonhoeffer insists that we must find a nonreligious interpretation of the Gospel for secular man. He is right. Pragmatism and profanity, like anonymity and mobility, are not obstacles but avenues of access to modern man. His very pragmatism and profanity enable urban man to discern certain elements of the Gospel which were hidden from his more religious forebears.

John F. Kennedy and Pragmatism

Urban-secular man is pragmatic. In the dictionary sense of the word, this means he concerns himself with "practical or material affairs" and is interested in the "actual working out of an idea in experience." He devotes himself to tackling specific problems and is interested in what will work to get something done. He has little interest in what have been termed "borderline questions" or metaphysical considerations. Because religion has concerned itself so largely precisely with these things, he does not ask "religious" questions.

The preceding paragraph could very well serve as a thumbnail sketch of the political style of John F. Kennedy. Once at a dinner party, a guest seated next to Walt W. Rostow, at that time planning director for the State Department, asked him what President Kennedy was "really like." After some hesitation Rostow replied, "Well, I would use one word to characterize him. He is a pragmatist." Though cryptic, Rostow's answer was actually exeedingly apt. Mr. Kennedy represented just that no-nonsense practicality and interest in workable solutions that is best characterized by the word *pragmatism*.

From Europe comes a similar judgment about the late President. Writing on the mastery of technological civilization, World Council of Churches staff member Harry O. Morton reminds us quite rightly that such mastery "requires the competence to isolate a problem, to exclude from view enough of the important but not immediately relevant data in order that one may study the problem by itself, and thus find for it a workable solution."[1] Morton concedes that all such solutions are only partial and temporary, that if they work they will in fact present us with a whole new series of problems, and this is just what we expect to happen. Most interesting for our purposes, Morton uses John F. Kennedy to illustrate this method. He describes the Kennedy administration as one which "springs from this approach rather than from a systematically developed ideology." Morton was especially impressed with Kennedy's flair for bringing together teams of experts "to study special problems and to work out an immediate coherent policy in a limited field."

To say that technopolitan man is pragmatic means that he is a kind of modern ascetic. He disciplines himself to give up certain things. He approaches problems by isolating them from irrelevant considerations, by bringing to bear the knowledge of different specialists, and by getting ready to grapple with a new series of problems when these have been provisionally solved. Life for him is a set of problems, not an unfathomable mystery. He brackets off the things that cannot be dealt with and deals with those that can. He wastes little time thinking about "ultimate" or "religious" questions. And he can live with highly provisional solutions. He sees the world not so much as an awesome enigma evoking a sense of hushed reverence, but as a series of complex and interrelated projects requiring the application of competence. He rarely ponders what we usually call religious questions because he feels he can handle this world adequately without them.

Technopolitan man's understanding of truth is therefore pragmatic. Does this exclude him from biblical faith? The core question we must ask is, What does the Bible, especially the Old Testament, mean by truth, and Can this truth be reconciled with the pragmatic meaning of truth which characterizes the technopolitan style?

To cast some light on this question we turn to the thought of C. A. van Peursen, a sociologist and lay theologian who now occupies the chair of philosophy at the University of Leiden in the Netherlands.[2] Although relatively unknown to the English-speaking world, van Peursen's profoundly original work on numerous subjects is beginning to arouse notice. Certainly in the field of the theology of secularization, he makes an indispensable contribution. Deeply interested in the relationship between types of societies and ways of perceiving reality, van Peursen believes that we now find ourselves in a period of transition from what he calls the "ontological" to what he calls the "functional" period of human history. The ontological era replaced an earlier one which he calls the "mythical." These three eras, with their respective ways of grasping reality, correlate very closely to what we have called the tribal, town, and technopolitan epochs, each with its characteristic *manière d'être*.

In the period of myth, says van Peursen, the world is one of "fascination," a world of what he calls "socio-mythological space." It corresponds with what we have called "the enchanted forest." In this period the subject is merged with the object in what is essentially a magic world. In the period of

ontology, man is freed from the fear of magic. The gods retire
to some supernatural abode and leave the world to man. The
sacred is separated from the profane. An interest develops in
the "nature of things" and objects are slowly organized into a
hierarchy, a "great chain of being." Things are viewed as
essences, having a kind of substantial being. This is the period
of the appearance of the polis or town. It witnesses the emergence of what van Peursen calls "ontological thinking" and its
peculiar danger, he says, is that it becomes "substantialistic,"
isolating the substances, dealing with "things in themselves."

In our emerging functional period, thinking is no longer
reflection on isolated substances, but is "a tool of concrete
human lives, of the functioning of human society." In fact,
secularization itself, van Peursen believes, can be viewed in
this light:

> In a secularized world, there is no longer an ontological
> way of thinking, a thinking about higher . . . metaphysical
> beings. . . . Now we are liberated from all these unreal
> supernatural entities; . . . Only that which is directly related
> to us is real. Things do not exist in themselves; they are no
> longer substances, but they exist in and for the sake of
> what they do with us and what we do with them.[3]

In the functional era, corresponding to technopolis, things
become things to do. "The nouns of the ontological era,"
says van Peursen, "become the verbs of the functional era."
We are concerned with thinking rather than with thought,
with acting justly rather than with justice, with the "art of
loving" rather than with love. To sum up the whole sequence,
van Peursen says:

> In the period of myth, the main issue was *that* something
> is; in the period of ontological thinking, it was *what* some-
> thing is; in the period of functional thinking, it is *how*
> something is, how it functions.[4]

Clearly, van Peursen has described in philosophical terms
what we mean here by pragmatism. The question remains,
however, whether the functional-pragmatic view of truth con-
tradicts the biblical tradition. Must pragmatic man discard the
Bible?

Van Peursen does not think so. He believes quite strongly
not only that the view of truth emerging in the functional era
does *not* depart from the Bible, but that it actually coheres
much better with the Bible than did the mythical or ontological definitions it displaces. He demonstrates his case by a
careful study of how the Hebrew word *'emeth,* usually trans-

lated "truth," as used in the Old Testament. The word designates something that can be counted on, something that is found to be dependable. It is used to refer to a vine which bears fruit, as expected, in the fall. God is spoken of as true because He does what He says He will do. He delivers the slaves from captivity and is thus true to His people. Performance is the yardstick of truth. There is no necessary contradiction between the biblical view of truth and that which is emerging in our functional society.[5]

Van Peursen's verdict should not surprise us. The Jews had no gift for ontology at all. Asked about Yahweh, the average Old Testament Israelite would never have answered in terms of metaphysical categories—omniscience, omnipresence, and the like. He would have told his interrogator what Yahweh had *done*: brought him up out of the land of Egypt, the house of bondage. This is a functional, not an ontological, way of speaking and conceptualizing.

There is still another way, however, in which the pragmatic style of technopolitan man coheres with the biblical images of truth. That the pragmatist works at his problems one at a time testifies to his belief in the order of things. Conversely, it is a mark of unbelief in the ontologist that he must always scurry about to relate every snippet to the whole fabric. One suspects that he fears the universe will fall into pieces unless his conceptualization constantly fixes everything in place. In the article mentioned earlier, Harry Morton eloquently expresses the confidence inherent in the pragmatic approach:

> . . . the fact that we approach life today without feeling the need for a big key that fits everything together as one great whole, and are able to concentrate instead on isolating particular issues and dealing with them as they come up, shows that we have a basic confidence that the world is held together, is strong, is self-consistent, has regularity in it and can be put to the test without everything in life going to pieces.[6]

He goes on to suggest that operating in this fashion is to believe what Paul said to the Colossians, that it is God who in Jesus Christ holds the world together. So we do not have to be afraid that if *we* do not, it will splinter into fragments.

This is not to say of course that we should have no interest in unifying and organizing the diverse congeries of factual information by which we are inundated in the modern world. But the way we unify truth today is not through subsuming it in a metaphysical system—we unify it by bringing it to bear

on specific human problems. Truth is unified pragmatically.
The teams of specialists from various fields who bring their
disparate specializations to bear on the problem of cancer,
or synthesizing protein, or planning a new downtown area for
a city, or simply confronting a community problem—these
people are unwittingly doing what the metaphysical systems
of the past tried to do. They are pulling the various strands of
knowledge together into a cord that will serve a particular
human need. In this experience, they find that they are all
human beings, that they need each other, and that as a group
they need the teams which are at work on other problems. It
is through this pragmatic process that technopolitan man
unifies the truth he is doing.

So understood, pragmatic truth does not seem such a sheer
contradiction to biblical categories. We may begin to see why
the New Testament word for truth, *aletheia,* constantly appears in syntactical contexts we once found jarring. Jesus says
he *is* the truth and that his followers should *do* the truth. He
constantly gauged truth by what people did rather than what
they said. These passages become considerably less puzzling if
we stop trying to read them with an ontological view of truth
and interpret them instead as expressions of that effective
truth which is found both in the Bible and in the emerging
functional era.

But pragmatism as a style and a method should never be
allowed to degenerate into pragmatism as a new ontology.
The danger of functional thinking is that it narrows into "op-
erationalism." This hazard arises when, having isolated some
particular aspect of a phenomenon for special attention, we
then forget that there *are* other aspects. It results from taking
a helpfully restricted view of something and then deciding
there is nothing more to it—the age-old temptation to forget
that there are an infinite number of ways to look at the same
blackbird.

The same aberration must be guarded against in a society
like ours which judges everything in terms of "usefulness."
The secular man asks most frequently of the stranger he
meets *not* who he *is* but what he *does.* Or, to be more accurate, when he asks who someone *is* the answer he expects is a
description of what that person *does.* Thus the question of
meaning is identified with the question of purpose, human
serviceability.

There is nothing intrinsically wrong with seeing meaning
and value in terms of human purpose. The existentialist claim

that our culture is meaningless or purposeless is simply wrong. Our culture does *not* lack purpose; it lacks only the particular purpose the existentialists had grown used to. Our culture *is* a teleological, or purpose-oriented, culture, and man is the fashioner of purposes. We size things up by asking what they are *for,* and to say of something or of someone that he is useless is about the worst thing we can say.

But usefulness, like pragmatism, must not degenerate into a new closed world view. To write off artistic beauty, poetry, or even whole groups of people because they appear useless constitutes a terrible threat. Hitler wanted to gas Jews, invalids, and mentally retarded people because they could not make a contribution to the New Order of the Third Reich. People whose outlook *is* influenced by technological utopianism (for instance some of the scientific and business elites in the U.S.A. and the U.S.S.R.) tend to denigrate abstract art and music as worthless because to them it serves no useful function. Students and young adults with compulsive career orientations shun any hobby, recreation, or pastime which does not make a direct contribution to their professional development. So there are dangers here, but the dangers do not lie in the subsuming of worth and meaning under purpose. They lie rather in the catastrophic *narrowing* of the idea of usefulness and thus of worth to the purposes and programs one's own group considers important. The peril lies in an unwillingness to widen and deepen the purview of significant human purposes to include those outside the orbit of one's group or nation.

Thus neither Nazis nor technological utopians are really secular or pragmatic. They represent groups which are still to some extent bogged down in the mythical or metaphysical stages of human development. For Hitler it was sometimes "God" and sometimes the *Zeitgeist* which had called him to fulfill Germany's destiny. The meaning of history was to be consummated in a Thousand-Year Reich. For the orthodox Communist there is an inner logic in history which is not dependent on man, a meaning to which man must adjust his personal projects or suffer the consequences. So long as it preserves elements of this fatalism, communism will continue to be a kind of godless "religion." Likewise, for the American business careerist, success is a residual religious vocation. It is *the* meaning, not *a* meaning, of life—and he cannot tolerate suggestions that there may be highly divergent patterns of life within which people find significance in ways totally different from his. Hence, for example, the bureaucrat's fear and resentment of the beatnik.

The rejection of meanings which do not contribute to those of one's own group is the opposite of secularization. It is a remnant of the metaphysical period when *"the* meaning of history" seemed discernible. It is a leftover of tribal and town culture in which radical inclusiveness had still not emerged. Augustine's God or Adam Smith's invisible hand or Karl Marx's dialectic as *the* pattern moving behind and within all the events of history entails for the devotee a necessary intolerance of other views and purposes.

On the other hand, when history *is* seen to be man's responsibility, the justification for inquisition is called into question. If men rather than metaphysical phantoms bear the meaning of historic life, then purposes other than those of one's own clan can be appreciated rather than repudiated. Separate world views present the occasion not for mutual destruction but for fashioning a societal framework within which such variance can be encouraged and nourished. Ideally the secular city is such a society. It provides a setting in which a hodgepodge of human purposes and projects can thrive because each recognizes itself as provisional and relative. Authentic secularity demands that no world view, no tradition, no ideology be allowed to become *the* officially enforced world view beside which no others are tolerated. This in turn requires pluralistic social and political institutions.

We should not be dismayed by the fact that fewer and fewer people are pressing what we have normally called "religious" questions. The fact that urban-secular man is incurably and irreversibly pragmatic, that he is less and less concerned with religious questions, is in no sense a disaster. It means that he is shedding the lifeless cuticles of the mythical and ontological periods and stepping into the functional age. He is leaving behind the styles of the tribe and the town and is becoming a technopolitan man. As such he may now be in a position to hear certain notes in the biblical message that he missed before. He may be ready, in some respects, to "do the truth" in a way his superstitious and religious forerunners were not.

Albert Camus and Profanity

When the Nobel Prize committee named Albert Camus recipient of the award for literature in 1957, they cited him correctly as the one who "illuminates the problems of the human conscience in our time." Camus addressed himself to the most salient issue of the modern consciousness: how to live with direction and integrity in a world without God. For Camus, however, the absence of God was not simply a lamentable fact; it was a necessary reality. Hopes and values which reach beyond this world he rejected as a betrayal of this world and therefore of one's fellow man. Unlike Voltaire, who said, "If God did not exist, we should have to invent Him," Camus would say, aligning himself with Bakunin, "If God *did* exist, we should have to abolish Him."

For Camus there was an unavoidable contradiction between the existence of God and human responsibility. He had to be an atheist. But every atheist must be a particular kind of atheist: He must disbelieve in some particular God. Camus was plainly a classical "Christian atheist." He found the God of orthodox Christian theology irreconcilable with human freedom and justice. Therefore he had to reject him. Yet he did not do so in a mood either of vindictiveness or of despair, and this is what propelled Camus far beyond the anguished existentialism of many of his contemporaries. Though he began with a declaration that the world was absurd, he refused any forlorn or crestfallen response to such a reality. Instead, he celebrated the joy of what he called "the invincible summer" within, the sheer beatitude of human reciprocity.

Camus did not allow his atheism to deteriorate into a fanatic antitheism, which would have been a new religion. He soon lost the stridency of his early novel *The Stranger,* and modulated his tone. He was more interested in this world, its hopes and its pains, than he was in the nonexistence of some other world. In this sense he was like Kennedy who, though he was a Roman Catholic, did not allow his belief in some other world to divert him from a passionate concern for this one. Both Kennedy and Camus were secular men; both focused on the issues which torment men within the terrestrial horizon. For Kennedy these were problems of politics, for Camus they were the issues of ethics and meaning.

Camus knew that there is an essential contradiction between the traditional Christian doctrine of God and the full freedom and responsibility of man. He faced this contradiction in all its seriousness, and we must face it too. In grappling with the issue, Camus is a true child of the French Revolution. He follows in the footsteps of Pierre Joseph Proudhon (1809–1865), who first enunciated many of the themes Camus picked up. "God is *the* evil," Proudhon once wrote, since he deprives man of his own creative power and prevision. Therefore, for Proudhon, "the first duty of free and intelligent man is to chase the idea of God out of his conscience incessantly."[7] History is a contest between God and man, and man will achieve his victory only by casting the divine enemy from his throne.

There is a good deal of posturing and hyperbole in Proudhon, but he really believed that he and his radical associates were carrying on the work of "defatalization" begun by the early Christians. He saw, as we have noted, that the first Christians were secularizers, and he believed that the time had come to push their work still further. They had banished the pagan gods and freed man from the furies. They were accused by their contemporaries of being atheists. Proudhon saw himself as their successor, and Camus is the successor of Proudhon. Toward the end of his life, even Proudhon tempered his style somewhat, so that the similarity of his mood to Camus' becomes even more striking. The following passage from his *Positive Philosophy* vividly recalls the atmosphere of Camus' *The Plague*:

> Today civilization is indeed in a critical stage. . . . All traditions are used up, all beliefs abolished. . . . Everything contributes to sadden people of good will. . . . We shall struggle in the night, and we must do our best to endure this life without too much sadness. Let us stand by each other, call out to each other in the dark, and do justice as often as an opportunity is given.[8]

Camus could easily have written these words. Free of the vivid rhetoric of his predecessor, and without his adolescent promethianism, Camus nevertheless quietly insisted that man must choose between the tyrant God of Christian theology and being a full man. Having made this choice, man could then turn his full attention to striving for justice "as often as the opportunity is given."

I believe that the choice Camus presents us with is an unavoidable one, and that given the choice as he understood it, we can only choose with him. A God who emasculates man's creativity and hamstrings his responsibility for his fellow man must be dethroned. Nietzsche and Marx as well as Proudhon saw this. The difference is that in our period the issue is being forced not by a few scattered intellectuals who style themselves atheists, but by the whole character of urban-

secular civilization. Camus spoke not for a tiny conventicle
but for the entire emerging generation.

The central question is: What are the sources of meaning
and value by which man lives his life? Are they created and
imposed by God, or does man invent them himself? It is
characteristic of urban-secular man that he perceives himself
as the source of whatever significance the human enterprise
holds. His perception is confirmed by modern cultural anthropology and by the sociology of knowledge. Symbol systems, the constellations of meaning by which human life is
given value and direction, are seen as projections of a given
society. They change when the society changes and in predictable ways. There is nothing timeless or divine about them.

But does not this theory of the source of meaning in human
life rob God of His divine prerogative? How can we accept
this grandiose assessment of man's place in the universe without at the same time limiting or degrading God?

In answering these questions, it is important to emphasize
again that Camus was a particular kind of atheist. The God
he rejected, rightly I believe, is the God of traditional Christian theism. But I believe both Camus' rejection and the
Christian defense of this God are misplaced. Both Camus'
atheism and Christian theism stem from a deficient doctrine
of God, itself a remnant of the metaphysical era. They arise
because of a concept of God that is not biblical but essentially
Platonic or Aristotelian. If we allow the traditional metaphysical categories by which we have conceptualized God to
be corrected by the Bible, I believe Camus' objection to the
tyrant God can be met at least in part. In fact, an authentically biblical doctrine of God not only survives the view that
man himself is the source of cultural meanings, but actually
supports and encourages such a view. An examination of the
ancient Yahwist account of Creation, dating from 950 B.C.
and found now in Genesis 2:4–24, substantiates this claim.

In one of the most picturesque sequences from this provocative story, Yahweh decides that it is not good that the
man He has created should be alone. So Yahweh forms out of
ground "every beast of the field and every bird of the air"
(2:19). But then comes the theologically decisive segment.
Yahweh brings all these creatures to man "to see what he
would call them." Man gives them all names—the cattle, the
birds, the beasts, and, as the Yahwist writer concludes, "whatever man called every living creature, that was its name."

This is a truly remarkable passage. Every syllable is loaded with rich theological overtones. The passage indicates that man has a crucial part to play in the creation of the world. The world is not really finished, not really "the world" until its components are "named." For the Hebrew, naming did not mean simply attaching an arbitrary label. It meant conferring on something its meaning and significance. As Gerhard von Rad says, the naming of the animals is the way man "incorporates them into his life."[9]

The act of naming here is an original and creative one. Man does not "form" the animals, but he does give them their names. Yet naming and forming must not be too widely separated. As God begins his activity in Genesis 1, the earth is described as "without form" and "void." God's creative activity includes forming, separating, and naming. Then, after He creates man, He enlists him in this creating activity. Thus the world does not come to man already finished and ordered. It comes in part confused and formless and receives its significance from man. Since man names the animals, the meaning they have comes from the fact that they are incorporated into his life. Their significance arises from their being a part of his projects and purposes. Von Rad goes on to remind us that "name-giving in the ancient Orient was primarily an exercise of sovereignty, of command."[10] For this reason he holds that the animal naming passage must be read in close connection with Genesis 1:28, where man is commanded by God to "have dominion over the fish of the sea and over the birds of the air. . . ."

Here is a truly exalted view of man. God does not simply insert man into a world filled with creatures which are already named, in relationships and meaning patterns already established by decree. Man must fashion them himself. He doesn't simply discover meaning; he originates it.

Compare this biblical description of the relation between God and man with the Platonic version. Part of Plato's concern in devising his famous theory of Ideas was precisely this problem of "naming" things. He wondered how the words *man* or *dog* or *tree,* which are attached to numerous different things, had any reality. Where was *the* "dog" of which all these poodles and Pekingese were merely expressions? His answer was his theory of Ideas. Plato asserted that the objects of our knowledge are not the physical things we perceive in this world of appearances, but a series of changeless, perfect, and eternal ideas all of which are eventually ordered and subordinated under what he called the Idea of the Good.

These timeless ideas can in no sense be man's creation. He perceives them, rather, by an act of intuition. The "names" precede men, not vice versa.

The identification of Plato's Idea of the Good with the idea of God as *ens realissimum,* the most real of all entities in Christian theology, has been a basic element of Christian philosophy down through the centuries. A. E. Taylor, the distinguished British Platonic scholar, once wrote:

> The distinguishing characteristic of the "Form of the Good" is that it is the transcendent source of all the reality and intelligibility of everything other than itself. . . . It is the supreme value and the source of all other value. . . . Thus, it seems to me, metaphysically the Form of the Good is what Christian philosophy has meant by God and nothing else.[11]

Although Taylor's opinion is not unanimously held, it reflects a long tradition in Western philosophy in which the biblical God and the Platonic Idea of the Good have been melted down and coalesced into a new alloy. But in the process something essential to the biblical God has been lost. Even when Aristotle urged, in criticism of Plato, that the ideas had no anterior existence (*ante res*) but were to be found *in* the things themselves (*in rebus*), the task of man was still restricted merely to discovering, not inventing, the images by which the world is understood.

For the Greeks, man's role as creator of meaning was not very significant. In fact man, for the Greeks, is not a creator at all. Even God does not really create. Yale philosopher John Wild correctly senses the woodenness and lack of real creativity in the Aristotelian version of "creation," later adopted by St. Thomas, when he says that it "confuses creation with causation." But the fatal consequence, as Wild sees it, is that the human mind is not regarded as an active source of meanings; it is rather the passive receiver of a timeless structure of things that has been established once and for all."[12]

Because St. Thomas follows Aristotle, the relationship of God and man in the Thomistic theological tradition bears only a vestigial resemblance to the biblical account. The world is no longer something to be shaped and celebrated but is a hierarchical cosmic order "fixed and finished for all time."[13] A careful study of the traditions of Athens and Jerusalem demonstrates that Hellenistic man bears far *less* responsibility than biblical man in the creative work of God. Our urban-secular man is more biblical than Greek, and the distance between him and the Bible is not so impassable as some have imagined.

It is ironic in view of the comparison just made between the status of man in Plato and Aristotle and in Genesis that Greek philosophy, rather than the Bible, has frequently been read by Western philosophers as the source of the loftiest humanism. I think this represents an inaccurate interpretation. Naturally there are many other biblical images which have entered into the consideration, mainly the doctrine of the Fall, but much of this questionable reading has been due precisely to the attempt to fuse Greek and biblical images into what A. E. Taylor referred to as "Christian philosophy." It has produced an endless succession of insoluble conundrums and has seriously adulterated the biblical view to the point where it is simply incompatible with our experience. Only now, with the emergence of the secular city and its culture, do we begin to see how ambiguous the whole matter has become.

Generations of biblical scholars, charmed by the spell of the Greeks, have overlooked or minimized the astonishing fact that the Creation is *not* completed by God in the Bible until after man is formed and begins to work as God's partner in ordering the chaos. This means, in effect, that creation is *never* really "complete." The Genesis stories depict something that man and God are always doing. Part of the error of Christian philosophy has arisen from a rather mechanical insistence on a *creatio ex nihilo*. Without denying that God does bring the world into being out of nothing, we must go on to see, with Gerhard von Rad, that this is not the real point. The concern of the Genesis narrative "moves not so much between the poles of nothingness and creation as between the poles of chaos and cosmos."[14] God orders the chaos by giving it names ("God called the light Day, and the darkness he called Night," v. 3). Man participates along with God by naming the living creatures (2:20) and the woman (3:20). Together God and man devise the emblems and meanings by which anarchic confusion becomes a world. When we read the record this way, the tyrant deity of both atheism and theism disappears, and the partnership of Yahweh and man comes into focus.

The willingness of the classical philosophers to allow the Holy One of Israel to be blurred into Plato's Idea of the Good or Aristotle's Prime Mover was fatal. It has resulted in a doctrine of God which in the era of the secular city forces men like Camus to choose *between* God and human freedom, between Christian faith and human creativity. It has led Christianity into a cautious unwillingness to abandon the values and institutions of previous eras and has produced a mentality more given to the reshuffling and rearranging of what is than to the imaginative projection of what might be. Since classic Greek philosophy necessitated a changeless objective order to which we must constantly strive to assimilate, radical human inventiveness seemed impossible. But the confusion seems to have run its course. As John Wild says in his ringing rebuttal of Plato, "We may doubt whether the objective universe is in any sense prior to the human life-world and independent of it."[15]

Professor Wild is not, of course, denying the existence of a physical solar system before the appearance of the anthropoids. He means that the ordered, objective, knowable world is not simply "there" awaiting man's pedestrian efforts to uncover it. Rather, the meaningful ordering of the world is itself a human enterprise, an undertaking which man assumes as God's partner. His statement reminds us once again that the Genesis accounts of the Creation are not concerned with the geologic origins of the universe. They have to do with the creation of a "world," a cosmos of meaning which is wrestled out of a chaos of disorder.

The extraction of the biblical doctrine of God from the metaphysical solvent in which it has been suspended provides one of the most important theological challenges of our day, one we shall treat further in a later chapter. It would be patronizing to suggest that if it were accomplished, men like Camus would suddenly become Christians, however. It is not correct to imply that the difference between men of faith and serious skeptics is merely verbal. There are genuine differences between the two which cannot be overlooked. But it is precisely to uncover and clarify these real differences that we must expose and discard the unreal ones. Whether or not he gives credence to the tenets of classical theism is not what separates the Christian from Camus.

We have found technopolitan man to be pragmatic and profane. But in taking him seriously in his pragmatism and profanity, we have found that he stands at these very points closer to the biblical view of man than did his religious and metaphysical predecessors of preurban culture. Still, it might be suggested that there is something ironic in our having

called upon John F. Kennedy and Albert Camus as personifications of the buoyant reasonableness and calm sense of assurance which characterizes the best in our epoch. Not only
are there other, darker currents in our time, but both these
men have become for some people symbols of blind fate and
human futility. Both were dashed into oblivion by eruptions
of irrationality. The careers of both were terminated just as
they had begun to flower, one by an assassin's bullet and the
other in an automobile crash. Do not their meaningless early
deaths conjure up the dark irrational fears of our world and
call into question the notions of adulthood and reasoning
responsibility they championed?

I think not. Though Kennedy was an artist in the application of reason to politics, and his alleged assassin seems a
character from the pages of a Dostoyevski novel, it is still the
spirit of Kennedy which triumphs, not that of his murderer.
In the same way for Camus, not even the terror of wars and
concentration camps could cause him to change the judgment
with which he ends *The Plague*—"there are more things to
admire in men than to despise."

Tillich, Barth, and the Secular Style

Our affirmation of the pragmatism and profanity of secular
man raises some troublesome questions about the approaches
used by two well-known systematic theologians who have
vigorously attempted to speak to the man of our age. In their
own ways, both Paul Tillich and Karl Barth launched ambi-
tious efforts to grasp the nettle of modern man's secularity
and to bring the message of the Bible to him. Tillich has done
it by a daring utilization of existentialism and depth psychology; Barth has done it by trying to penetrate the layers of
idealism and ideology which have clung like barnacles to the
inherited Gospel and find again the authentic Word of God.
How does our diagnosis of the style of secular man comport
with what they are doing?

It coheres somewhat better with Barth than with Tillich,
although at important points it departs rather widely from
both. Tillich was the great pioneer of theological analysis of
culture. He invented and refined some of the methods used
in this book. There can be little doubt, however, that much
of the foregoing analysis calls Tillich's theological method
into radical question. Tillich's approach has no place

for pragmatic man. It is built on the assumption that man by his very nature *must* ask these "ultimate" or existential questions. Admittedly, Tillich said such questions are asked in different forms by different ages. First-century man was concerned about death and immortality, sixteenth-century man about guilt and punishment; twentieth-century man is disturbed by the threat of meaninglessness. But the question, he insisted, is always asked; and beneath each of these formulations lurks the same basic question of "ultimate concern." We must uncover and bring to consciousness this ultimate concern, Tillich argued, for it poses the question for which the Gospel is the answer.

Tillich spoke to those who still feel the need to ask "religious" questions even when they are asked in nontraditional ways. These are questions he believed to be inherent in the very structure of human existence. The difficulty, however, is that they are obviously *not* questions which occur to everyone, or indeed to the vast majority of people. They do not trouble the newly emergent urban-secular man very frequently. They arise, in fact, not from the structures of existence at all but from the erosion of inherited world views and cultural meanings. They express the shock and terror of those who wake in the night to find that their whole theistic faith has been built on a conjecture. Like existentialism, which is its formal philosophical expression, the "ultimate question" Tillich wants us all to ask arises from Western man's realization that the Hegelian synthesis held no title to foundation in reality, that Christian civilization is gone and that its God is dead. Tillich's life spanned the years of this frightening realization, and he spoke with unparalleled power to those whose spiritual life is defined by the same transition. He was thus the theologian's theologian, the indispensable comforter of those who grew up in a faith they can no longer believe.

But today's urban-secular man has not lived through this loss of innocence. He was never innocent to begin with. He has never been shaken by the cruel discovery that the meanings he took to be designed by God, or at least written into the nature of things, turned out to be humanly conceived and replaceable. Since to him the world has always appeared devoid of any built-in meaning, he tends to be puzzled by Tillich's fascination with "meaninglessness." Also Tillich's "God above God" who appears, as he said in *The Courage to Be*,[16] when the traditional theistic God "has disappeared in the anxiety of doubt," never gets a chance to appear, since the traditional God was never there to disappear in the first place. As for "the anxiety of doubt" about the God of theism, the closest today's man gets to such a state is a mild curiosity or at most a kind of wistfulness. Urban-secular man came to town after the funeral for the religious world view had been held. He feels no sense of deprivation and has no interest in mourning.

Both philosophical existentialism and Paul Tillich's theology are expressions of the mourning period which began with the death of the God of metaphysical theism and Western Christian civilization, but the wake is now over. That is why existentialist theologies and philosophies do not partake of the spirit of the emerging age but symbolize rather the passing of the old. There is a certain validity to the Marxist assertion that existentialism is a "symptom of bourgeois decadence," since its categories of *Angst* and vertigo seem increasingly irrelevant to the ethos of the new epoch. In the age of the secular city, the questions with which we concern ourselves tend to be mostly functional and operational. We wonder how power can be controlled and used responsibly. We ask how a reasonable international order can be fashioned out of the technological community into which we have been hurried. We worry about how the wizardry of medical science can be applied to the full without creating a world population constantly hovering on the brink of famine. These are pragmatic questions, and we are pragmatic men whose interest in religion is at best peripheral.

It *is* true that at the center of our pragmatic questions we can hear echoes of older ones about how to be saved, how to overcome guilt and insufficiency, how to discern significance, and how to live purposefully. But there is a real difference. In former ages, man looked to muses, gods, or "values" for the answers to his problems. Secular man relies on himself and his colleagues for answers. He does not ask the church, the priest, or God. This is not because he has no respect for religion. He is probably not an anticleric. He simply feels that the issues he is concerned with relate to a different field. Like all contemporaries, he is a specialist, usually scrupulously tolerant of those with a different specialty. So it is pointless and unfair to try to force secular man into asking religious questions, consciously or otherwise, before we can converse. We begin by accepting pragmatic man as he is, and this means we must part company with Tillich.

If it is in our acceptance of secular man's pragmatism that

we seem to cross swords with Tillich, it is in our second point, affirming his profanity, that we seem to be denying the characteristic contribution of Barth. Barth's whole emphasis in his earlier theology was to write a question mark next to man's capacity to bridge the gap to God. He wanted to reaffirm the utter and unquestionable initiative of God in acting for man in contrast to the various forms of culture-religion and religious humanism which had begun to appear. For this reason Barth's earliest work displayed a mood of sharp diastasis. The Gospel had to be separated from religion, God from man, heaven from earth. In his preface to the second edition of his famous *Epistle to the Romans,* Barth says: "If I have a system it consists in the fact that I keep . . . before me . . . what Kierkegaard has called the 'infinite qualitative distinction between time and eternity.' "[17]

Unfortunately, many Americans believe this is as far as Barth went. If it were, then the things we have just said about the partnership between man and God in the creative work of ordering and naming the world would be in sharp contrast to his theology. But in actuality, the diastasis formed only the preliminary stage in Barth's work. For years now he has emphasized ever more strongly that the most important thing to say about that yawning gap between God and man is that it has been bridged. God has crossed the chasm in Jesus Christ.

The two moments of Barth's theology form a necessary unity. The kindness of God in liberating man becomes even more glorious in the light of the "infinite qualitative distinction." But more important, by insisting with curmudgeonly stubbornness on the transcendence and total freedom of God, Barth set the stage for an understanding of human creativity which does not have to be atheistic. A God who is dependent on man turns out to be a terrible limitation on man's freedom and creativity. Whereas, as Paul Ramsey once wrote, "the transcendent God who lives his own life and creates man in his own image already has deity enough and is in no need of intrinsically limiting man's cultural life."[18]

The triumph of Barth's theology is a God who doesn't need man; therefore He can let man live. Only when God and man have been fully differentiated from one another can God come near to man without limiting and oppressing him. This may have been what Bonhoeffer meant when he wrote that ". . . we must not gloss over the ungodliness of the world, but expose it in a new light. Now that it has come of age, the world is more godless, and perhaps it is for that very reason nearer to God than ever before."[19] As the last stages of myth and ontology disappear, which they do in Barth's theology, man's freedom to master and shape, to create and explore, now reaches out to the ends of the earth and beyond.

In executing these two complementary movements in his theological development, it is not surprising that Barth did not succeed equally well with both. He does not work out so completely as he might have, for example, the full weight of the fact that God has chosen man to be his *partner*. If the partner is also the one who is created in God's image, then although original initiative is God's, derivative initiatives from man should find a larger place in theology and life.

Even so, no one can claim today that Barth has erected a theological edifice which denigrates the role of man. This typical quotation from his *Church Dogmatics* should show that man has an exalted place in Barth's system:

> It is apparent that the formula, "God is everything and man nothing" . . . is not merely a shocking simplification but complete nonsense. . . . By the grace of God man is not nothing. He is God's man. . . . He is recognized as himself a free subject, a subject who has been made free once and for all by his restoration as the free covenant partner of God. . . . We cannot say and demand and expect too much or too great things from man. . . .[20]

We cannot possibly expect too great things from man! Here stands the basis, admittedly not worked out to the full, of a theological view of man that would celebrate rather than deprecate his responsibility as creator of the meanings he lives by, as fashioner of the symbols that give direction to history. Barth himself has called for a "change of direction in the thinking of evangelical theology,"[21] which could mean a more thorough working out of the celebration of man which his theology makes possible.

We have affirmed technopolitan man in his pragmatism and in his profanity. To do so we have not abandoned the Bible; we have found, on the contrary, that its views of truth and of creation display important areas of similarity with the style of the secular city. We have found, however, that we have had to differ with Tillich at certain points and to go further than Barth was willing to go. There is no pathos in this. Theology is a living enterprise. The Gospel does not call man to return to a previous stage of his development. It does not summon man back to dependency, awe, and religiousness. Rather it is a call to imaginative urbanity and mature secularity. It is not a call to man to abandon his interest in the problems of this world, but an invitation to accept the full weight of this world's problems as the gift of its Maker. It is a call to be a man of this technical age, with all that means, seeking to make it a human habitation for all who live within it.

NOTES TO CHAPTER 3

1. Harry O. Morton, "The Mastery of Technological Civilization," *The Student World,* LVI (First Quarter 1963), 46.
2. C. A. van Peursen, "Man and Reality—the History of Human Thought," *The Student World,* LVI (First Quarter 1963), 13.
3. *Ibid.*, p. 16.
4. *Ibid.*, p. 17.
5. C. A. van Peursen, "The Concept of Truth in the Modern University," *The Student World,* LVI (Fourth Quarter 1963), 350.
6. Morton, *op. cit.*, p. 48.
7. Quoted in Karl Löwith, *Meaning in History* (Chicago: University of Chicago Press, 1949), p. 63.
8. *Ibid.*, p. 66
9. Gerhard von Rad, *Genesis, A Commentary* (Philadelphia: Westminster Press, 1961; London: SCM Press), p. 80.
10. *Ibid.*, p. 81.
11. A. E. Taylor, *Plato, the Man and His Work* (New York: Meridian, 1959), p. 289.
12. John Wild, *Human Freedom and Social Order* (Durham, N.C.: Duke University Press, 1959), p. 161.
13. *Ibid.*, p. 159.
14. Von Rad, *op. cit.*, p. 49.
15. Wild, *op. cit.*, p. 63.
16. Paul Tillich, *The Courage to Be* (New Haven: Yale University Press, 1952; London: Fontana Books), pp. 189–190.
17. For a good brief account of the development of Barth's theology, see Helmut Gollwitzer's introduction to selections of excerpts from Barth's *Church Dogmatics* (New York: Harper & Row, 1963; Edinburgh: T. & T. Clark).
18. Paul Ramsey, preface to Gabriel Vahanian, *The Death of God* (New York: Braziller, 1961), p. xxxvii.
19. Dietrich Bonhoeffer, *Letters and Papers from Prison* (New York: Macmillan, 1962), p. 224.
20. Karl Barth, *Church Dogmatics* (Edinburgh: T. & T. Clark, 1958), pp. 89, 90.
21. Karl Barth, *The Humanity of God* (Richmond: John Knox Press, 1960; London: Collins), p. 37.

CHAPTER 4

The Secular City in Cross-Cultural Perspective

The epoch of the secular city is breaking in all over the world, not alone in the West. The seeds of secularization, borne by traders and adventurers, missionaries and revolutionaries, have long since taken root, flowered, and begun to bear fruit. The urbanization of Latin America and India and the industrialization of Africa and China are proceeding with accelerated pace. As all this happens, it becomes clear that although secularization does exhibit certain common features wherever it occurs, the wide differences in the historical backgrounds of the cultures in which it takes root cause a marked diversity in the whole *manière d'être* of various technopolitan areas. No one secular city is quite like any other.

In this chapter, four cities representing four distinctive regions will illustrate the rich variety of the secularization process. It is clear that this heterogeneity is a valuable feature of the modern world, and should be guarded. A secular civilization need not be monochrome or homogenous. But the color and character lent by diversity cannot be left to chance. Like everything else in the secular city, variety must be planned for or it does not happen. This is something regional planners and urban-renewal experts must keep in mind. Contrast and diversity are an essential ingredient of a human environment. As man takes over from nature in shaping this environment, dissimilarity must be nurtured.

The four cities we shall visit in this chapter are New Delhi, Rome, Prague, and Boston. The author has firsthand acquaintance, in some cases brief, with all four. They represent the march of secularization and urbanization in, respectively, Southeast Asia, Western Europe, Eastern Europe, and the United States. Each of the four has felt the pressure of secularization differently, in part because of their diverse histories. The careers of these cities prove that the emergence of a worldwide urban civilization need not obliterate the distinctive coloration of particular cities or erase the uniqueness of their character.

This tour will also demonstrate an important distinction made in an earlier chapter—the difference between *secularization* as a historical movement and *secularism* as an ideology. The two should never be confused. Secularization is a liberating process. It dislodges ancient oppressions and overturns stultifying conventions. It turns man's social and cultural life over to him, demanding a constant expenditure of vision and competence. Secularism short-circuits the secular revolution by freezing it into a new world view. It clips the wings of emancipation and fixes a society on the pin of another orthodoxy. The objective of our round-the-world examination is to show that the polymorphic tone of secularization in different places calls for a decidedly different strategy on the part of the Christians who live in these areas, that diversity is a value worth defending and planning for, and that secular*ism* is a danger which must be fought in whatever guise it appears.

New Delhi and India

The mere existence of "New" Delhi is an evidence of the jarring changes that have come to India through its contact with the West. Built by the British between 1912 and 1929 to replace Calcutta as the capital city, New Delhi still presents a certain raw, unfinished look. It suggests what Washington, D.C., must have looked like during its early years. Fused with Old Delhi into the territory of Delhi, it is nonetheless a striking and even grandiose city. Ruins dating back to the centuries before the Mogul period silently recount the many eras through which Delhi has lived, but today it is in no sense a city facing the past. Delhi also throbs with more visible signs of cultural dislocation and social change than any other city I have seen.

In New Delhi and around its edges there are hungry people. Nowhere else does the specter of famine dog the steps of economic progress so relentlessly. Here the two pivotal indices are food production and population. Assuming that the birth rate does not decline significantly, India's population will reach five hundred million by 1971. Although some demographers expect a downward trend to begin about 1966, that may well be too late to head off the major gap between food needs and food production which seems to be in the making. A study by the Ford Foundation Agricultural Production Team pointed glumly in 1960 to the 3.2 per cent yearly rate of foodstuff increase and declared that the gap between supply and demand would reach twenty-eight million tons per year by 1966. It stated bluntly that "no conceivable program of imports or rationing could meet a crisis of this magnitude" and urged "an all-out emergency food production program."[1] Today Indian demographers and economists are less hopeless, but far from sanguine. India remains the last great testing ground of the capacity of a more or less democratic nation to solve the problem of hunger without restorting to totalitarian practices.

In addition to population and hunger, India still faces the challenge of unassimilated language, religious, and caste groups. A pitched battle still rages over whether Hindi, identified by all South Indians with the North, shall become the official language. Riots between Moslems and Hindus flare up periodically. Many observers believe that only the charismatic leadership of Nehru managed to hold India together through the past decade.

The future of India depends on continuing secularization. Tribal, caste, and religious interests must be subsumed by broader policy needs. They must be relativized—not discarded, but subordinated to the more crucial and more inclusive objective of achieving a balance between productivity and population. This raised—until his death in 1964—the problem of the so-called secularism of Nehru himself, and of the major elements of the Congress party. It provides also a particularly good example of the critical difference between secularism and secularization mentioned earlier.

Nehru, though a devoted disciple of Gandhi, was certainly not a religious man. He always grimaced painfully whenever he had to go through even the most perfunctory religious observance. Once at the dedication of a dam, he angrily waved away a Hindu *sadhu* who tried to anoint him with holy water. Nehru was in one sense a very "secular" man. But was he really a secularist in the sense we have described?

Nehru, ruled a country in which fratricidal religious battles have shed more blood than anywhere else in the world, yet a country justly known for its "spirituality." His view of religion sprang from a variety of sources. It had its roots in the bitter struggle for independence against a "Christian" nation, in the sophisticated this-worldliness of Harrow and Cambridge where Nehru was educated, and in the Marxism which once prompted him to break with his master over whether India should industrialize. Nehru's position was also forged in the fire of a lifetime of political combat against the Muslim League on the one side and the various Hindu parties on the other. In opposing these religious parties, Nehru always favored the "secular state," one in which public religious observances play no role, no faith is given even the smallest element of state support, and relations among the various religious groupings are managed with scrupulous impartiality.

In this sense, Nehru went at least as far as many of those who are so feared and despised as secularists by church leaders in many other countries. Why, then, did "secularist" Nehru win the consistent support of Indian Christians year after year?

The answer is that Nehru, however secular his personal convictions might have been, was never a dogmatic "secular*ist.*" He wanted India to be a secular state, and the overwhelming majority of Indian Christians have agreed. The alternative, especially since the partitioning of Pakistan, would probably be a Hindu sacral society. But even if it were not, India's vast variety of sects and religions, beside which North America's so-called pluralism must appear dully homogeneous, can survive only within a secular state. Also, since the deeply divisive castes represent remnants of kinship and tribal groupings, only further secularization will release Indians from the social fetters that caste imposes.

In India it is nearly indisputable that Christians should struggle for a "secular state." This may also be the case in Burma and Thailand, where the danger of sacralizing the state is always present. Thus in cultures where the emergence of a "secular state" from the dim history of sacral societies is beginning to occur, it is meaningless for Christians to murmur darkly against secularization. Such societies show with unusual clarity how secularization functions as emancipation, and Christians, as numerous pronouncements by Indian church leaders have indicated, should support it.

Rome and Western Europe

One can streak from New Delhi to Rome by Air India in a matter of hours. Again he finds himself in a city which, like New Delhi, displays for all to see evidences of the various periods through which it has lived. There are many Romes: There is the Rome of the spare and virtuous Republic, peopled by the lean-flanked children of Romulus and Remus.

There is the Rome of the top-heavy Empire, racked by intrigue and decay. There is the Rome of the Catholic centuries, where the popes, like the ghosts of the Caesars, reigned over a spiritual empire. There is the Rome of the revolution, where Garibaldi and Mazzini fought to liberate Italy from foreign and clerical control. There is the Rome of Mussolini, decked out in pseudo-Roman insignia and marching in lockstep to punctual trains which rushed a whole nation to catastrophe. Finally, there is the postwar Rome, first of *Open City* and then of *La Dolce Vita*, the official residence of film magnates, Fiat roadsters, and ennui.

All of these Romes can be seen in today's Rome. The city hides no secrets. One can wander from the imperial Forum to the Vatican Museum to the Via Veneto on foot, strolling from epoch to epoch with only the glut of traffic to hinder one's pilgrimage. The rampant secularization of Rome symbolizes in a particularly graphic way what has happened to all of Western Europe. It shouts a message we can hardly miss. Rome, though occupying the same seven hills it always has, is in actuality a very different entity than it was when Julius Caesar fell at the foot of Pompey's statue, or when a monk named Brother Martin recoiled in shock at the pomp and decadence of the Renaissance papacy, or when Henry James wrote from his sunlit balcony on the Corso in 1873 ". . . in Rome, in May, everything has an amiable side, even popular uprisings."[2] True enough, murders and decadence and even amiable uprisings are still a part of the Roman temper. But secularization, which has been thriving in Rome at least since the Renaissance, has recently come into its own; because this has happened in the capital city of Christendom, it provides an unusually fruitful case study. It also places all single-minded enemies of secularization on the defensive, for modern Rome remains one of the most humane and habitable places in the world.

But what about its rampant secularization? Should it not give us some pause to see secularization so undisguisedly operative in the cradle of Christendom? Hardly. Sacral civilizations, whatever their complexion, should cause no Christian tears when they depart. Since our eyes have been opened to the worldwide scope of the biblical faith, we can see now what we might not have noticed a few decades ago—that although it never became a *fully* sacral society, European "Christian civilization" in the medieval period bears a close resemblance to such classical sacral cultures as Inca Peru or Buddhist Tibet. Christianity was the religion of Europe. It was tied to European culture and identified as such by non-Europeans. But the so-called Constantinian era is over now and Christians should rejoice that it is. Slowly, ever so slowly, non-Europeans are beginning to accept a gospel which is not simply the religious sanctification of Western cultural values. The secularization of Europe has enabled us to see more clearly the truly "catholic" breadth of a faith which was once unimaginable without Greek metaphysics, Latin rituals, and Gothic architecture. Time was when to "be a Christian" meant simply to be born (and baptized) within the boundaries of Christendom. But since the discovery by Abbé Michonneau and Cardinal Souhard that France, as well as Mozambique, was a "land of mission" and the analogous awakenings of churches in Britain and Germany, this geographic theory of mission no longer holds. As Cardinal Souhard once said, France is a land full of baptized pagans.

There can be no authentic Christian sacral societies Spain to the contrary notwithstanding. There is no more "Christendom." The church exists everywhere in a "missionary situation," and this is precisely as it should be. Every parish is either what Abbé Michonneau calls a *communauté missionaire* or it is not a Christian parish at all, but a vestigial remnant of cultural Christendom.[3]

More than a hundred years ago Kierkegaard asked how it was even possible to be "a Christian in Christendom." He wondered how a man could say yes to the Gospel when its message was so obfuscated by its compromised involvement with European culture and bourgeois values.

Increasingly, the process of secularization in Europe has alleviated Kierkegaard's problem. Marxism of various kinds, existentialism in its different forms, the passionate humanism of Camus, and a kind of "what-the-hellism" associated with *la dolce vita* have increasingly presented Europeans with genuine, live options to Christian faith. More and more, "being a Christian" is a conscious choice rather than a matter of birth and inertia. The change can hardly be viewed as unfortunate.

The young European Christians one meets now in the German ESGs (Protestant Student Christian Movements) or the French JOCists (Young Catholic Workers) are not mourning the passing of Christendom. Many of them find the atmosphere of the new "post-Christian" Europe a bracing one.

They can now present the claims of the Gospel in university and trade union without having to apologize constantly for the bourgeois baggage of a decaying Christendom. Of course, there are dangers in the new European climate. Its affluence combines with the disorientation that haunts any transitional period to produce the kind of anomie reflected so well in, for example, the films of Jean-Luc Godard. But it is idle to suppose that the lostness of which these are the symptoms could be cured by hauling Europe back to one of its previous cultural syntheses—Victorian, Hapsburg, or medieval. The Christian church now has the opportunity to help forge a new spiritual fabric in Europe, one which will be truly humanistic and urbane, but in which the Christian faith, instead of supplying the ruling ethos, will provide one of the living options in a genuinely pluralistic culture.

Prague and Eastern Europe

When I visited Prague in 1963, I made these notes in my travel diary, the sentiment of which still holds today:

> Travelers all rave about Prague. "The most exquisite city between Florence and Leningrad," say some. I do not believe they exaggerate. My first full day began with a car trip through the center of the city to the venerable Carolinium of the University of Prague, the great assembly hall which is used only for very important academic occasions. It was a splendid day. The sun burned jagged spots into the minted roof of St. Vitus Cathedral. The river Moldau seemed to be humming the broad bars of Smetana's anthem, and I could imagine the ghost of a thin, coal-eyed Franz Kafka picking his way through the labyrinthine streets of the ageless ghetto.[4]

Prague has always been a city in the middle. The heterogeneous capital of a composite state since 1918, it has always been either the most westerly Eastern or the most easterly Western city in Europe. The cohabitation of peoples and cultures has always been culturally productive if politically uneasy. Even today, the Germans and Slavs in Prague, and the Czechs and Slovaks in Czechoslovakia, alternate between periods of cool antipathy and intensive interaction. Prague today would like nothing more than to regain its role as broker between East and West. Its geographic and cultural position, along with its own tumultuous internal history, combine to make it a leading candidate for the part.

Prague has spawned an incredible variety of religious and intellectual movements. Here the Reformation led by John Huss began a century before Luther nailed his theses to the door in Wittenberg. Here Tycho Brahe and Johannes Kepler pioneered a breakthrough in modern mathematics and astronomy. Between the world wars an active German-Jewish culture flourished here, of which Franz Kafka is perhaps the prime example.

An unforgettable turning point for Prague came on that grim day in September 1938 when France and Britain agreed that Nazi Germany could take over the Czech Sudetenland. This event remains like a scar burned into the brain of every Czech who remembers it. They consider it the basest kind of betrayal. Some think of it as the surest evidence of the weakness and irresolution of the Western democracies. The Munich agreement gained enormous support for the Czech Communists, and when the coup came in 1948, Czechoslovakia had one of the largest Communist parties in Europe.

In Prague, as everywhere in Eastern Europe today, secularization is proceeding apace. The situation all over Eastern Europe is complicated, of course, by the presence of a militant secularistic world view. But even this monolith has feet of clay. Communism plays an ambiguous role in the process of secularization. We have already noted how its atheism and its relativization of values provide some of the cultural preconditions of secularization. In some places, however, communism has sought to become a quasi-religious world view with all the trappings of a new state church. This is especially evident in East Germany, where the Communists have attempted to take over the traditions and observances of the vanishing Lutheran *Landeskirchen,* including *ersatz* confirmation, wedding, and burial services.

In the Eastern European situation, marked by a Marxist quasi-religious establishment, Christians become, in effect, the real advocates and protagonists of secularization. For example, it is the Catholic intellectuals, writing in such journals as *Slowe Powszechne* in Warsaw, who are the most articulate supporters of "cultural pluralism" in Poland today. The same is true in other East European countries. One East German theologian says, "We do not oppose communism because it is rationalistic, but because it is not rational enough; not because it is materialistic, but because it is metaphysical. We want communism to be what it says it is, scientific and socialistic, and to stop being a new holy orthodoxy."

Astute students of the history of communism, such as Helmut Gollwitzer of the Free University of Berlin, are becoming increasingly convinced that it is a curious conglomerate of political analysis and action with an added nimbus of Messianic utopianism. It is a program for one kind of economic development plus an ecstatic sectarian cult complete with saints and a beatific vision.[5]

The Christians of Eastern Europe form one of the forces now splitting this basically unstable compound. By granting to Communist regimes political allegiance and, at the same time, withholding any acceptance of their closed, atheistic world view, Christians contribute to what some scholars have termed the "de-ideologization" of communism. Another way to describe the process would be to call it the secularization of communism. Christians in Eastern Europe want communism to be really "secular." They want it to purge itself of its holistic, quasi-religious aura and become what it really is, one way among others of relating economic institutions to state power. It will then have to demonstrate its mettle in a peaceful competition with other societies, a competition in which thus far its performance has been indeterminate.

Many Western churchmen are deeply suspicious of Eastern European Christians who grant even a modicum of political allegiance to a Communist regime. They believe real Christians should either flee to the West or organize a resistance movement. But in staying in their countries and presenting Communists with the perplexity of a movement which is politically loyal but ideologically deviant, Christians perform a service both for their own societies and for an eventual "de-ideologization" of the Cold War. Their attitude also bears a striking resemblance to that of the early Christians toward the emperor discussed in Chapter i. They are counting on the possibility of communism's eventual secularization and the disestablishment of the Marxist orthodoxy. For this reason, when Christians issue wholesale condemnation of secularization in all its forms, they only confuse the issue.

Boston and the United States

We land at Boston's Logan International Airport, not because Boston is either the political or the commercial capital of the United States, but because along the shores of Massachusetts Bay the contrast between the epochs is more point-

edly evident than in any other city in America. Boston is at
once the oldest city in America and the newest. It is both the
historic site of the puritan colonizers and the launching pad of
the new electronic civilization. It combines, in a proportion
lacking in any other North American metropolis, just enough
Old-World elegance and space-age streamlining to make it the
most transparent American example of the emergence of the
secular city.

Martin Meyerson and Edward C. Banfield, two authorities
on urban problems, have called Boston "one of the few beautiful cities in America." They suggest that the reason for its
special position is that it was built up largely in the preindustrial period and therefore possesses a great many structures
"with the simplicity and charm of an age which could afford
nothing less." Also, Boston was governed for a long time by
an aristocracy of wealth and taste. It remains true that most
of the really beautiful cities of the world were laid out by such
people, not by popular referendum. They were designed "by
monarchs, nobles and prelates who had absolute power and
who cared not a whit for the convenience or welfare of ordinary people."

But Boston, the "good gray lady," had sunk to an abys-
mally low ebb before her current astonishing rebirth. Picturesque streets became clogged with gasoline buggies. The
frontal collision between Yankees and Irish drove many
people with money and civic interests to the suburbs. As Mr.
Justice Brandeis reported, at the turn of the century the
wealthy citizens of Boston told their sons: "Boston holds
nothing for you except heavy taxes and political misrule.
When you marry, pick out a suburb to build your house in,
join the Country Club, and make your life center about your
club, your home and your children."[6] The advice was taken
not just by the sons of the wealthy, but by everyone with
enough savings to flee to Newton or Belmont.

But urban renewal, the great political fact of the 1960s for
American cities, has come to Boston in an extra large pack-
age. Under one of the most vigorous mayors in her history,
aided by one of the toughest urban renewers in the business,
Boston has bitten off a huge chunk of self-redevelopment.
Early in the process a couple of serious errors were made. The
old West End was ruthlessly demolished and its lower-class
families scattered to the winds to make room for the futuristic
Charles River Park, where both the apartment buildings and
the rents soar to the upper reaches.[7] A public-housing project

on Columbia Point, land reclaimed from the harbor and accessible only over a narrow peninsula, is now also commonly conceded to be a mistake of the first magnitude. But in several other areas, renewal authorities are trying with real success to make up for a bad start. The design for the new Boston City Hall, chosen by an objective jury from 256 entries, has been acclaimed by several architects as one of the boldest and most inventive plans yet devised for a civic building in America. In the so-called gray areas of the city, a program called "neighborhood conservation" has begun to replace the bulldozer as the pathway to new metroplitan life. Most significantly, however, the master plan for Boston's redevelopment envisages the preservation of the distinctive character of such sections as Beacon Hill, Back Bay, and North End. This is important. The nourishment of the local color accumulated in diverse quarters *within* a city is just as important as safeguarding variety *among* cities.

But all this activity in the "new" Boston has not simply materialized full-blown out of the brows of Boston's eager urban renewers. The economic basis for it lies mainly in the spectacular growth of a whole new technical and industrial complex in and around Boston. The city and its environs have become what *The New Yorker* has called "the center of a new world." It is the new world of the electronic computer and that peculiar brand of industry which goes along with it: research-oriented, highly skilled bands of specialists working in laboratory-factories on projects which change even faster than automobile designs. The nerve center of this renaissance is Cambridge, just across the Charles River from Boston, but its tentacles spread out for miles in every direction, especially along Route 128, the circumferential highway around Boston that has become synonymous with the electronics industry.

But technopolis in Boston is far from achieved. The tensions between the old and the new are raw and nerveracking. Wealthy Bostonians, heeding the advice of their fathers, not only left Back Bay but resisted all Boston's efforts to annex them. The town of Brookline presents the most ludicrous anomaly of all. Almost completely surrounded by the city of Boston, it nonetheless clings to its independent status, pretending to spurn all involvement with the corruption of The Hub. Metropolitan Boston exhibits a more serious imbalance between the size of the city proper and the size of the metropolitan area than any other urban region. Suburbanites gleefully utilize the city's harbor, hospitals, and highways, to say nothing of its concerts, films, and theaters, but they retire behind zoning laws and economic ramparts when it comes to the urgent issues of the city itself. Consequently Bostonians groan under an oppressive property-tax burden, which still cannot seem to support an adequate school system, pay the police, or keep the streets clean.

So Boston presents not only a starkly etched contrast of old and young; it also typifies in a particularly glaring way the same crisis faced by every urban region in America—the civic abdication of the middle classes and their withdrawal into a parasitic preserve on the periphery of the city. Like every American city, but in exacerbated form, Boston is impaled on the hyphen in techno-polis. Technically and sociologically, it is a metropolitan region, interdependent in every respect. Politically it is a congeries of fiefdoms and protectorates engaged in the legalized looting of the center city, all the while groping ineffectually with the colossal problems of metropolitan living.

Part of this anarchic miasma stems from the unwillingness of substantial groups within the populace to accept the reality of the secular city. They still want to cling to town and even tribal styles of living. Within the city, clan feuds between Irish, Italian, and Yankee political war parties rage on, while in the suburbs harried escapees from the issues of the inner city deck out their modern homes with wagon wheels and fake colonial furniture. They keep the spotlight shining on the old white church on the green in an effort to convince themselves that they really do live in the simple self-sufficient village founded there three hundred years ago.

But it is all a disastrous self-delusion. Efforts to live in an eighteenth-century town or to maintain the purity and power of the tribe will eventually be exposed for the charades they are. The actual interdependence and technological unity of the urban region will eventually require a political expression.

Besides exemplifying the urban crisis exceptionally well, Boston also portrays with unusual clarity the distinctively American version of the contrast between secularization and secularism. What city better symbolizes a country where a venerable quasi-sacral Protestant culture is just now breathing its last? Its departure, though lamented by some romantics and arcadians, has been greeted by many Protestants with the same relief with which European Christians accept the death of Western Christendom. Protestants may for the first time stand free enough of their culture to be against it or for it selectively, as the guidance of the Gospel suggests. But unfortunately, just as this promising possibility has emerged, the sly temptation of a new sacral society has also appeared. It is the danger of what Martin Marty calls "American shinto."[8] He refers to the "American religion" with three denominations, Catholic–Protestant–Jew, laid open so neatly by Will Herberg and others. It is one of the hidden pitfalls of the present ecumenical movement that we will be urged to remember, à la Brotherhood Week posters, that after all we are all Americans and have a common religious heritage.

As Franklin Littell has made potently clear in his book *From State Church to Pluralism*,[9] this "religious past" is really a myth that badly needs demythologizing. People of a variety of religions (and none) came to America for a multiplicity of reasons, not all of them pious. The Protestant sacral culture was imposed on them. The secularization of American society has been a healthy development. It brought about the much-needed emancipation of Catholics, Jews, and others from an enforced Protestant cultural religion. By freeing them it also freed Protestants from important aspects of their culture bondage. It would be too bad if Catholics and Jews, having rightly pushed for the de-Protestantizing of American society and having in effect won, should now join Protestants in reconstituting a kind of tripartite American religion with Americanized versions of Moses, Luther, and Saint Thomas sharing the haloes in its hagiography. At this point, Christians should continue to support the secularization of American society, recognizing that secularists, atheists, and agnostics do not have to be second-class citizens.

We have yet to measure the enormous contribution made by the brief administration of John F. Kennedy to the desacralizing of American society. His election itself marked the end of Protestant cultural hegemony. But in the way he fulfilled the office, in his quiet refusal to function as the high priest of the American religion, Kennedy made an indispensable contribution to the authentic and healthy secularization of our society. He was a supremely political leader. Though there can be little doubt that his Christian conscience informed many of his decisions, especially in the area of racial justice, he stalwartly declined to accept the semireligious halo that Americans, deprived of a monarch who reigns *gratia dei*, have often tried to attach to their chief executive. In thus divesting his office of any sacral significance, Kennedy did, in his place, what the Christians of Eastern Europe do when they seek to distinguish between the political or economic and the ideological claims of Communist regimes.

The secularists of America may be God's way of warning us that the era of sacred societies is over. Christians have contributed to its demise, perhaps more so than most of us realize. By separating pope from emperor and thus granting a certain provisional autonomy to the secular arm, Western Christianity introduced a process which has produced the modern open society and the ecclesiastically neutral or secular state. But, as we have seen, the seeds of secularization go back still further: to the Creation story in which man is made responsible for the care of the world; to the separation of the kingly from the prophetic office in Israel; to the New Testament injunctions to respect those in authority so long as they do not make religious claims.

The task of American Christians vis-à-vis their nonreligious fellow citizens is not to browbeat them but to make sure they stay secular. They must be helped to be true to their own premises and not to allow themselves to be perverted into a new fideism, the intolerant religion of secularism. In this respect the decision by the California State Board of Education that the schools should have no hesitation in teaching *about* religion was a welcome one. The board paid its teachers a welcome compliment by suggesting they "are competent to differentiate between teaching about religion and conducting compulsory worship." Significantly, the board added that it would be just as illegal to teach a "point of view denying God" as it would be to "promote a particular religious sect."

This is a decision which points toward maturation in American society. It recognizes that the public school is no place for required prayers and hymn singing. But it also recognizes, as so many disciples of secularism do not, that atheists and agnostics have no more right to propagandize their sectarian views through the schools than anyone else does.

NOTES TO CHAPTER 4

1. Selig S. Harrison, *India, The Most Dangerous Decades* (Princeton, N.J.: Princeton University Press, 1960), pp. 333f.
2. Morton Dauwen Zabel (ed.), *The Portable Henry James* (New York: Viking, 1963), p. 499.

3. Abbé Michonneau, *Revolution in a City Parish* (Westminster: Newman Press, 1949).

4. Harvey Cox, "A Theological Travel Diary," *Andover Newton Quarterly* (November 1963), pp. 27–28.

5. See Helmut Gollwitzer, "Die Marxistische Religionskritik und Christlicher Glaube" in *Marxismusstudien*, Vierte Folge, No. 7 (Tübingen, 1962).

6. Quoted in Lewis Mumford, *The City in History*, p. 495.

7. See Herbert Gans, *The Urban Villagers* (New York: The Free Press, 1962) for the sad tale of Boston's West End.

8. Martin Marty, *Second Chance for American Protestants* (New York: Harper & Row, 1963), p. 72.

9. Franklin Littell, *From State Church to Pluralism* (Garden City, N.Y.: Doubleday, 1962).

PART TWO

THE CHURCH IN THE SECULAR CITY

CHAPTER 5

Toward a Theology of Social Change

The starting point for any theology of the church today must be a theology of social change. The church is first of all a responding community, a people whose task it is to discern the action of God in the world and to join in His work. The action of God occurs through what theologians have sometimes called "historical events" but what might better be termed "social change." This means that the church must respond constantly to social change, but it is hampered from doing so by doctrines of the church deriving from the frayed-out period of classical Christendom and infected with the ideology of preservation and permanence. They are almost entirely past-oriented, taking their authority from one or another classical period, from an alleged resemblance to some earlier form of church life, or from a theory of historical continuity. But this will no longer do. A church whose life is defined and shaped by what God is *now* doing in the world cannot be imprisoned in such antiquated specifications. It must allow itself to be broken and reshaped continuously by God's continuous action; hence the need for a theology of social change.

Two incidents in the early 1960s will illustrate this imperative need. The first took place when leaders of the World Council of Churches returned from a large Christian youth conference in Africa. Despite the crowds at the conference, the leaders confessed gloomily that in ten years they expected that most of the young Africans would have severed all relationships with the church. Our present Christian ethics simply do not make contact with the issues faced by African young people. Caught up in the excitement of nation-building, the struggle against new and old colonialism, the problems of economic planning, the organization of political institutions, and the fashioning of a real African culture, they find individualistic ethics and the middle-class morality now identified with the church entirely uninteresting and useless. They need

91

a theology and an ethic that will enable them to make sense of a wholly new world. They are leaping from tribal culture into technopolitan civilization, hardly pausing at the stage of town culture. But it is town culture which remains the real home base of most Christian theology.

Cuba and Latin America present another striking illustration of the need for a theology of social change. Many Cuban Christians, especially Baptists, were very active in the Castro movement before and during the period of its victory over the Batista regime. This should not be surprising since Oriente province, where the 26th of July Movement based its first operations, has the island's largest Protestant minority. Also, the Cuban Catholic church, heavily influenced by the Spanish hierarchy and led by large numbers of priests from Spain, had achieved a deservedly bad reputation for supporting Batista. But after the seizure of power in January 1959, the Christians found themselves in an exceedingly difficult position. Castro's control of the instumentalities of power was in no sense secure. A counterrevolution or a new coup was possible at any time. A radical reorganization of the entire society, including a complete turnover of leadership in thousands of posts of private and public power, seemed called for. But there were no existing juridical means for accomplishing these ends, and certainly no Christian principles to guide such actions. Cuban Christians found themselves in a revolutionary situation with no theology of revolution. Confused and paralyzed before such an unprecedented challenge, they left one by one, or were replaced. Some went back into Oriente and silence. Others eventually fled to North America. Their places were often taken by Communists who, although they had once bitterly opposed Castro's movement, were now able to exploit it to full advantage. Again, Christians were unable to participate responsibly in rapid social change because they had no theological basis for understanding or appreciating it.

The Cuban conundrum holds in only slightly different form for all of Latin America today. Christians find themselves swept along by a seething eruption of social ferment. They are searching desperately for a theological perspective which will make sense of their convulsive continent. But their dilemma differs very little from the one now faced by the whole Christian church. The nations of North America and Europe are no exception. We are all trying to live in an age of accelerating change with a static theology. Since the phrase *rapid social change* serves often merely as a euphemism for *revolu-*

tion, the issue could be put even more bluntly: we are trying to live in a period of revolution without a theology of revolution. The development of such a theology should be the first item on the theological agenda today.[1]

In part, the growing interest among modern theologians in a theology of history relates closely to the need for a theology of revolution. The phrase *theology of history* can often be a very misleading one. For most people, history refers to what is already past. The concept of a theology of politics comes closer. It has been said that history "is merely past politics," and there is real truth in the claim. This means, however, that politics is also present history, so our task is that of developing a theology of politics, and in particular a theology of revolutionary social change.[2] All questions about the formulation of a new social ethic or the reshaping of the structures of church life must depend for their answers on the answer we give to a previous problem: How is God acting for man in rapid social change?

Theologies of history and politics in the past have frequently fallen prey to one of two classical errors. Some have been so skittish about the danger of idolatry that they have hesitated to point to any tendency in history as being the work of God. There is something to be said for this scrupulosity. The value of the traditional Lutheran doctrine of the "two kingdoms," for example, is that it prevents the church from blessing causes indiscriminately or elevating political programs into holy crusades. In actuality, however, this position frequently functions in a conservative way. It implicitly favors the "powers that be" and movements of change are guilty until proved otherwise. At its worst, a two-kingdoms theology can become an ideology of reaction.

Some theologies, on the other hand, have been more than willing to identify all sorts of human programs with God's action. The Calvinist Puritans, for example, who fervently believed that God was building a holy commonwealth, often pointed with little hesitation to where God was surely at work in their midst. They had fewer reservations about identifying this or that course of events with the will of God. The strength of this type of theology is that it offered clear political guidance. Its weakness was that it sometimes discerned the hand of the Almighty at work where we would feel there was room for real doubt. We can be grateful today, for example, that William Lloyd Garrison opposed slavery so stridently on specifically theological grounds, but we should not forget that he also advocated absolute prohibition and total sabbatarianism on the same grounds. This is the problem of any theology of history, and it holds even more true for a theology of politics. How can we pick out the narrow passageway between fanaticism and irrelevance, between proclaiming a divine program to which all men must be subjected, and pronouncing the political order devoid of any theological significance whatever? A theology of politics must draw man into purposeful participation in the political process without tethering him to some overarching meaning to which he must comply. Can we fashion such a theology for our day?

Perhaps the symbol of the secular city provides the starting point. Clearly we have already begun to use it this way in the earlier chapters of this book. We have viewed the emergent secular city, technopolis, not as a static fact but as an emergent reality. Secularization and urbanization have been seen as a process. We have interpreted the emergence of this new form of human community in the light of such biblical categories as the Creation, the Exodus, the Sinai Covenant. We have examined it in view of other biblical motifs, including the tension between Law and Gospel and the struggle between Yahweh and the Canaanite Baals. Now we propose to move one step further. We propose to test the symbol of the secular city itself as a category by which to make theological sense of rapid social change.

Why should the secular city provide a key to understanding social change that avoids the two classic errors? First, it is the *secular* city. When we look at history as a process of secularization, it becomes for us at the same time meaningful *and* open-ended. It suggests that history has a significance for man, but it does not impose a meaning on him. In fact, it topples inherited metaphysical and religious meanings and turns man loose to compose new ones. It also suggests, as we shall see later, a whole range of images—growing up, assuming the responsibilities of an heir, executing an accountable stewardship—which appear throughout the New Testament.

Second, it is a secular *city*. Urbanization is included, and this brings to the symbol the enrichment of an impressive heritage of city symbols from the New Jerusalem and the City of God to the New Creation as Metropolis, defended so skillfully by Professor Gibson Winter in his 1963 book.[3] It also suggests a long tradition of social utopias in Western thought including Erewhon and Atlantis. There is no reason why

Christians cannot make use of the aspirations set forth in these fictional cities. As an interpretive model, the city usefully complements the freedom and liberation of secularity with the idea of reciprocity and interdependence. But the city too is an open-ended image. No street plan is provided. Every utopia which does prescribe specific remedies quickly becomes an impediment to change rather than a spur. The emerging city signifies a purposeful process, not an achieved goal. The pattern of the secular city is not revealed from on high. It must be painfully worked out by man himself.

The idea of the secular city exemplifies maturation and responsibility. Secularization denotes the removal of juvenile dependence from every level of a society; urbanization designates the fashioning of new patterns of human reciprocity. Combined in the symbol of the secular city, they portray man's continuing effort to find a basis for common life as archaic order and sacral ties disappear. The secular city emerges as tribes and towns vanish—and the process is never over.

THE KINGDOM OF GOD AND THE SECULAR CITY

The idea of the secular city supplies us with the most promising image by which *both* to understand what the New Testament writers called "the Kingdom of God" *and* to develop a viable theology of revolutionary social change. This contention must be defended from objections directed at it from two different sides, theological and political. On the theological side we must demonstrate that the symbol of the secular city does not violate the symbol of the Kingdom of God. On the political side, we must prove that the concept of the secular city, while remaining faithful to the doctrine of the Kingdom of God, still lays open and illumines the present ferment of social change. It must prove its mettle as a viable revolutionary theory.

If we begin with the theological objections against discerning in the secular city the same eschatological reality once expressed by the idea of the Kingdom of God, three principal retorts must be considered:

1. Whereas the Kingdom of God is the work of God alone, the secular city is the accomplishment of man.

2. Whereas the Kingdom of God demands renunciation and repentance, the secular city requires only skill and know-how.

3. While the Kingdom of God stands above and beyond history (or exists in the heart of believers), the secular city is fully within this world.

We must reject all of these objections, but nonetheless they are understandable, and no discussion of the Kingdom of God and the secular city can proceed without replying to them satisfactorily. Let us then take them up in order.

First, what about the contention that the secular city is constructed by man, while the Kingdom is the work of God? This objection is made all the more serious by the fact that American theology, especially during the period of the Social Gospel, allowed the phrase *building the Kingdom of God* to gain wide circulation, implying sometimes that the Kingdom was a human accomplishment. This mistaken idea has rightly been discarded by more recent theologians who base their rebuke on a sharp insistence that God and God alone brings in the Kingdom. Their corrective was much needed. The idea of the Kingdom of God had become fused with notions of progress and social betterment. But, like most correctives, it was pushed too far in the other direction.

Professor Amos Wilder, in his interesting book *Eschatology and Ethics in the Teachings of Jesus,*[4] draws attention to a crucial feature of the Kingdom of God theme in the New Testament which may help redress the balance somewhat. He points out that Jesus identified himself so closely with the Kingdom that its meaning is represented in his person. Jesus *is* the Kingdom. He is its representative, its embodiment, and its central sign. The theological problem of the Kingdom thus becomes a Christological one, and all questions about whether it is to be interpreted as a divine or a human act must be answered in terms of the person of Jesus. Thus both the older man-centered and the younger God-centered theologies of the Kingdom are called into question.

If Jesus personifies the Kingdom of God, then the elements of divine initiative and human response in the coming of the Kingdom are totally inseparable. Is Jesus God or man? Does his life represent an act of God for man or the full response of a man to God? The perennial answer of theologians has always been that he is both, and that the amounts of one or the other are not measurable. When the problem was discussed in the language of Greek substance philosophy, the formulation of the Council of Chalcedon held that Jesus was fully God *and* fully man. When the same discussion is translated into the vocabulary of contemporary social change, the issue is whether history, and particularly revolution, is something that happens *to* man or something that man *does*. Social determinists have battled with advocates of something called the "freedom of the individual" over this question for years. Is man the subject or the object of social change?

The only convincing answer is that he is both, and efforts to sort out amounts of one or the other inevitably fail. True, there are moments when man seems to step out and launch vast new initiatives. There are other periods when the tides of history seem to sweep man along despite all he can do. But the secular city, the fusion of secularization and urbanization, stands for that point where social movement and human initiative intersect, where man is free not in spite of but because of the social matrix in which he lives. Just as some theologians have interpreted the deity of Jesus as his readiness to accept and execute God's purpose for him,[5] so the secular city signifies that point where man takes responsibility for directing the tumultuous tendencies of his time.

The Kingdom of God, concentrated in the life of Jesus of Nazareth, remains the fullest possible disclosure of the partnership of God and man in history. Our struggle for the shaping of the secular city represents the way we respond faithfully to this reality in our own times.

The second objection to seeing in the secular city a present-day sign of the Kingdom of God is that while the Kingdom demands renunciation and repentance, the secular city does not.

Again, Amos Wilder's analysis of the Kingdom helps answer this objection. Wilder maintains that the coming of the Kingdom presented itself in the form of claims requiring the renunciation of certain things and the acceptance of a new discipline of discipleship. This new way of life entailed first of all a radical break with the past, so radical in fact that it might even involve breaking family ties or waiving the filial duty of burial. Another New Testament scholar underlines the revolutionary import of this latter demand. It is "unthinkable for the Jewish mind, a scandalous outrage . . . it bursts every custom that might bind the disciples. . . ."[6] Those responding to the appearance of the Kingdom were expected to be ready to sever all past ties, however intimate, and set aside all past values, however sacred, to enter into the new activities and responsibilities required by the Kingdom.

Our idea of the repentance demanded by the Kingdom has tended to be entirely too moralistic. Wilder shows us that repentance involves a far more sweeping and inclusive act of sacrifice. If he is right, then the Kingdom of Jesus came when God's doing something wholly new *coincided* with man's laying aside previous values and loyalties, and freely entering the new reality. Life in the emerging secular city entails precisely this kind of renunciation. So it does require penitence. In fact, the emergence of the secular city may help us discard our moralistic perversion of repentance and return to a more biblical version.

But a third question remains about the relationship between the secular city and the Kingdom of God. Isn't the Kingdom of God somehow beyond or above history, while the secular city is "within" it?

Here the traditional discussion has revolved around the question of whether the Kingdom will come *sometime in the future* or if it has *already come*. The words of Jesus himself can be interpreted in either way. Recent New Testament scholarship, however, has now moved beyond this stalemate. It has suggested that the debate over futuristic versus realized eschatology posed the question falsely and that we should speak instead of an eschatology which is *in process of realizing itself*. German scholars call this a *sich realisierende Eschatologie*. If we accept this interpretation, then we live today in a world where what the New Testament writers describe as the coming of the Kingdom still occurs. It still presents us with an objectively new social situation and provides the occasion within which we are summoned to discard the old and take up something different.

The main objections that might be put forward against the secular city as a viable concretization of the ancient symbol of the Kingdom of God do not, as we have seen, stand up to careful scrutiny. The problems of whether God or man brings the Kingdom, whether there is a need for repentance, and whether the Kingdom touches our *present* crisis can all be set aside by a thoughtful examination of the idea of the Kingdom in the Bible.

ANATOMY OF A REVOLUTIONARY THEOLOGY

Let us turn then from theological to political considerations. Does the coming of the secular city provide us with the necessary basis for a theology of revolution?

Any workable revolutionary theory must exhibit four essential features. It must include (1) a notion of why action is now necessary, and this notion must be capable of catalyzing action; therefore we call this first ingredient the *catalytic*. It must include (2) an explanation of why some people have *not* acted so far and still refuse to act, an interpretation of their inability to see or to move. Webster defines catalepsy as a mental disease characterized by rigidity and inability to move. What we see here is a kind of social catalepsy, a political paralysis; hence we call this second feature of an adequate revolutionary theory its *interpretation of catalepsy*. But the theory must also have (3) a view on how people can be changed, how they can be brought out of their cataleptic stupor and encouraged to act. It must have an *idea of catharsis,* the purgative process by which the hindrances to action are eliminated. Since this purgation always occurs by means of a radical alteration of the environment of the social cataleptic, every revolutionary theory must have it, and (4) finally, an *understanding of catastrophe*—again according to Webster, "an event overturning the order or system of things." It is the catastrophe, the social denouement, which makes possible a change in those who are unable to move and thereby facilitates purposeful action.

The catalytic factor in most revolutionary theories appears in the form of what might be called a *catalytic gap,* the idea that a lag exists which must now be closed, and that closing it is the action required. Awareness of the gap provides the catalytic agent which releases change. In most revolutionary theories, this catalytic gap is viewed as a lag between one aspect of civilization and another. Thus for the French *philosophes*, the Age of Reason had already dawned among thinking people, but the priests and princes were still purveying superstitious absurdities. For the Russian Bolsheviks, the dialectic of history had opened the door to a classless society while both the czars and their ineffectual social-democratic successors still dawdled in the vestibule. Both theories provided a potent source of accelerated social change.

Today the catalytic gap suggested by the theorists of the French and Russian revolutions no longer fills the bill. In fact, we lack any potent revolutionary theory. Scientific technology and medical research have ushered us precipitately into a civilization for which neither our political nor our cultural institutions are prepared. Though our predicament can be partially illuminated by Marx's diagnosis of the economic substructure outrunning the political superstructure, in reality our dilemma is a vastly more complex one. We are entering an era in which power is based not on property but on technical knowledge and intellectual skills. We are rushing headlong from the production line to the linear computer, from work to leisure values, from an industrial to an automated society—and our political processes as well as our cultural and religious symbols still reflect the bygone pretechnical society. Our infant republic has sprouted and shot up in every direction, and we can no longer button its clothes around it. We are still trying to dress a rapidly growing technological society in political rompers. This lag should have provided us with the catalytic gap we need, but so far it has not. Our accumulating crises in mass transit, housing, and growing unemployment dramatize our inability to deal politically with the problems created by technological change. We need a new revolutionary theory, pertinent to the pressures of the times.

This is why the word *technopolis* suggests both the possibilities and the problems of our new urban civilization. *Techno* symbolizes the technical base on which the secular city rests, *polis* recalls the social and cultural institutions without which the technical environment becomes an unlivable monstrosity. Together they suggest the tension out of which social change can emerge. We are now choking on a serious imbalance between the technical and the political components of technopolis. This should create our catalytic gap. The challenge we face confronts us with the necessity of weaving a political harness to steer and control our technical centaurs.

Again the biblical image of the Kingdom of God, transcribed for our times into the symbol of the secular city, the commonwealth of maturity and interdependence, provides a catalytic gap. God is always one step ahead of man. Man repeatedly encounters God in the Bible as the One who beckons him to come from where he is to a different place. Motion, from here to there and from now to then, fixes the crucial axis of the Bible. The Kingdom of God has never come in its fullness and perfection, so man can take his ease. Yet it is never so distant and unattainable that man can only surrender in despair. Rather, the Kingdom of God is always just arriving. It is always the "coming Kingdom," the new reality which is beginning to appear. Its initial marks are always *becoming* visible.

The catalytic gap from the biblical viewpoint is provided by the semicolon in the phrase which is the very first sentence attributed to Jesus by the oldest Gospel, Mark: "The time is fulfilled, and the kingdom of God is at hand; repent, and believe the Gospel" (1:15). When this epochal announcement is utilized, as the community of faith does, not just to comprehend Jesus but also to illumine the whole of historic reality, we can see that man is placed in a permanent catalytic gap. The Apostle Paul caught the same mood when he summarized the life of faith with the following phrase: ". . . forgetting what lies behind and straining forward to what lies ahead, I press on toward the goal. . ." (Philippians 3:13). The Bible places this present age in the crevasse between what was and what will be. For this reason the ethical tension seen by the Bible is somewhat different from the tension between what is and what ought to be, as it is usually stated in philosophical ethics. The grammar of the Gospel is not a categorical imperative; it first of all points to what *is* occurring, only secondarily does it call for a consequent change in attitude and action. The Kingdom of God is at hand; therefore repent.

The syntax of the secular city is identical. Through its irrepressible emergence it establishes a new situation which renders former ways of thinking and doing wholly obsolete. When called to man's attention, secularization summons him to action. It creates its own gap, catalyzing man to close it if he wishes to remain man and not be overwhelmed by the forces of history.

Then why does man *not* act? When the ancient imagery of a kingdom is translated into contemporary idiom, why does he still turn away? Even when he hears the Gospel as a summons to leave behind the society and symbols of a dying era and to assume responsibility for devising new ones, why does he refuse? Here we need to explore the *social catalepsis*, the blindness and paralysis which prevent men from acting to close the gap.

Theologians have insisted that man always remains capable of saying no to the Gospel, if he wishes to. He may cling tenaciously to the patterns and purposes of a previous era the way insecure children sometimes continue to clutch to themselves a blanket or bib that comforted them in infancy, but this refusal clearly represents a flight from maturity. It condemns a man to live in what the New Testament calls "this dying age." It will result in an increasing disorientation and a growing sense of unreality. This in turn will produce mountingly frantic and ultimately fruitless efforts to grasp the import of events in terms that are no longer adequate.

But the question remains, Why do people who are caught in the catalytic gap still stalwartly refuse to change? The

Marxists' answer to the problem of social catalepsy remains a classic one. They explain it with their notion of "false consciousness." They suggest that consciousness itself springs from a social matrix, in particular from one's relationship to the means of production. Therefore a person whose ties to property place him within the patterns of the passing era has his view of the world poisoned, so to speak. He perceives things wrongly. Though he is caught in the hiatus between past and future, he cannot change because he cannot *see* that he is caught. The only way to change his viewpoint is to change the point from which the view originates; this means to separate him from his property. As we shall notice when we discuss the Marxist catharsis, depriving a man of his property is really a liberation. It releases him from his interest in a society marked for destruction and thus acts as an antidote to the poison that contaminates his vision. Logically, the total abolition of all private property cures everyone of this social trachoma and all false consciousness disappears.

Biblical thought also delves into the dilemma of why men do not respond to the coming of the Kingdom. Men are "sinners"; they suffer from a deformed and distorted vision of themselves, society, and reality as a whole. The sinner is infirm. His sickness festers into a fatal incapacity to see or hear properly what is going on in his environment. Hence he is in the middle of the catalytic gap but does not know it. He is like a person living in a trance induced by posthypnotic suggestion. The Bible describes this condition with a wide variety of figures, including lameness, deafness, sleep, and death. Paul suggests that persons in this condition have been mesmerized. In scolding the backsliders of Galatia he pointedly asks them who has bewitched (hypnotized) them. In other places such people are described as being in chains, in prison, in darkness. The similes combine to depict a condition in which the person is unable to see his world clearly or to respond to it appropriately. He has a jaundiced view of reality and his capacity to react is crippled. This is why when Paul writes to the early Christians he often tells them to "wake up!"—to snap out of their trance. When the followers of John the Baptist come to Jesus and ask him point-blank if he is the promised one or should they wait for another, he replies, significantly, by telling them to look around them at what is happening: the blind see, the deaf hear, the lame walk, and the poor have the Gospel preached to them.

But now comes the problem of *catharsis*. What caused

these people to wake up from their stupor, to see what they had been missing before? The process is called in the New Testament *metanoia,* a very radical change. The former self dies and a new self is born. It is a total change for the person involved: ". . . all things become new." No one is seen any more from simply a human point of view. It is like being "born again" or coming alive from the dead. It is conversion, a sweeping change in one's perception of self and world. It results in a life in which one is now able to see, hear, walk, and leap for joy. Obstacles to perception and to response are both removed. Man can now see what is happening in his world and react appropriately.

Another important group of New Testament images for conversion, or the transformation of one's perception of reality, are those denoting the achievement of maturity, coming of age and adulthood. "When I became a man," says Saint Paul, "I put away childish things." In the letter to the Galatians he compares the man of faith with a person who has been under the governance of a tutor during his minority but now attains the age of accountability and becomes a full heir to his father's estate. As heir the son must now bear full responsibility for the administration of the estate.

These images of maturity and responsibility are crucial for our argument here since secularization itself can be viewed as a process of maturing and assuming responsibility. Secularization signifies the removal of religious and metaphysical supports and putting man on his own. It is unlocking the gate of the playpen and turning man loose in an open universe. Consequently it is important to notice that maturation and responsibility symbols are in no sense exceptional in the New Testament. They appear for instance in several of the parables attributed to Jesus in which he speaks of stewards who are given charge of an estate while the master goes away. Their assignment includes not just the care of sums of money for which they will be held accountable. It includes also a responsibility for the mature and judicious treatment of the master's servants. Thus the drunken stewart who beats the servants is judged with great severity. He has betrayed an assignment, the stewardship of power. Entirely too much has been said in most churches about the stewardship of money and too little about the stewardship of power. The modern equivalent of repentance is the responsible use of power.

But what brings about the catharsis? What causes man to change, to repent, to revolt, to accept responsibility for power? A revolutionary theology, like a revolutionary theory, must make a place for catastrophe, in the technical sense of an event which overturns the order of things.

For Marx the catastrophe was the objective condition growing out of the development of industrialization which placed the power in the hands of the workers. Revolutionary action merely brought the political superstructure in line with the existing reality of the substructure. Though Marx may seem to dodge on the issue, his view of revolution is a clear example of man's doing something and his having something happen to him all at once. The revolution is no more paradoxical than the Incarnation.

For Marx, this catastrophe, this overturning, provide the essential prerequisite for catharsis. He saw that an objective condition, the removal of their property, was the indispensable precondition for correcting the false consciousness of capitalists. This is why Marx was so impatient with intellectuals who wanted to argue or persuade people out of their political ideas or religious beliefs. People's opinions, Marx believed, could only be changed by altering the social reality on which they were based. He was tired of those philosophers who had spent their lives interpreting the world. "The time has come," he said, "to change it."

Similarly, for the Bible the coming of the new order of the Kingdom is the catastrophe. It provides the indispensable precondition for waking up. Paul never believed that just a shout from him would wake up the entranced Galatians. What enabled them to slough off their sleep was the new reality in which they had been placed by God's action in Christ. Paul's words had power only because they were uttered in the context of the Kingdom, which he referred to more often as the New Creation or the new era.

Our perception of reality is highly conditioned. It is influenced by our personal careers, our social location, the job we hold, and the web of meanings arising from all of these by which the ideas and experiences we encounter are screened and selected. Hence our perception of reality can be changed only as these conditions themselves are changed.

This is an immensely important fact for any theology of social change, any revolutionary theology, to take into consideration. It implies that people simply cannot be expected to see or react responsibly to emerging social and political problems merely by hearing sermons or reading articles. Something else has to change first. The summons they hear must occur within the matrix of a new social situation, a new objective context which provides the basis for a changed perception of reality. The catastrophe precedes the catharsis. The Kingdom of God precedes repentance. In fact the reality of the emerging Kingdom is the essential presupposition for the preaching of the Gospel. Within the reality of the Kingdom, the Gospel becomes a call to discern the signs of the Kingdom and to respond appropriately.

Likewise, the coming of the secular city supplies the new occasion. In face of its coming, attitudes which have been brought along from yesterday must be discarded, and a new orientation which is in keeping with the new social reality must be initiated. Today, the Gospel summons man to frame with his neighbor a common life suitable to the secular city. He responds by leaving behind familiar patterns of life that are no longer apropos and by setting out to invent new patterns.

The summons in no sense requires a thoughtless novelism, a scurrying after the new simply because it is new. It means rather that antiquity is no longer *per se* a mark of authenticity. Old ideas and practices must compete on an equal basis with new ones. What one has accepted must be constantly tested in the light of a world which never stops changing. Thus the past is celebrated and appreciated, but it can never be allowed to determine the present or the future.

The coming of the secular city is a historical process which removes adolescent illusions. Freed from these fantasies man is expected to assume the status of sonship, maturity, and responsible stewardship. His response to the call must include a willingness to participate in the constant improvisation of social and cultural arrangements which will be changed again and again in the future. The acceptance of provisionality is part of maturity. So is the need to exert one's own originality. No one supplies the steward with a handbook in which to look up procedures by which to cope with every problem in the garden. He must be original. No one provides secular man with surefire solutions to the ever-new problems thrown up by the tireless historical process. He must devise them himself. His maturity lies in his sensing the vast ambience of his assignment, in his willingness to let go of obsolescent patterns, and in his readiness to evolve ways of dealing with the emerging realities of history.

Catastrophe and catharsis come again and again. Just as the Bible sees God's Kingdom coming to man time and again, demanding a new response each time, so in our terms the secularization of history keeps going on. The human world is never fully humanized; therefore, again and again we must "cast off the works of darkness." We must be ready to react to new realities in history by discarding even our most cherished ideas and accepting new ones, later to be sacrificed again. "We are always *becoming* Christians," observed Kierkegaard wisely. We are always becoming mature and responsible stewards. Permanent revolution requires permanent conversion.

Without a doubt the kind of conversion described here must arise in response to a very different kind of preaching than we now have. We have departed today from the preaching of the Apostles. They followed the practice of presenting the hearer with something that had happened and would soon be happening, the raising of Jesus from the dead and his coming again with power. In the same way Jesus presented people with himself as a decisive event in their own biography and in the history of which they were a part. In the context of this new event, both Jesus and the Apostles issued a summons to respond. This summons was always highly specific, especially with Jesus. He expected people to drop their nets, get out of bed, untie a horse, invite him to dinner. No one could doubt either that something momentous had occurred or that something quite definite was required of him.

Our preaching today is powerless because it does not confront people with the new reality which has occurred and because the summons is issued in general rather than in specific terms. It is very doubtful, however, whether proclamation which is not highly specific can be thought of as preaching in the biblical sense at all. Only where an event which has changed the whole character of the situation becomes the occasion for a word which requires a specific responsive action does the biblical Gospel come through.

We have suggested that the message of Jesus, ". . . the Kingdom of God is at hand; repent and believe the Gospel," includes God's action and man's response coming to a focal point in Jesus himself. In our terms, *secularization,* though it is a human action, represents the objective reality, the new era in which we find ourselves. It happens to us. We are uprooted from traditional sources of meaning and value. As John the Baptist cried, "The axe is laid to the root of the tree." *Urbanization,* though it also happens *to* man, represents here the human effort to come to terms with the new historical reality, the formulation of ways to live more equably with other human beings in a system of increasing reciprocity. The fact that secularization not only precedes urbanization but also follows and is produced by it need not trouble us here. Any effort to extricate the action of God from the response of man fails finally as the traditional Christological formulations have amply shown. At the intersection of the action of history on man and the action of man on history is the phenomenon of conversion or what we have called responsibility, the acceptance of adult accountability.

NOTES TO CHAPTER 5

1. Two excellent books on the challenge of social change deserve special mention, although neither attempts to construct a theology of social change. They are Paul Abrecht, *The Churches and Rapid Social Change* (Garden City, N.Y.: Doubleday, 1961) and Egbert deVries, *Man in Rapid Social Change* (Garden City, N.Y.: Doubleday, 1961; London: SCM Press).

2. See Wolfhart Pannenberg (ed.), *Offenbarung als Geschichte* (Göttingen: Vandenhoeck & Ruprecht, 1961) for a provocative attempt to work toward a theology of history from a starting point defined by Gerhard van Rad's Old Testament theology. See also Pannenberg's *Was ist der Mensch?* (Göttingen: Vandenhoeck & Ruprecht, 1962), and his article in James Luther Mays (ed.), *Essays in Old Testament Hermeneutics* (Richmond, Va.: John Knox Press, 1963; London: SCM Press). For a criticism of Pannenberg's work, see James Robinson, "The Historicality of Biblical Language" in Bernhard W. Anderson, *The Old Testament and Christian Faith* (New York: Harper & Row, 1963; London: SCM Press).

3. Gibson Winter, *The New Creation as Metropolis* (New York: Macmillan, 1963).

4. Amos Wilder, *Eschatology and Ethics in the Teaching of Jesus* (New York: Harper & Row, 1950). For a more recent study see Norman Perrin, *The Kingdom of God in the Teachings of Jesus* (Philadelphia: Westminster Press, 1963). [Both books, London: SCM Press.]

5. D. M. Baillie, *God Was in Christ* (New York: Scribner, 1955; London: Faber & Faber).

6. Quoted by Wilder, *op. cit.,* p. 173, from Schlatter's *Der Evangelist Matthäus.*

CHAPTER 6

The Church as God's Avant-garde

It is no oversight that we have waited so long to deal with the place of the church in the secular city. The theologians of our generation have tended to be inordinately obsessed with various aspects of the doctrine of the church. Because of this they have pressed for answers to questions about the church before other questions have been dealt with. M. M. Thomas, a noted South Indian sociologist and lay theologian, writing for a World Council of Churches publication, says:

> . . . we have overdone the idea of the church in the last fifty years of ecumenical theological thinking. I do not think we can go back to any non-church understanding of Christianity, but we have to look at the question of how the church as a congregation is different from the traditional idea of a religious community.[1]

Thomas is right; a doctrine of the church is a secondary and derivative aspect of theology which comes *after* a discussion of God's action in calling man to cooperation in the bringing of the Kingdom. It comes after, not before, a clarification of the idea of the Kingdom and the appropriate response to the Kingdom in a particular era. Consequently, we are ready to ask some questions about the church now only because we have already dealt with the secular city.

The church is not in the first instance an institution. It is a people. The Bible calls it the *laos theou*, the "people of God." It is a people whose institutions should enable them to participate in God's action in the world—the liberation of man to freedom and responsibility. Archie Hargraves puts it graphically. He compares the work of God in the world, where Jesus Christ is present, to a "floating crap game" and the church to a confirmed gambler whose "major compulsion upon arising each day is to know where the action is" so he can run there and "dig it."[2] Thomas Wieser expresses the same thought in more scholarly language when he says that accord-

108

ing to the book of Acts the *Kyrios,* the risen Christ, always
goes *before* the church into the world. He appears here and
there and the church simply follows.

> . . . the way of the church is related to the fact that the
> Kyrios himself is on his way in the world . . . [and] the
> church has no choice but to follow him who precedes.
> Consequently obedience and witness to the Kyrios require
> the discernment of the opening which he provides, and the
> willingness to step into this opening.[3]

Theology, in these terms, is concerned *first* of all with finding
out where the action is, the "discernment of the opening."
Only then can it begin the work of shaping a church which
can get to the action. This is why the discussion of a theology
of social change must precede a theology of the church.

The key to locating the action is, of course, that the same
God who was there yesterday is present in the action today.
To locate today's action we need to know the lead actor, and
this actor has disclosed himself in the life of Jesus of Nazareth. As we noticed in discussing the Kingdom, here too the
location of the action is a Christological problem. After the
action has been uncovered, when we know where and what
God is doing, then we can ask about the appropriate shape
and style of church life.

Phrased in more traditional terms, the forms of church life
are dependent on the function, or mission, of the church.
They must be designed to facilitate locating and participating
in the "mission of God." They must effectuate rather than
hinder the congregation's capacity to discover and cooperate
in the work of God in the world. This means that the content
of the church's ministry is simply the continuation of Jesus'
ministry. It cooperates and participates in the ministry of
Jesus. But what is the character of Jesus' ministry? Jesus
himself described it in these terms:

> The Spirit of the Lord is upon me,
> Because he has anointed me to preach good news to the
> poor
> He has sent me to proclaim release to the captives and
> recovering of sight to the blind,
> To set at liberty those who are oppressed,
> To proclaim the acceptable year of the Lord. (Luke
> 4:18, 19)

Jesus thought of his task as threefold. He was to announce
the arrival of the new regime. He was to personify its mean-

ing. And he was to begin distributing its benefits. Similarly the church has a threefold responsibility. Theologians call it *kerygma* (proclamation), *diakonia* (reconciliation, healing, and other forms of service), and *koinonia* (demonstration of the character of the new society). The church is the avant-garde of the new regime, but because the new regime breaks in at different points and in different ways, it is not possible to forecast in advance just what appearance the church will have. It is not even possible to delineate the mission of the church "in the city." Cities differ, and the visage of the church in any given urban environment will differ. There are, however, certain basic facts about urban secular life that will need to be taken into consideration by any church. Let us take the three elements of the church's task as avant-garde—kerygma, diakonia, and koinonia—and see how they work out in a typical urban setting.

The Church's Kerygmatic Function:
Broadcasting the Seizure of Power

The word *kerygma* means "message." The church, like any avant-garde, has a story it is trying to get across. It is telling people what is coming, what to expect next. Employing political terminology, the church broadcasts the fact that a revolution is under way and that the pivotal battle has already taken place.

This broadcasting function of the church is crucial. It makes the church different from any other avant-garde. It has no plan for rebuilding the world. It has only the signal to flash that the One who frees slaves and summons men to maturity is still in business. It flashes this signal not in the form of general propositions but in the language of specific announcements about where the work of liberation is now proceeding and concrete invitations to join in the struggle.

In traditional language, the message of the church is that God has defeated the "principalities and powers" by Jesus and has made it possible for man to become the "heir," the master of the created world. This sounds foreign to us now, but nothing could be closer to the center of human existence in twentieth-century urban society. These "principalities and powers" actually signify all the forces in a culture which cripple and corrupt human freedom. In various ages men have experienced these forces in different ways. Sometimes they have denied their existence, but this has not happened often. In the tribal era which colors much of the New Testament, they were perceived as demons, spirits, and astral forces. They were believed to be linked up with individuals and especially with rulers. Each person had his own "star" (we still read horoscopes today) and astronomical symbols were often associated with kings. In the transition period to town culture these forces were either denied or were reduced to regular movements and predictable patterns. Newton's spheres and Adam Smith's invisible hand are good examples. Still, the nineteenth century as a whole was skeptical about such forces, and only in our own time have they been rediscovered under such concepts as the id, the collective unconscious, the dialectic of history, or even statistical probability. One could sum up all these fields of force insofar as they impair or imperil man's free exercise of responsibility in the single word *fate*. When Proudhon claimed, as we saw in a previous chapter, that the impact of biblical faith is to "defatalize" the world, he was right. What is meant by the kerygmatic assertion that Jesus has defeated the "principalities and powers" is not that they have been annihilated. Ids and economic pressures still roam through history. What is meant is that these forces do not have the power to determine man. Rather, man has the power and the responsibility to rule over them and use them in responsibility before God.[4]

These principalities and powers, according to the New Testament, were originally intended to be a part of the world, to be dominated and utilized by man. But man's freedom is so complete that he "worshipped and served the creature rather than the Creator" (Romans 1:24). Man thus fell captive to forces over which he was intended to "have dominion." Things he was meant to control controlled him. He had to be extricated. God's action, which goes on all the time but was made known in Jesus of Nazareth, is to call man to freedom *from* the powers and principalities, and to summon him at the same time to responsibility *over* and *for* them.

This is no sequential story. Man is always tempted to surrender his freedom to the powers. God is ever at work making freedom and personhood possible. There is no neutral ground. Man either masters and manages his environment or he is mastered and managed by it. The call to freedom is at the same time a call to responsibility. In terms of modern urban life, this means that we should never seriously ask "Is New York City governable?" or "Can nuclear war be prevented?"

or "Can racial justice be achieved?" The fact is that man is placed in an environment of problems which he is called to master. God has not stacked the cards against man the way fate does in Greek tragedy or a Thomas Hardy novel. To believe the kerygma is to believe that man not only *should* but *can* "have dominion over the earth." For the Bible, there are no powers anywhere which are not essentially tameable and ultimately humanizable. To deny this, in word or deed, is to "worship the creature rather than the Creator," to open the door and readmit the banished furies, to genuflect before some faceless Kismet.

The fusion of freedom and responsibility appears in the biblical symbol of sonship, which has been explored at length in the theology of Friedrich Gogarten. He believes that one of the key passages in understanding man's relationship to the "powers" can be found in Galatians 4:1, where Paul discusses man's coming to maturity. Paul argues that under the old regime, man, though he is designated the heir, is actually no better than a slave. But under the new regime, Paul says, man becomes the owner of the whole estate. "So with us," Paul continues, "when we were children we were slaves to the elemental powers of the universe . . .," but he insists that now ". . . through God you are no longer a slave but a son, and if a son then an heir" (Galatians 4:4f.). He implores the Galatians not to return to slavery to "the weak and elemental spirits of the universe."

Again let us not be distracted by the mythical conceptualizations. Paul was using his own language to describe the forces which impair human responsibility, including genes and glands and early toilet training. He is saying that although these things exist, no one *has* to be determined by them. Man may be free—if he chooses to be. But freedom entails responsible sonship.

Sonship, as Gogarten understands Paul's usage, means not a physical descent but a relationship in which man recognizes that he is a son and therefore has a father. Without a father before and to whom one is responsible, this idea of sonship would be meaningless. He points out that the Greek word used in Galatians specifically means "son" and not child. It refers to an adult offspring who now assumes the role once played by the father. He has come of age. He is free from the world only insofar as he exercises his mastery over the world.[5]

All this still sounds very abstract and general. As such it is not the kerygma, but only a discussion of the kerygma. The kerygma itself is articulated only when a man knows that he really is free from dependence on the fates and recognizes that his life is now being placed in his own hands. The kerygma comes to a people when they stop blaming economic forces or psychological pressures for social injustice and family strife and begin to do battle against the causes of woe. The taming of the powers means that man is invited to make the whole universe over into a human place. He is challenged to push forward the disenchantment and desacralization which have expelled the demons from nature and politics.

Because the avant-garde announces the coming of a new era which has already begun but is not yet complete, its message is in the indicative mood, not the imperative. It does not urge or exhort people. It simply makes known what has happened, that "the acceptable year of the Lord" has arrived. Recurring to the floating-crap-game figure, it gives out word of where the action is.

The church's announcement produces what theologians call the "crisis of the Kingdom." It results in a catalytic gap in which people have to make a decision. It is the coming of the new regime into the midst of the old which requires this response.

To express it in wholly political terminology, the revolutionary regime has seized power but the symbols of authority are still in the hands of the old displaced rulers. Like the inhabitant of a country torn by revolution, each man is confronted by a choice, a crisis. Shall he obey the new authority announced by the avant-garde, though it does not yet possess the symbols (legal legitimation, ceremonial inauguration, etc.), or shall he obey the "duly constituted authorities" who still claim the right to govern?

The illustration is a particularly apt one because the citizen cannot answer the question theoretically. He must cooperate either with the new regime or with the old. His choice is expressed in what he *does*. Nor can he merely evade the issue. Even neglecting to oppose one regime, for example, could at some time be interpreted as collaboration.

A biblical theology begins by viewing all of history since the coming of Jesus as the beginning of a new regime. But the new regime takes shape in the midst of the old. Consequently, a crisis of choice is presented which eventually confronts every man who hears about the new reality. In this respect it is essential to notice that Christian theology, unlike the Old

Testament vision, claims that the seizure of power *has* already
taken place. The revolutionary deliverer *has* come and *has*
won the decisive battle. For this reason, all of human history
takes place between the achievement of *de facto* power and
the appearance of visible *de jure* authority. History does not
take place between the black noon of Good Friday and the
bright dawn of Easter. It takes place, rather, between Easter
Day and the Last Day. History is a permanent crisis in which
the defeated old regime still claims power while the victorious
new regime has still not appeared publicly on the balcony.
The New Testament looks forward not to the victory of Jesus,
since that has already been won, but to the day when "every
knee shall bow and every tongue confess" that Jesus is victor.

Exodus and Easter remain the two foci of biblical faith, the
basis on which a theology of the church must be developed.
The Exodus is the event which sets forth "what God is doing
in history." He is seen to be liberating people from bondage,
releasing them from political, cultural, and economic captivity, providing them with the occasion to forge in the wilderness a new symbol system, a new set of values, and a new
national identity. Easter means that the same activity goes on
today, and that where such liberating activity occurs, the
same Yahweh of Hosts is at work. Both Exodus and Easter
are caught up in the inclusive symbol of the Kingdom, the
realization of the liberating rule of God. In our terms, God's
action today, through secularization and urbanization, puts
man in an unavoidable crisis. He must take responsibility in
and for the city of man or become once again a slave to
dehumanizing powers.

The Church's Diakonic Function:
Healing the Urban Fractures

Some scholars translate *diakonia* as "service." But service
has been so cheapened that it retains little significance.
Diakonia really refers to the act of healing and reconciling,
binding up wounds and bridging chasms, restoring health to
the organism. The Good Samaritan is the best example of
diakonia. In the case of the secular city, diakonia means the
responsibility of the church for effecting what Gibson Winter
has called a "ministry of communication" which will bring
back into reciprocity the fragmented pieces of what is essentially a functioning whole. Healing means making whole, re-

storing the integrity and mutuality of the parts. In order to be a healer, the church needs to know the wounds of the city firsthand. It needs also to know where and how these abrasions are being healed, so that it can nourish the healing process. For the church itself has no power to heal. It merely accepts and purveys the healing forces which God, working with man, sets loose in the city.

What are the major cleavages in the age of the secular city? Where is healing going on? We cannot deduce answers to this question from the Bible or theology. We must depend on specialists in the study of urban life. Let us first locate the fissures.

Edward C. Banfield and James Q. Wilson of the Harvard–M.I.T. Joint Center for Urban Studies, in their excellent book *City Politics,*[6] mentioned these salient cleavages in the fabric of urban life: (1) center-city versus suburbs; (2) haves versus have-nots; (3) ethnic and racial tensions, especially white versus Negro; (4) the competition between political parties. These cleavages can be found in almost every modern city, though the form and intensity in which they appear vary widely, and they always cut across each other. Particular ethnic groups, for example, are found not only in the suburbs, but also the center-city, not only among the haves but also among the have-nots, and in both political parties. This means that alliances are always shifting and reforming from issue to issue. This shifting helps to mitigate some of the tension. Thus Irish and Polish immigrant groups in the center-city may be hostile to each other. But they frequently pool their hostilities in opposition to Negroes; and they join in a political coalition with Negroes against the political power of the suburbs. This changing pattern is probably good, and for this reason it is ominous when opposed groups begin to polarize. This could happen if, for example, the tendency of many white immigrant groups to flee the city center as soon as possible continues, leaving it to Negroes, who have more difficulty buying suburban homes. If the center-city were to become a largely Negro, have-not, one-party ghetto, the balance-of-tensions theory of Banfield and Wilson would be seriously threatened. Unfortunately, this polarization seems to be precisely what is happening in many urban regions, and good urban planning must include some effort to arrest it.

The church has the responsibility to be the servant and the healer of the city. It might be objected at this point that Jesus cured souls while we are here discussing the "curing" of a whole urban region. The two are not to be separated. The cleavages of the secular city correspond to the cleavages in the soul of urban-secular man. The way man arranges the life of the city reflects the fears and fantasies of his own inner life; his own inner life is in turn molded by the cities he devises. Thus the operative segregation of Negroes in most cities, which one writer likens to an urban concentration camp watched over by the ramparts of suburban power and exclusion, expresses the fear and prejudice of the white man. But it also reinforces them. His refusal to permit himself or his children to have normal contacts with Negroes permits his racial stereotypes to go unchallenged. It means that the Negroes he does see will be largely domestics who often feel that to challenge the stereotype might endanger their jobs. At the same time it contributes to the locking of Negroes into ghetto areas, producing all the sicknesses that go with segregation.

In any case, the church's task in the secular city is to be the *diakonos* of the city, the servant who bends himself to struggle for its wholeness and health.

But how are the wounds on the body of the city to be healed, how are the gaps enumerated by Banfield and Wilson to be closed? Again there are no specifically Christian replies. Christians struggle for answers along with people who have no faith. Cities themselves vary. A strategy for Cleveland will differ from a strategy for San Antonio. Three things can be said about the urban issue in America, however, which point to a possible strategy. First, the modern city suffers from a *decentralization of authority,* a lack of political structures which can be used to deal with metropolitan problems. Second, *city problems must be dealt with on a society-wide basis.* The sores on the body come from the poisons in the bloodstream of the total society. The city serves as a kind of drain in which issues accumulate that cannot be dealt with in the drain alone but must be faced throughout the whole system. Third, *the powerlessness of oppressed peoples* is the key issue. The real illness of the American city today, and especially of the deprived groups within it, is voicelessness, the lack of either the readiness, the capacity, or the channels to make their legitimate needs felt throughout the whole system.

In one sense, it is the stubborn residue of tribal and town ideology which prevents the technopolis from being realized. This can be seen quite clearly in the issues we have just enumerated. To advocate the centralization of authority in any government runs directly counter to the prejudices of bourgeois and small-town attitudes as they are enshrined in suburb, county seat, and Congress. Town ideologies were developed to oppose divine-right kings and it is natural that they should be suspicious of governmental power. But our problem today in the technical city is just the opposite. Within the city, power is divided among the mayor, the city council, the various semiautonomous boards, the urban renewal authority, the state government, and some metropolitan port and transit authorities. In the metropolitan region it is broken into hundreds of municipalities. This fragmentation of power often creates a situation of sheer immobilism in which only marginal problems can be dealt with because an attempt to cope with a major issue will annoy or threaten one of the power blocs needed in any effective coalition. Cities are forced by this anarchy to deal with single problems as they emerge one by one, enlisting whatever coalition can be harnessed at the time. This makes long-range planning very difficult. Just as the various ethnic, class, and religious groups within the city divide and reassemble, depending on the issue in question, so the various power centers in a city find themselves in varying alliances as they deal with such typical urban issues as where some facility is to be located, how taxes are to be apportioned, or which agency will be in charge of a particular program. This is why references to *"the* power structure" which have recently come into circulation can be very misleading. The further one stands from the context in which decisions are made in a city the more monolithic "the" power structure looks. But the closer one comes, the more it appears to be a congeries of shifting structures, changing somewhat from issue to issue, never stable enough to be pinned down once and for all.

The truth is that even before one fights a battle with "the" power structure, an effective structure of responsible power must first be created in the American city. As Banfield and Wilson say, "In order for anything to be done under public auspices, the elaborate decentralization of authority . . . must somehow be overcome or set aside. The widely diffused *right* to act must be replaced by a unified *ability* to act."[7] This can be accomplished in many different ways, but it is the prerequisite to any possible political mastery of technical society. How it is done depends largely on the given history of the city in question. It is doubtful that utopian paths for the massive annexation of suburban areas (to overcome the suburban–central-city cleavage), or thoroughgoing charter reforms (to combine disparate city authorities into one framework), can be expected very often. The actual situation calls for the enlargement and strengthening of existing metropolitan boards such as port, transit, and park authorities, especially those which include areas overlapping state and city jurisdictional lines. Within the city, it will also be necessary to strengthen existing movements toward centralization rather than merely replace existing mechanisms. This may appear to be political drudgery, but it is also diakonia.

No one should be naïve enough to believe that once a measure of centralized authority is attained in American cities, the problems will be solved. A centralized authority can also be oppressive and unjust. Chicago, the American city with the highest degree of centralized power, amply demonstrates this. But, on the other hand, we cannot begin to deal with the pressing issues of technopolis until some progress has been made in fashioning politically effective instrumentalities.

As effective political channels begin to emerge in the city, it will become increasingly clear that the city cannot be expected to solve its own problems. This brings us to the second general principle in a strategy for the diakonia of the urban church: *The problems of the city are the problems of the whole society.* They must be faced on the state and federal as well as on the city level. Cities always have a higher percentage of the aged, the ill, recent immigrants, and the culturally disadvantaged. Just because they happen to be located in the physical boundaries of a city does not mean that they must be wholly the city's responsibility. All of the injustices and abuses of America drain into a place like, for example, East Harlem. The wreckage and castoffs of ruthless competitiveness find themselves bunched together with the old, the infirm, the mentally deficient, the victims of racial and ethnic persecution. Only structural changes in the larger society will ever enable East Harlem to deal with these problems.

A large part of the difficulty is simply lack of money. Here the outlandishly anachronistic tax base on which our urban age tries to operate must come to light. Nothing illustrates more vividly the gap between town-age sentiments and technopolitan realities. Seven out of every eight local tax dollars are still collected from real-property tax. This tax is a remnant of colonial days. At that time property meant wealth. Income came from land; also, land by its very nature was evenly distributed. But as Senator Joseph Clark has shown,[8] a tax levied on a man's real estate no longer accurately measures his relative ability to pay. Property represents only a small fraction of wealth. Only poor and lower-middle-class people accumulate the majority of their wealth in mortgaged houses. Better-off people will own additional wealth in stocks or other forms of intangibles. "In short," Senator Clark says, "while the rich man pays local property taxes on what may amount to a tiny fraction of his accumulated wealth, the average-income man pays on what may be two to ten or more times his accumulated wealth." All this means that the limits of property taxing are reached very soon, long before most cities can raise enough money to pay their bills.

Even though corporations pay property taxes, the way they do so is highly inequitable. A giant plant may pour all its property taxes into the coffers of the tiny village or suburb in which it is located and not give so much as a penny to the school districts in which the children of its employees are educated. Wage and sales taxes also reach a limit fairly soon. This is in part a result of the fact that the wage earner is taxed for all his income while the person whose income comes from rent or dividends pays on only a part. Recognizing the plight of the cities, most states share in the expense, but even states operate on tax bases that are outdated.

In our system of overlapping local, state, and federal tax systems, only the federal system is equipped to touch the types of wealth needed to help cities pay the bills. This is why we have begun to see in recent years the appearance of a coalition of city and federal power against rural and "upstate" power. This coalition of cities, united without reference to state boundaries, represents the newly emergent electoral alliance which first spoke clearly in 1960 with the election of John F. Kennedy. Kennedy was the first really urban President. Of the fourteen major metropolitan areas of the United States, only two of which went for Stevenson in 1956, Kennedy won every single one—by majorities ranging from 65.7 in Boston to 51.8 in Minneapolis–St. Paul. It was Kennedy who sought to organize a department of urban affairs at cabinet level. His short term of office indicated that the urban regions have a degree of political power which can be swung together despite regional differences. We can look forward with some measure of confidence to an increased utilization of federal funds, raised by the federal tax structure, to grapple with urban problems. But the maintenance of the urban alliance will be no mean political feat. It is a volatile and highly unstable mixture which, because of the internal cleavages mentioned before, could fall apart easily. But if the problems of the city represent a cencentrate of the problems of a technical-industrial society, then the nourishing of urban power is a clear need in the emerging technopolis. At our stage in history, the birth of the urban coalition is a healing force which the healing church should foster.

This brings us directly to the third problem of urban regions which calls for an intelligent exercise of diakonia on the part of the church—the comparative *powerlessness of certain groups in the cities.* Political apathy, defeatism, and cynicism are the canker sores of the slums just as much as rats and roaches. We have emphasized that the healing of urban wounds demands a redistribution of power and a measure of centralization in metropolitan authority. The reason they are slow in coming stems in part from the resistance of people still living by town and tribal ideologies, and also from the apathy and inertia of people who live in inner-city ghetto areas.

How has the church related itself to these areas? Its first response, as is well known by now, was simply to run away as quickly as possible. The mass emigration of the Protestant churches from the city in the first half of the twentieth century is by now a shamefully documented fact. Recently conscience pangs have begun to set in. Since shortly after the Second World War these same churches have begun to notice the inner-city again. They have established and financed missions. They have helped support inner-city ecumenical parishes such as the ones in East Harlem and Cleveland. They have sometimes exchanged leaders and Sunday school teachers. Youth groups have been sent in for weekend work camps. By and large this has added up to a flimsy and even self-deluding series of efforts. It has not only been too little and too late; it has also been largely ill-conceived and patronizing. What is needed in these areas are not incursions of rescue bands from outside, but a basic redistribution of power so that there is no longer any need for condescension. But this is asking for a sacrifice on the part of suburban churches that very few are willing to make.

Work camps provide the best example of the clear abuse of a well-intentioned gesture. For years, religious groups have been sponsoring work camps in which high school and college students from suburban areas come to a slum and work, often together with the local residents, to repair and paint dilapidated property. Much is made of the cooperation engendered

and of the personal relationships formed. The work camps
have the advantage of bringing young people into an area they
might never have seen otherwise, but the psychology of the
situation is so unfavorable that, on balance, work camps
probably do more harm than good. The visitors play the role
of those who bring health and soundness to an area marked
by decay and deterioration. The whole operation, despite a lot
of rhetoric to the contrary, suggests to the youthful suburban
participants that they are showing by their example how
houses and neighborhoods can be maintained. They learn
through the experience, though it is rarely stated openly, that
truly compassionate suburbanites should bestir themselves and
do something for their inner-city brethren. Inner-city people
are expected to be grateful for the service rendered.

But the weekend work camp, one of the main aspects of the
church's diakonia in the city, is wrong in nearly every way. In
a city, the way a neighborhood is best maintained, especially
where the vast majority of people do not own their own
homes, has more to do with learning how to apply political
pressure on landlords than with learning how to apply putty
with a knife. Suggesting otherwise often does real harm. Furthermore, visits of suburban paint brigades sometimes even
create in the landlord a cynical belief that he doesn't need to
keep things up himself.

The psychology of the weekend work camp is wrong because it perpetuates an attitude of dependency on the part of
those who ought to be stimulated to protest and action; and it
perpetuates an attitude of condescension in those who should
be confronted by their guilt in the structural inequities of
metropolis. How many suburban youngsters, coming to an
inner-city work camp, are sent back to ask their fathers
whether they should change the discriminatory zoning regula-
tions which prevent low-income families from building or buying in the suburbs and thus produce the ghetto? How often is
the iniquitous tax structure explained to them so they realize
that they benefit every day from the hunger and hardship of
the people they see? How frequently do they hear that the
banks in which their parents deposit their salaries and on
whose boards they sit really make these areas slums by mark-
ing them as places where mortgages and home-improvement
loans are almost impossible to obtain? Leaders of weekend
work camps usually want their charges to have "a good experience" and to return to their homes with less rancor and

prejudice against inner-city people, especially Negroes. Therefore discussions are kept on a personal level and controversial topics are resolved on the personal level. But the recent civil rights revolution in America has proved at least one thing: Negroes are not so much interested in winning whites to a less prejudiced attitude as they are in preventing them from enforcing the prejudice they do have. The Negro revolt is not aimed at winning friends but at winning freedom, not interpersonal warmth but institutional justice.

Work camps are not popular with inner-city Negroes intent on changing rather than ameliorating the ghetto situation. In light of this unfavorable attitude, one ghetto congregation recently presented a group which proposed a weekend work camp with a counter suggestion. The white suburbanites were invited to come to the inner-city for a weekend, not to do something for the slum dwellers but to be taught by inner-city youngsters how to engage in direct nonviolent action. After the training, the two groups were to take such action not only in the city but in the very suburban areas from which they came. The issue selected was the improvement and integration of the inner-city schools. The action involved knocking on doors and urging people to participate in a school stayout. The project was carried through, but whether it will ever happen again remains a question. Suburban parents who allowed their teen-agers to come to a slum for a work camp blanched at the sight of teams made up of their own plus Negro youngsters ringing their neighbors' doorbells to acquaint them with the plight of the urban schools. But the response of the inner-city Negroes was extraordinary. Confronted for the first time with the challenge of teaching something *to* white youngsters, and taking action in the community, many of them disclosed a level of imagination and ability they themselves barely knew they had.

The lesson of this political substitute for painting tenement kitchens is that metropolitan problems must be dealt with on a metropolitan level, not simply in the inner-city itself. They must be dealt with politically, not only privately. Most important, they must be tackled by groups of people from all sectors of the city who recognize each other as co-responsible for finding solutions, not as those who *do* and those who are done *for*.

The most interesting and controversial example of the jump from drift and torpor to bold community action in a slum is probably represented by the organization set up in 1960 in

Chicago's Woodlawn section. Named The Woodlawn Organization and including some ninety community organizations (of which thirteen are churches), TWO was formed with the assistance of Saul D. Alinsky, executive director of the Industrial Areas Foundation. It was sparked, however, by Protestant ministers and a Catholic priest, and represents, according to Charles E. Silberman of the *Fortune* board of editors, ". . . one of the most meaningful examples of Protestant–Catholic amity and cooperation to be found anywhere in the United States."⁹ A genius in getting people to do things themselves and to begin to exercise power, Alinsky had already helped turn Chicago's "back-of-the-yards" area into a desirable neighborhood several years ago. He never enters an area unless a real cross section of the population wants him, and he will not come unless the community itself will accept full responsibility for financing the whole program within three years. Through a mixture of pyrotechnics and politics, Alinsky helped Woodlawn to organize and fight back against the coalition of the University of Chicago and the powerful South East Chicago Commission, which is really the University's bridge to the centers of financial and political power in the city. He helped organize rent strikes and picketing, and he eventually won representation for the community in the groups that were planning the "renewal" of Woodlawn.

The organizing of Woodlawn has had a spectacular impact on Chicago politics. It has convinced a whole community of inner-city Negroes that they do not have to ask people to do things for them but can take their lives in their own hands. Alinsky does this by his steadfast refusal to coddle, patronize, or override. He forces the community to become adult, to stand up and demand what it rightly deserves, and to apply pressure at those points where the blood flows nearest the surface in the body politic. Many Woodlawn residents say that because of TWO they have now lost their fear of expressing themselves: "We don't have to go, hat in hand, begging anymore." Besides giving residents of the community a new sense of identity and dignity, says Mr. Silberman, TWO has also "given many people a sense of direction and purpose and an inner discipline that have enabled them to overcome the disorganization of the Negro slum."¹⁰

The Woodlawn experiment holds many clues for strategy for an urban church. Where is the new age breaking in? It is appearing wherever men are summoned to dignity and accountability, where defeat and resignation give way to freedom and responsibility. If that is so, then Woodlawn is certainly a sign of the Kingdom, an instance of the emergence of the true secular city, the city of man. City mission societies and councils of churches would do well to examine this program and either launch or support similar experiments elsewhere. This would mean a complete change from much of the present approach to inner-city missions now taken by churches, however much it is honeyed o'er with sweet words about "personal contact" and "seeing persons as persons." People trapped in the prison house of urban injustice are not interested in friendly guards who drop down from the suburban ramparts to fraternize on occasion with the inmates, re-reating after a warm experience behind a carefully maintained wall. Inner-city people represent the oppressed to whom Jesus said he had come to bring not warm words but liberty. The inmates of the urban concentration camp do not long for fraternization with the guards; what they want is the abolition of the prison; not improved relations with the captors but release from captivity.

Of course this demands a lot of suburbanites. It suggests that they participate in a revolution which, in terms of "this world," is against their best interests. Increasing the relative power of the inner-city means decreasing the relative power of the suburbs. Changing bank practices, zoning laws, school financing, and tax structures means they will have to foot a larger if more equitable portion of the bill for supporting an urban society. But no one ever claimed that the summons of the Kingdom did not entail sacrifice and responsibility. In the preceding chapter we pointed out that these constitute the heart of what the Bible means by repentance. But sacrifice and responsibility in the church have not been equally distributed, by a wide measure. Middle-class suburbanites have exercised responsibility but have rarely sacrificed, and therefore their responsibility has hardened into an elaborate form of self-protection. Suburban politics is often antimetropolitan and self-centered, directed toward keeping taxes down and "undesirables" out. Lower-class inner-city people, for their part, have sacrificed a lot, but they have not been willing or able to take political responsibility. Therefore their sacrifices have tended to engender only bitterness and resentment. Suburbanites must now be called upon to sacrifice parochial interests for the health of the whole; and inner-city people must be called upon to assume responsibility, not just for themselves but for the metropolis of which they are a part.

This discussion of summoning and calling brings us back to the kerygmatic function of the church, and reminds us again that kerygma, diakonia, and koinonia can never be fully separated from each other.

The Church's Koinoniac Function: Making Visible the City of Man

The Greek word *koinonia* is usually translated "fellowship." In our discussion it will designate that aspect of the church's responsibility in the city which calls for a visible demonstration of what the church is saying in its kerygma and pointing to in its diakonia. It is "hope made visible," a kind of living picture of the character and composition of the true city of man for which the church strives.

Actually there is a considerable amount of consensus among contemporary theologians on this element of the church's life, albeit expressed in widely various ways. Using the Greek New Testament word *eschaton,* meaning the "last things" or the "new age," Rudolf Bultmann calls the church the "eschatological community." It is that portion of the world which already lives in the ethos of the new era, which already orders its life according to the style of the new regime. This coheres with J. C. Hoekendijk's suggestion that the church is the avant-garde of God, that group whose ties to particular political and cultural arrangements are sufficiently tenuous that it is always ready to move to the next stage in history. It lives in tents, not in temples. It is a people whose life is informed by its confident expectation that God is bringing in a new regime and that they are already allowed to taste its fruits.[11]

Karl Barth calls the church "God's provisional demonstration of his intention for all humanity." More than simply a community of hope, the church participates in a provisional reality: It is where the shape and texture of the future age come to concrete visibility. Gerhard Ebeling suggests that the "marks of the church" are

. . . the overcoming of the separation between Jews and heathens (as the prototype of religiously based particularity), and the overcoming of the distinction between

clean and unclean (as the root of the cultic view of
reality). . . .[12]

Thus Ebeling puts the traditional "marks of the church"
discussion in a much-needed contemporary framework. The
insistence by the Reformers that the church was "where the
word is rightly preached and the sacraments rightly administered" will simply not do today. It was useful in a period
when the church had to be distinguished from heresies. But
we must define the marks of the church today in ways which
suggest that the "true church" occurs where its functions
(kerygma, diakonia, koinonia) occur. The "signs" of this sort
of occurrence, as Ebeling suggests, are the abolition of religious
and cultic boundaries—and the world views that go along
with them. The church appears where tribal and town chau-
vinism are left behind along with their characteristic mythologies, and a new inclusive human community emerges. The
church is a sign of the emergent city of man, an outrider for
the secular city. The story of one unusual city may illustrate
the meaning of the koinoniac function of the church as an
eschatological community.

Shortly after the Communists came to power in Poland in
1945, they constructed a spanking new model city. They
named it Nova Huta (New City). Replete with verdant parks,
spotless day nurseries, and gleaming sport and cultural facilities, Nova Huta was designed to serve as a visible embodiment
of the direction of history as the Communists envisioned it. It
was the embodiment of the dialectic in its fulfillment, a living
demonstration of what the Communists said they were working for. The people to live in Nova Huta were selected on the
basis of their "ideological maturity" and freedom from the
remnants of so-called bourgeois attitudes. It was clearly designed to be a Communist equivalent of a "sign of the Kingdom."

Unlike Nova Huta, the eschatological community of the
church does not locate itself in only one place. It dis-
perses itself, living within the structures of the old society,
participating there in erecting models of the Kingdom.
These signs have both a symbolic and a substantive function. They are *instances* of the coming of the Kingdom, just
as Jesus' coming was; they are also signs or clues as to where
history is going, what the City of Man is really like.

Wherever cogent and tangible demonstrations of the reality
of the City of Man appear today, these are signs of the King-

dom. Such signs sometimes appear among people who reject religious idiom. One excellent example of a sign of the Kingdom were the Freedom Schools which took place in several Northern cities during the school boycotts of 1963 and 1964. As a protest against scrimping school budgets and racial separation, the boycotts were justifiable on their own merits. But the Freedom Schools introduced a positive note to the protest which strengthened it immeasurably. Boycott leaders were objecting to oversize classes, segregation by residential patterns, paternalistic and authoritarian instruction, a curriculum lacking in Negro history or the philosophy of social protest. In the Freedom Schools that were well planned and administered, all of these conditions were corrected—if only for one day. Children were placed in small groups on a racially inclusive basis. They were taught by volunteers (some of them losing a day's pay from work somewhere else) who had participated in a careful training period. Teachers relied heavily on discussion rather than rote even with the youngest students, and used teaching materials which included pictures of dark-skinned as well as light-skinned people. In addition, teachers tried to help each child realize that he was even now participating in a movement of social protest and that he *could* have some impact on the status quo.

The Freedom Schools provided a sign of the coming Kingdom, a portrait of the City of Man. But signs of the Kingdom anywhere succeed only as they call to repentance, as they summon people to let go of previous ways of organizing urban education and to find new patterns which will cohere with the emerging urban reality.

The relationship between the church and these signs of the Kingdom is twofold. The church is one of the signs, and it points to and supports the other signs. It is wrong to identify the church with the Kingdom. Its whole existence is a derivative one, dependent entirely on the prior reality of the Kingdom. The church's koinoniac or demonstrating function dovetails with its kerygmatic functions. Its job is to proclaim and to show the world what the signs of the Kingdom are: harbingers of a reality that is breaking into history not from the past but from the future. They are warnings of a future for which we had best prepare, making whatever sacrifices are necessary. The avant-garde of God makes its announcement by allowing its own life to be shaped by the future Kingdom (not past tradition) and by indicating with its lips and its life where other signs of the Kingdom are appearing.

The koinoniac function of the church cannot be executed unless the church itself includes all the elements of the heterogeneous metropolis. In the secular city, a church divided along ethnic, racial, or denominational lines cannot even begin to perform its function. The character of such a church is still shaped by forces emanating from the tribal and town epochs. It is a prisoner of what the Bible calls "this passing age." Such a so-called church is not a breakthrough point into the future but a bastion of the past, and as such it is not a church at all. It is not a part of the eschatological community. With considerably less restraint than has been exercised here, the Reformers called such groups "antichurches" and their leaders representatives of the anti-Christ. Such language is not popular today, but the point should not be missed. Jesus Christ comes to his people not primarily through ecclessiastical traditions, but through social change. He "goes before" first as a pillar of fire and then as the presence which moved from Jerusalem to Samaria to the end of the earth. He is always ahead of the church, beckoning it to get up to date, never behind it waiting to be refurbished. Canon and tradition function not as sources of revelation but as precedents by which present events can be checked out as the possible loci of God's action.

NOTES TO CHAPTER 6

1. M. M. Thomas, quoted in "From Letters Concerning 'The Missionary Structure of the Congregation,' " in *Concept* V, Papers from the Department on Studies in Evangelism, World Council of Churches (mimeographed document), p. 4.
2. Archie Hargraves, "Go Where the Action Is," *Social Action* (February 1964), p. 17.
3. *Concept* (April 1963), p. 3.   ,
4. In his excellent book, *The Militant Ministry* (Philadelphia: Fortress Press, 1963), Hans-Reudi Weber points out that the Greek verb *katargeo*—which is used to describe what happens to the "powers"—in no sense suggests they are annihilated. Rather, it means they are dethroned and tamed. "These powers are being disarmed by Christ as enemies and at the same time mobilized for God's service." P. 103, note 14.
5. Friedrich Gogarten, *Der Mensch zwischen Gott und Welt* (Stuttgart: Friedrich Vorwerk Verlag, 1956), pp. 13, 14.
6. Edward C. Banfield and James Q. Wilson, *City Politics* (Cambridge, Mass.: Harvard University Press, 1963).
7. *Ibid.*, p. 101.

8. Joseph Clark, "Cities in Trouble," *New University Thought* (Spring 1961), p. 4.

9. Charles E. Silberman, "Up from Apathy," *Commentary* (May 1964), p. 57.

10. *Ibid.*, p. 58.

11. The extraordinarily fresh thinking of J. C. Hoekendijk underlies much of the present writer's thinking about the church. Unfortunately most of his writing appears in Dutch. Two articles in English are "The Call to Evangelism" in *International Review of Missions* (1950), pp. 161ff., and "Christ and the World in the Modern Age" in *The Student World* (1961), Nos. 1–2, pp. 75ff.

12. Gerhard Ebeling, *Theologie und Verkundigung* (Tübingen: JCB Mohr–Paul Siebeck, 1962), p. 94. My translation. See also Ebeling's *Nature of Faith* (Philadelphia: Fortress Press, 1963) and his *Word and Faith* (Philadelphia: Fortress Press, 1963).

CHAPTER 7

The Church as Cultural Exorcist

We have discussed the church as the avant-garde of God, the representative of the new regime instituted by Jesus. We have said that where the kerygmatic, diakonic, and koinoniac functions of the church converge, there it most faithfully continues what Jesus did. But in our discussion so far we have quite obviously left out one of the most puzzling aspects of Jesus' ministry. Though it frequently embarrasses us today, Jesus was viewed by his own age as a great exorcist. His power to cast out demons was central to his ministry. It focused all his various roles. As the one who announced the New Age, he commanded the "evil spirits" to depart, a kerygmatic function. As a healer and reconciler, he exorcised them to restore people to their places in the community, a diakonic function. As the personification of the Kingdom, he was recognized and feared by the demons he cast out, the koinoniac function.

All of this sounds extremely peculiar to modern ears. Most of us would prefer to forget that for many of his contemporaries Jesus' exorcism was in no way peripheral, but stood at the heart of his work. How does the church carry on this function today? Or should the church simply forget exorcism?

Even in the twentieth century, exorcism remains that point at which the three aspects of the church's ministry come closest to fusing. But to understand what the responsibility for exorcism means in the secular city, we must get behind the prescientific images of spirits and demons to the reality they expressed. Men of New Testament times used this language to designate the subpersonal forces and suprapersonal influences which warped and twisted human life. They represented the "principalities and powers" as they functioned in a particular personality, something that is still very much with us.

Anthropologists who investigate magical beliefs among tribal peoples today report that violating a tabu can cause death, and that people who have been killed in effigy by voodoo techniques do in fact die with more than accidental frequency.[1] The reason for this is that a personality system includes organic, social, and cultural components. A person whose whole view of himself includes the cultural meanings inherent in a magical society will literally die if that culture indicates he should. Culture has a powerful effect on persons, far more than we were willing to admit during the eighteenth and nineteenth centuries, when rationalistic individualism laughed at such things.

Even in the emerging secular city, massive residues of magical and superstitious world views remain. In his fascinating book *Life against Death*,[2] Norman O. Brown has uncovered a lengthy catalog of sacred sediments which still encrust our supposedly rational modern life. One of the best examples of this magicosacral hangover is our attitude toward money. Brown demonstrates that this attitude projects onto our "filthy lucre" esoteric attributes and talismanic properties which belie earlier economic theories about the utter rationality of money. Utilizing psychoanalytic categories, Brown attributes these and other magicosacral distortions to repression, our unwillingness to entertain certain feelings and desires on the conscious level.

By now, the psychoanalytic theory of repression and projection, though it has undergone certain modifications in detail since first elaborated by Freud, is widely accepted in its main outlines. Roughly, the theory states that, because societies forbid men to accept and express feelings of hostility and sexuality, we either redirect them into some other form of activity (sublimation) or transfer them onto other persons and groups, or even onto mythical realities (projection). Thus the escapades of the gods in the Greek myths can be understood as a projection of the conflicts and aspirations of the Greeks themselves at particular stages in their historical development. Projection also operates, however, between persons and social groups. Parents project attitudes onto children which the children themselves soon accept and emulate. Karl Adorno, in his famous work *Authoritarian Personality*,[3] shows how the Germans, unable to accept their own sexual and acquisitive desires, projected them onto the Jews and then punished the Jews for their own failings. The same phenomenon can be seen in relationships between white and Negro Americans. The Negro has become one of the receptacles into which the unresolved sexual and economic problems of the white majority have been poured. John Dollard in *Caste and*

Class in a Southern Town[4] has shown how the popular images of the Negro as lazy and sexually virile find their sources in the unaccepted feelings of the white man.

Needless to say, this sort of activity encourages certain forms of behavior in the groups onto which the stereotype is projected, which in turn serve to corroborate the images. This can be explained through role psychology, or the mechanism called "self-fulfilling prophecy." Thus Negroes or Jews, where they are given no other identity images than those served up to them by the white majority, tend to enact the expectation, which in turn reinforces the prejudice. Swiss playwright Max Frisch has explored this fatal process in a brilliant play entitled *Andorra*.[5] It tells the story of a young man who is thought by the residents of the town to be a Jewish foundling, although he is actually the illegitimate son of one of the townspeople. Slowly, through the open and devious suggestions of his fellow residents, the young man painfully assumes more and more "Jewish" characteristics. As Freud would say, he "introjects" the role until he becomes in fact a Jew. As with the New Testament demoniacs who really believed they were possessed of demons and the witches of Salem who confessed to being witches, the mechanism of projection and introjection had done its work.

Thus the presence of repressed and projected feelings probably explains the demons of the New Testament period, the witches of colonial New England, and the cultural stereotypes of the modern epoch. Cultures concentrate repressed feelings into roles which are forced on given individuals who in turn enact them. Consequently, casting out of demons necessitates dealing both with those who have projected the spurious identities and with those who have introjected them. As Martin Luther King put it, equality for the Negro must include *both* changing the prejudice of the white man *and* overcoming the "slave mentality" in the Negro. Dealing with such problems is the modern equivalent of casting out demons.

The achievement of health in place of neurosis on the individual level cannot be separated from the restoration of wholeness to the entire society. Various cultures have their ways of encouraging some neuroses while punishing others. Our culture, for example, is easy on obsessive greediness and compulsive achievement but it punishes sexually expressed neuroses—sometimes very sternly. Freud concentrated on the sick individual in his therapy, Marx on the sick society; the two cannot be separated. As Erich Fromm has written, the realization of the individual's full potential as a human being may contradict the social ideal of normalcy, but this merely calls for a "pathology of normalcy." Thus such a realization *is* possible and "the interest of the society and of the individual need not be antagonistic forever."[6]

The world in which the interests of the society and of the individual are not antagonistic catches up elements of the vision of the secular utopians and the promise of the Kingdom of God. It is symbolized in the image of the secular city, the Commonwealth of Man which is always appearing but never complete, the focal point of the partnership between God and man. But religion, instead of freeing man to play his part in the making of the secular city, has frequently served as precisely that vehicle which has kept him in bondage to his past, which has tied him to the childhood of the species. Norman Brown is aware of this. Like Freud himself, Brown sees a close link between history itself and the history of religion. The maturation process in cultures and in individuals is analogous. Consequently, the cultural equivalent of infantile regression and childhood fears and fantasies can be found in the religion of a given culture. Religion is, in a sense, the neurosis of cultures; secularization corresponds to maturation. As Freud put it in *Moses and Monotheism:*

> In the history of the species something happened similar to the events in the life of the individual. That is to say, mankind as a whole passed through conflicts of a sexual-aggressive nature, which left permanent traces . . . and created phenomena similar in structure and tendency to neurotic symptoms.[7]

Freud saw that this "archaic heritage" in every culture functioned as a kind of neurotic constriction, limiting its freedom and creating a phantom world through repression and projection.

Jesus dealt in his exorcism with the neurotic constrictions of individuals, but his whole life represented a kind of sweeping exorcism of the neurosis of a whole culture. He confronted demonic images and legalistic compulsions in such a way that people were liberated from both into clearheaded and productive ways of life. Both on the individual and on the cultural level, neurotic constriction is expressed in the fusion of demons and ritual obedience—in psychoanalytic terms, of fantasies and obsessive behavior patterns. In the New Testament, Jesus' confrontation with the demons represents his battle against projected fantasies, and his attack on the Scribes and Pharisees who were the custodians of ritual meticulousness dramatizes his struggle against compulsive behavior patterns.[8]

In his splendid book on the Gospel of Mark, the New Testament scholar James M. Robinson has shown that these two elements of Jesus' ministry are inseparable.[9] He demonstrates that Jesus' casting out demons and his debates with the Scribes were really two episodes in the same titanic struggle. "Mark not only presents the debates in a form similar to that of the exorcisms," Robinson concludes, "but also envisages the meaning of the debates in a way similar to the exorcisms."[10] The writer of Mark saw, in his own terms, a close connection between repression with its resultant illusory projections, on the one hand, and the obsessive performance of ritual requirements with its resultant lack of personal freedom on the other. Jesus had to defeat both the demons and the Pharisees. In order to make men free for concrete obedience and responsible decision making, men had to be liberated both from the archaic heritage which distorted their vision of reality and from the anxious legalism which constricted their behavior.

Jesus calls men to adulthood, a condition in which they are freed from their bondages to the infantile images of the species and of the self. Exorcism is that process by which the stubborn deposits of town and tribal pasts are scraped from the social consciousness of man and he is freed to face his world matter of factly. The British scientist and lay theologian John Wren Lewis has argued that a belief in occult powers, whether crude or subtle, represents the very opposite of biblical faith. It ". . . diverts people's attention from the concrete problems of this world . . . wherein alone the true call of God can be found, into an activity of imagining things that go on behind the scenes."[11] Lewis believes quite rightly that the impact of Jesus is to call this irresponsible dodge into question, so that we are no longer able to avoid "facing up to the call of God in our immediate situation by engaging in ritual activity of one form or another. . . ."[12]

The ministry of the church in the secular city must include a contemporary extension of exorcism. Men must be called away from their fascination with other worlds—astrological, metaphysical, or religious—and summoned to confront the concrete issues of this one, "wherein alone the true call of God can be found." They must be freed from the narcotic vagaries through which they wrongly perceive the social reality around them, and from habitual forms of action or inaction stemming from these illusions. This is the work of social exorcism. It was carried out by Jesus; his church should be expected to carry on this same work.

But the work is not carried on by the churches alone. Jesus refused to think of himself as the only legitimate exorcist. When his disciples reported in annoyance that other people were also casting out demons and asked him to call down fire upon them, he would not do so. He reminded them that "those who are not against us are for us." In the modern world, there are many allies who are contributing to the work of social and cultural exorcism. John Wren Lewis counts the modern scientific revolution itself one of these allies. It contributes to cultural exorcism by virtue of its ". . . loss of interest in the occult, [its] preparedness to look at things as they actually are for their own sake, to look and see what is really there, to throw overboard any amount of theory in the light of experience. . . ."[13]

The ministry of exorcism in the secular city requires a community of persons who, individually and collectively, are not burdened by the constriction of an archiac heritage. It requires a community which, if not fully liberated, is in the process of liberation from compulsive patterns of behavior based on mistaken images of the world. In performing its function the church should be such a community and should be sensitive to those currents in modern life which bear the same exorcising power. The church should be ready to expose the fallaciousness of the social myths by which the injustices of a society are perpetuated and to suggest ways of action which demonstrate the wrongness of such fantasies.

One would not have to look very far in a modern metropolis for demonic distortions, for myths seeping into the present from an archaic heritage. We have already mentioned the humiliating role in which our culture has cast the Negro. So long as the distortion remains, both white and Negro will be caught in a debilitating fiction that can be dissolved only when the imagery is discarded and we look at things as they really are. Our attitudes about the poor partake of the same destructive make-believe. With our mental outlook still grounded in nineteenth-century Horatio Alger images of independence and initiative as a sure remedy for any economic hardship, we are incapable of dealing with the utterly new kind of poverty which has arisen in the technological age, a

poverty which grows out of structural dislocations in the
economy for which no one person is responsible. As Alan D.
Wade of the University of Chicago School of Social Service
Administration has written:

> The growth of our population, coupled with urbanization,
> automation and integration, have so outstripped our human
> imaginations that, instead of developing new social ar-
> rangements that can supplement or take the place of the
> old measures by which we protected those who fell along
> the way, we face *new realities* armed with little more than
> *immensely dangerous and costly myths.*[14]

Professor Wade's diagnosis comports precisely with the notion of sociocultural neurosis. Like an individual who cannot
cope with an adult problem because of anxieties and patterns
imported from childhood, our society is trying to grapple with
new and complex social issues with inflexible behavioral
myths and rigid cultural reflexes. Confronting people with
"what is really there" is always a painful process, but it is the
unavoidable prerequisite to maturity. It was what Jesus was
always doing, and it represents an indispensable element of
the church's function in the secular city.

In discussing the kerygmatic, diakonic, and koinoniac functions of the church in the secular city, we have said that these
functions converge in the church's role as cultural exorcist.
All of this clearly has significant implications for the institutional form of the church in such a society. Recently a spir-
ited discussion of the forms of church life has broken out,
partially under the auspices of the Department of Studies in
Evangelism of the World Council of Churches. The issues are
skillfully summarized in Colin Williams' little book *Where in
the World.*[15] As Williams sees it, the church today is ensnarled in a form of institutional life—the residential parish—
which dates from the preindustrial era. The residential parish
recalls a time when people worked and resided, prayed and
played in concentrated communities of shared life. The residential parish, in other words, dates from what we have called
town culture, before the onslaught of urbanization. Williams
contends that in an urban industrial world, where work and
politics and much of our leisure activity have emigrated out of
the residential area, we need new forms of church life commensurate with these new social arrangements. He recom-
mends that patterns be devised whereby the church can take
shape in such nonresidential social structures as business and
communication groups, the institutions of mass media,

"communities of need" (such as among drug addicts), and with reference to such social crises as race, poverty, and war.[16]

This exceedingly necessary discussion has opened many eyes, but it has also occasioned a considerable backlash of opposition from people who see it as a terrible threat to the existing forms of church life. Some even believe it displays a lack of realism about the way institutions really change and how much can actually be done outside the existing structures of church life. The less circumspect critics of Williams suggest that he exhibits a lack of faith in God's capacity to renew and revitalize the church.

Much of the uneasiness about the discussion of the need for "new structures of church life" comes, of course, from people who feel themselves theatened by what appears a downgrading of the present forms of church life. Some of it arises, however, from a certain lack of clarity in the discussion about the relationship between existing forms of church life and the ones which will certainly emerge, study or no study, in the coming years. The misunderstanding centers largely on the future of the standard residential parish. Some claim it is dead as a social form and should be discarded in favor of structures that are in keeping with an urban-industrial society where people come together more according to common functions than according to residential proximity. Others defend the parish church as the necessary base for any or all incursions into the nonresidential sphere.

The difficulty is that we are not moving from one stage of society in which a particular form of church life, the residential parish, was the characteristic form into a stage in which some other form of church life will replace it. The situation is far more complex. The key word to describe what is happening in our society is *differentiation*. We are moving into a stage in which we will need a widely differentiated range of different types of church organization to engage a society which is becoming differentiated at an accelerated rate. Church life in the secular metropolis will certainly include congregations based on residence, but since residence (as we saw in our discussion of mobility and anonymity) touches people today only in one segment of their lives, we shall also need other forms of church life *alongside* it. Not only will future forms of church life be differentiated and specialized, they must also be flexible and disposable, ready in their turn to give way to ever newer forms.

The church must be ready for differentiation if it wants to exist in a rapidly differentiating society. Defenders of the parish church would do better to see what it can realistically be expected to do in an urban-industrial setting instead of defending it against all critics. The truth is that the parish *can* do certain things, but it cannot do some of the other things that must be accomplished by industrial missions, lay academies, and issue-oriented groupings. Attackers of the residential parish, on their side, had best realize that imprecations will not kill social institutions. Much wealth and talent and leadership is still concentrated in residential parishes and will be for some time. The real question is how this fund of resources can be channeled into a ministry of exorcism in the city.

Besides the development of differentiated forms of church life, in addition to the residential parish, we can also expect to see a marked differentiation *among* residential congregations. This means two things. First, residential parishes will begin to play a somewhat different role than they have in the past. Relieved of the necessity of being all things to all men, of pretending to "serve the whole man," they can begin to concentrate on those areas of concern in which they really have some kind of entrée. Family problems, residential issues, and adult education seem to be among the things a local parish can deal with. In this regard, a local parish resembles sociologically a family. With the coming of industrialization, some sociologists confidently predicted that the family, shorn of its economc functions, would soon cease to exist. What has happened instead is that the family has assumed new functions in industrial society; it has begun to deal with problems that did not exist in earlier social epochs. The family has turned much of the socialization of children over to the school and the peer group, but it has retained some functions that make it almost indispensable to the society. In the same way the parish church, once it has ceased trying to be the whole church and has allowed other forms of church life to assume some of the responsibilities it once had, may be able to make a significant contribution within a plethora of differentiated ecclesiastical forms.

Second, the differentiation among forms of church life means that congregations will begin to develop specialities. They will not all try to do everything that every other congregation is doing. This means the end of uniform nationally planned programs. What any particular local church does will grow from what it discerns to be the action of God in that segment of the metropolis to which it has some genuine access. This will necessitate a survey of the composition of the congregation to determine what the members really have in common plus a study of the neighborhood to see how the various functions of the church can be executed. Judson Memorial Church in New York City is a good example of a local congregation that has developed a speciality, ministering to artists and intellectuals. The Blue Hill Community Church in Boston's Roxbury district specializes in work with people involved in the Negro freedom movement. Its entire program, including choir, Sunday service, youth program, and adult education, is geared into this effort.

No one could possibly deny that in urban-secular society, we shall see the emergence of radically new and unexpected forms of church life with no relationship whatever to residential congregations. The Detroit Industrial Mission is one such form. It exists entirely within the structures of the automobile industry and its derivative institutions. It makes no effort to operate from a residential "base." Experimental ministries, without residential bases, are springing up in the communications industries, in leisure and recreational areas, and among particular occupational groups. They have already emerged in hospitals and universities. The guild movement among Roman Catholics is an example of a variety of occupational congregation. These congregations tend to be transient and short-lived. Frequently they exist without benefit of permanent clergy. But this is not to be regretted. It would be deplorable if the promising appearance of new forms of church life in the disparate structures of modern life were to be hamstrung by forcing them into transplanted residential patterns. These new forms should not be expected to be permanent, to develop all the paraphernalia of traditional forms, or even to engage in cultic worship. Their *ad hoc* character, their willingness to disband after they have dealt satisfactorily with a given set of issues, may be an authentic characteristic of their appropriateness. They may be the kinds of "marks of the church" we will need in the secular city.

Two words of warning need to be issued. One is that the real ecumenical crisis today is not between Catholics and Protestants but between traditional and experimental forms of church life. If church leaders do not recognize this, within a few decades we shall see a cleavage in the church that will be comparable to the one that appeared in the sixteenth century.

There are both Catholics and Protestants who are suspicious
of new forms of church life—witness the way the Vatican
opposed the worker priests and the way the United Church of
Japan opposed the Non-Church Movement. There are also
both Protestants and Catholics who support and encourage
innovations in church structure. Here leaders in the established traditional forms must learn to appreciate the value of
the innovators and maintain communication across the newly
threatening abyss.

Second, there is a danger that *ad hoc* congregations, oriented around particular occupational groupings and specific
social issues, may lose sight of the interrelationships between
the various segments of a metropolis which have to be dealt
with together. They must guard against becoming just as insulated in their own ways as residential congregations are. *Ad
hoc* congregations represent the ecclesiastical equivalent of
contextual ethics. In recent years, Christian ethicists have
been reticent to deal with social philosophy in general and
have tended to deal with issues as they arose one by one. They
have eschewed attempts to bend problems into the terms of
ethical systems or preconceived plans for the betterment of
society. They have operated on a more or less piecemeal basis.

This contextual approach represents a real advance over
previous types of ethics. It has a flexibility and relevance that
rigid, systematic, and principal approaches lack. But one of
the great realities of the modern urban era is *planning*. Instead
of dealing with mass transit, education, housing, employment,
and crime on a piecemeal basis, urban planners today try to
pull all these factors together and plan for the development of
a city over a whole decade. Once again "the good city" is
being discussed, and issues are seen more in their relationship
to each other and as part of a social whole. How all these
various issues impinge on the individual and his family comes
to light in questions that sound very much like the traditional
queries about the "good for man." Urban planners debate
issues in terms of variant renewal programs, but they are the
same issues which were once debated in economics and before
that in theology: What is the path toward the fulfillment of
man's potential?

So social ethics and social philosophy may not be so old hat
as was once thought. But as Christians begin to enter into this
kind of discussion, it must be made clear again that there are
no specifically Christian answers to the inclusive problems of
social planning any more than there are to the piecemeal

problems with which we have usually been concerned. The Kingdom of God does not come in the same way everywhere. Mankind is not monochromatic. Men differ so widely in taste and temperament that the task of fulfilling human needs will require different kinds of cities in different cultural climates. Christians possess no blueprint for the heavenly city. They are free to struggle alongside people of many persuasions to devise a way of living together which allows man to be man.

In fulfilling its various functions in the secular city, the church will develop a wide variety of forms of life. Some will last. Others will disappear quickly. And the problem of "church unity," the issue that created such widespread interest among religious people in recent years, will not be a matter of the divisions between denominations but of the relationship between highly differentiated expressions of the same church.

In all its forms the church will continue to be a cultural exorcist, casting out the mythical meanings that obscure the realities of life and hinder human action. In the following chapters we shall indicate how the ethics of exorcism operate in a series of specific problem areas.

NOTES TO CHAPTER 7

1. For documentation of instances of death resulting from belief in the efficacy of magic, see Hutton Webster, *Magic: A Sociological Study* (Stanford, Calif.: Stanford University Press, 1948), pp. 486–488. Theoretical discussions of the link between psychosomatic sickness and death and cultural belief systems can be found in Lawrence Frank, "Cultural Control and Physiological Autonomy" in Kluckhohn and Murray (eds.), *Personality in Nature, Society and Culture* (New York: Knopf, 1959), pp. 119–122, and in Margaret Mead, "The Concept of Culture and the Psychosomatic Approach" in Douglas Haring (ed.), *Personal Character and Cultural Milieu* (Syracuse, N.Y.: Syracuse University Press, 1956), pp. 594–622.

2. Norman O. Brown, *Life against Death* (New York: Random House, 1959).

3. Karl Adorno, *The Authoritarian Personality* (New York: Harper & Row, 1950).

4. John Dollard, *Caste and Class in a Southern Town* (Garden City, N.Y.: Doubleday, 3d ed., 1957).

5. Max Frisch, *Andorra* [*Stück im zwölf Bildern*], (Frankfurt-am-Main: Suhrkamp Verlag, 1961).

6. Erich Fromm, "Individual and Social Origins of Neurosis,"

in Kluckhohn and Murray (eds.), *Personality in Nature, Society and Culture* (New York: Knopf, 1959), p. 521.

7. Sigmund Freud, *Moses and Monotheism* (New York: Vintage Books, Inc., 1955; London: Hogarth), p. 129.

8. I believe theologians must take the work of Freud on cultural analysis and religion even more seriously than they have taken his more therapeutic writings. On the last pages of his book *Civilization and Its Discontents* (New York: Cape and Smith, 1930; London: Hogarth), Freud even drops a hint about the role of Jesus in the maturation of culture.

9. James M. Robinson, *The Problem of History in Mark* (Naperville, Ill.: Alec R. Allenson, Inc., 1957; London: SCM Press).

10. *Ibid.*, p. 6.

11. John Wren Lewis, "Science, the World and God," *The Christian Scholar*, XLII (September 1959), 171.

12. *Ibid.*, p. 171.

13. *Ibid.*, p. 173.

14. Alan D. Wade, "Why We Hate the Poor," *Renewal*, IV (1964), 15. Emphasis added.

15. Colin W. Williams, *Where in the World?* (New York: National Council of Churches, 1963). For criticisms of Williams, see Truman B. Douglas, "In Defence of the Local Parish," *Christianity & Crisis*, XXIV (June 8, 1964), 115.

16. *Ibid.*, p. 84.

PART THREE

EXCURSIONS IN URBAN EXORCISM

CHAPTER 8

Work and Play in the Secular City

The twin tendencies of urbanization and secularization have an enormous impact on work. We shall restrict ourselves in this chapter to three basic alterations they produce: First, they separate the place of work from the place of residence; second, they transform work more and more into bureaucratic patterns of organization; and third, they emancipate work from the religious character it has retained from the period when it was interpreted as a spiritual discipline. All of these modifications of work have been viewed with alarm and criticized, frequently by religious people. Attempts have been made to reintroduce familial elements into the life of the modern corporation; objections have been voiced to the organization with its characteristic impersonality; laments have been sung over the disappearance of a sense of vocation in work.

Our objective here, however, is not to decry what has happened to work in the technopolitan era but to indicate how in each instance secularization, despite the problems it brings, has opened up new possibilities not present before. In the world of work, as in every other sector of human life, secularization is not the Messiah. But neither is it the anti-Christ. It is rather a dangerous liberation; it raises the stakes, making it possible for man to increase the range of his freedom and responsibility and thus to deepen his maturation. At the same time it poses risks of a larger order than those it displaces. But the promise exceeds the peril, or at least makes it worth taking the risk.

The Separation of Places of Work and Residence

Several trends in technopolitan society tend to separate the place one works from the place one resides. The growing specialization of work demands that those with comparable

145

specialties gather in more and more highly concentrated areas. The laws of efficiency, which point in most instances toward increased size, have with minor exceptions killed off the family farm and the small family business. Zoning and city planning have tended to segregate production areas from residential areas. Even where this tendency is being reversed, where a highly imaginative "mix" of land usages has been reintroduced, where offices, stores, and apartments share the same building, it has not meant a return to the undifferentiated small family business. The "psychological distance" between work and residence remains, even when work and residence areas are purposely near each other. Work is being steadily defamilialized.

The net result is that the workplace, the marketplace, and the school have moved away from residential areas. The butchers and grocers have set themselves up behind the glittering glass-and-steel showcases of shopping centers surrounded by endless acres of parking lots. Shoe salesmen, druggists, clothing and hardware dealers are following suit quickly. The Fuller brush man still rings the doorbell, as does the junior high student selling magazines. But most of the selling now goes on in the vast emporia of our air-conditioned bazaars. Other activities are showing the same tendency. Schools are placed in specially demarcated areas and consolidated into larger units. This is dictated by road safety and educational philosophy—and also by economics. Educators are finding ways to replace the endless locker-lined corridors and enormous chilly study halls which dwarf and alienate children. Still, the sheer equipment needed for modern education prevents any thought of going back to the little red schoolhouse. The chemistry laboratory of today's high school requires, at a minimum, equipment that would have seemed luxurious to a college chemistry professor two decades ago and is far too expensive to duplicate in numberless small schools.

The same principle holds for other services. The doctor who until recently had his office in one wing of his home, adding a note of nonresidential counterpoint to the monochromatic melody of hedges, lawns, and houses, has also become a commuter. With increasing frequency he is now found at a downtown professional building or in a medical arts center. Like everyone else, he needs expensive equipment he can better afford if he shares it, and he enjoys in the city the added advantage of having medical and dental colleagues close by for quick consultation.

One by one the workingman, the tradesman, the merchant, the doctor have packed their tools and emigrated out of the residential area. Few residential communities complain. They have little enough fondness for businesses mixed with family togetherness, and besides, the doctors and the businessmen are not arguing the point. Although they may occasionally complain about the commutation rat race, they really rather enjoy the psychic separation between workplace and home. The distance serves to insulate both areas, protecting each from unwelcome incursions from the other. The young oculist may genuinely look forward to an occasional visit to his office by his wife and even, at rare intervals, by his children. But it would be quite a different thing to have them living in the next room. Similarly, the account executive's long commutation to the suburbs or short trip to a high-rise apartment has a psychological as well as a logistical significance. During that time he tries to put behind him, at least in part, all the open questions he has left and concentrate on connecting his new woofer. The commuter-train tracks or the thruway connect his work with his home, but they also separate two sets of relationships which he feels are probably best kept somewhat apart.

Urban man's noticeable desire to keep these spheres from coalescing is both understandable and justifiable. He lives in so many different functionally defined relationships, in which he plays roles not always entirely self-consistent, that he must find ways to isolate the various circuits from one another, at least in part. This is why the insidious attempts of the corporation to annex family life are so resented.

One young accountant worked for a firm with what its well-intentioned management took to be very advanced ideas on personnel policy. Among these was a well-constructed scheme designed to inform wives of executives about their husbands' work and to enlist their enthusiasm for the corporation's objectives. Using an adaptation of the Harvard Case Study method, evening discussions were held monthly for husbands and wives on a case elementary enough to engage the interest of the women. Drinks were always served, on the company, and a dedicated young personnel executive steered the conversation in such a way that the wives would get the feel of the kinds of decisions with which their husbands often wrestled. The whole procedure was naturally highly democratic and permissive, with no single group-dynamics stone left unturned.

One evening during the height of the tax season, always the most hectic for accountants, a harried young CPA toiled until very late over ledger and trial balance and then caught the last train for his suburban retreat. Earlier the same week there had been a particularly hot session of the husbands-and-wives group. Since his wife was already in bed when the taxi brought him from the station, he began undressing quietly in the dark. Suddenly his wife's voice pierced the darkness. "You may turn the light on, dear, I'm not asleep yet. I'm just lying here wondering what *would* be the best way to handle the Havighurst case." The next morning over coffee the CPA suggested in an unusually decisive tone that it might be the best thing all around if they just stopped attending the Family Case Study Discussions.

The defamilialization of work which arises from the separation of work from residence provides needed insulation, and efforts to reverse it could be very damaging. It is true that some sociologists and urban planners still long for what they somehow believe were the convivial days before work and family life were differentiated from each other. They conjure a memory of "wholeness" before family life was shattered, an era when father, son, and grandson harrowed and reaped in the same field, or stood at the same coffee grinder; when the simple family business welded parents and children into a producing and not just a consuming unit. This was togetherness with a vengeance. Its virtues seem more and more indisputable as the era of the family business recedes further into the past. Nowhere does the fervor for this arcadian age reach such a crescendo as it does with the odes that are dedicated to the whooping crane of the American economic scene, the "family farm."

But the visionary economists who wish somehow to salvage the family farm, and the writers who want to abolish the hiatus between work and family, forget one thing. They forget that the very people who have lived through the experience of family businesses, living over the store, and houses snuggled next to factories are the ones who want nothing to do with it. These are the people who have been emancipated. They realize better than anyone else the human values of the work revolution which has severed once and for all the umbilical cord connecting family life and work life. For all their supposed values, the family farm and business often masked a tyrannical exploitation of family relationships and an abuse of child labor which continued long after it had disappeared from the factory. We should be glad these things are gone and set to work finding realistic ways to humanize the places in which we now work rather than longing for something that was never as satisfying as it now may seem. We should realize that most people *want* to keep their work lives and their family lives relatively distinct. We should respect that wish and recognize the new and valuable kind of freedom made possible by what we have often ruefully labeled the "fragmentation" of modern man.

In any case the facts of our economic situation in technopolitan culture are all on the side of further differentiation and against any reversion to a nineteenth-century idyll. The nearly unanimous verdict of the unsentimental agricultural economists who really know the family farm in America is that the faster it gives way to more economical units the better. Instead of trying to shore it up, our attention should rather be directed to the grim problem of how to solve our real agricultural problems—our outdated and inequitable parity arrangements, the insane and inhuman imbalance of world food distribution, our astronomical storage costs, and the shockingly exploited migrant labor force (in which, incidentally, family togetherness in work still binds parents and children).[1]

In the same way in the question of the small family business, our attention should not be diverted by those who seek to arrest the functionalization of work life in America by transforming the family or other centers of independent personal life into sources of organizational togetherness or extensions of the company country club. Its functionalism is precisely what makes the organization, as the key form of modern life, preferable to the guild or the family business.

As we have noted before, human beings cannot bear to have I–Thou relationships in all their connections with the various worlds of modern life. Urban man must be selective. He is exposed to so many different people making so many different demands that he must cultivate the "personal" qualities in some and discourage them in others. The humanization of our work life today is not to be accomplished by any "refamilialization." This results only in the ruination of both family and work. It is to be won by extending the process of genuine decision making so far as possible into the sphere of work. This means the sharing of power and responsibility and has nothing whatever to do with warmth and chumminess. Wherever a high incidence of "one big happy family" images appears in a company newspaper, one can be almost certain that paternalism is masking an inequitable power distribution. The humanization of work in the modern corporation requires discarding paternalism. The new science of personnel administration, which has sometimes done little more than provide management with a new rhetoric to justify old procedures, is no substitute for significant structural changes in the power distribution within the American economy.

The Bureaucratic Organization of Work

The secularization of work has produced the organization, and with it something called the "Organization Man." Already he has become the business equivalent of the supposedly faceless urbanite we discussed in Chapter 2. He has replaced the fat capitalist as the perennial villain of the steady glut of "social criticism" that flows from American presses. The "Orgman's" identifying symbols are as predictable as the arrows of Saint Anthony in a medieval fresco. In his beat classic *Naked Lunch,* William Burroughs portrays him: "Young, good looking, crew-cut, Ivy League, advertising executive type . . . the white teeth, the Florida tan, the two hundred dollar sharkskin suit, the button-down Brooks Brothers shirt. . . ."[2] From ladies' club rostrums, beatnik pads, and suburban pulpits there pours a flood of fulminations against gray flannel suits and attaché cases.

The irony is that the very people who buy these books and listen so avidly to these tirades *are* the organization. Beat poets, back-to-the-soil romantics, angry young (affluent) playwrights, sociologists with academic tenure or well-upholstered berths in foundations all depend on an organized society to deliver their mail, collect their garbage, and market their epithets. What is the real meaning of this noisy outburst against the organization, this orgy of ritual self-laceration?

To begin to answer this question, we must first realize that the organization is here to stay. There is simply no other way to run a world brimming with three billion people in the midst of an industrial epoch. Unless a nuclear war returns us to a culture of hunting and gathering tribes, our world will be increasingly organized as the decades go by. If we choose to live responsibly in the world, then we must face the issue of how we can harness organizational power for authentic human purposes.

We are right in refusing to allow organizations to identify

persons completely with the functions they perform. As individuals we do well to develop a degree of "technological asceticism," a discipline that will prevent our becoming captives of our gadgets. But we should never make the mistake of identifying this personal stance with the wishful thinking that hankers after Walden Pond. As David Bazelon says in *The Paper Economy,* "The problem of the individual should not be confused with the problem of the corporate system, because we have already made our commitment to the latter."[3] This same confusion, however, lies at the root of much of today's antiorganization thinking. It is the modern equivalent of the equally mistaken idea that social problems can be solved only by converting individuals one by one. The truth is that our freedom in the age of organization is a question of the responsible control and exercise of power—vast, towering, unprecedented power. Freedom in such a society is really a kind of power over power. The advent of the organizational age means that the mechanism of political democracy, which in the past three centuries has been applied to the state, must now be extended to the ponderous economic structures and service bureaucracies that have developed in the past decades. The sore point is *not* that these massive bureaucratic empires exist, but that we have not yet learned how to control them for the common welfare. We persist in living by stale ideologies deriving from a bygone age.

The problem is not that we do not know enough about man in society. Modern mass-persuasion techniques, "human engineering" in industrial management, psychotherapy, motivational research, brainwashing through group dynamics, all demonstrate that we have already acquired an awesome grasp of what makes homo sapiens tick. The question is one not of knowledge but of power. The fact is that the massive organizations of our society are not yet answerable to the population. We have developed a network of private governments whose rulers praise the virtues of competition while they in fact administer the flow of production, distribution, and services. We have a kind of "voluntary totalitarianism" by which we delegate vast segments of our society's decision making to managers who perpetrate the fib that we are still making these decisions ourselves, through consumption choices and shareholding. But everyone knows that stock voting is hardly more than a ritual. Corporations are run not by the so-called owners (the shareholders) but by the managers. My "consumer vote" is equally fictitious. The principle of "price leadership"

is an established fact. Recipients of welfare services have no
role in controlling these services. This produces a donor-client
relationship that is tyrannical and almost inevitably seethes
with hostility.

For years the keenest observers of our economic system,
from Thorstein Veblen to John Kenneth Galbraith, have
demonstrated that our cherished image of market competition
has precious little to do with the way our economy really
functions. If we would humanize the organizational world, we
must begin by demythologizing our sacred economic theologies. We must not be deceived by the frumpery of our socio-
economic house of mirrors; we must find out where the power
really lies. Only then can the mechanism be understood,
altered, and steered in the direction of human community.
The unvarnished fact is that our system is already a planned
and administered system. The only remaining questions are:
By whom is it planned? for whom is it administered? and how
well is it being done? The answer to all these questions is the
organization. Let us then turn to an unsentimental look at
what an organization really is.

As one aspect of secularization, the organization principle
derives in part from the impact of the biblical faith on Western culture. This point is well argued by the German sociologist Dietrich von Oppen.[4] He insists that in order to understand the "organization" we should compare it to the "order,"
the integrative principle it has replaced in Western society.
The difference in crucial. The order had a traditional, ethnic,
or sacral basis. The medieval guild, the Gothic tribe, the
Greek polis, the primitive clan are examples of orders. An
order encompasses all or most of the facets of social existence. It relates a person to a mythical past, a total way of life,
a secure identity. It corresponds roughly to certain aspects of
what we have designated as tribal and town society. In contrast to the order, the organization is flexible, future-oriented,
secularized, and limited in its scope. Although its predecessors
appeared long ago, only in the secular epoch has it become
the characteristic principle of social integration. In contradiction to its bucolic critics' claims, the organization offers many
more possibilities for choice and creativity than were available
in the age of the sacral order. Let us examine the four marks
of the organization.

1. The organization is *flexible*. It is consciously constructed
to accomplish specific purposes. Whether its purpose is to
build automobiles or to teach people how to dance, the organ-

ization as such makes no claim to ultimate origin or significance. It can be reorganized, merged, or disbanded if circumstances demand it. It must constantly change its practices to meet changing conditions. If it does develop a kind of tradition, the tradition plays a secondary and not a determinative role.

2. The organization is *future-oriented*. It is formed to achieve certain particular ends. An order views the present in terms of the past. An organization remolds and utilizes past experience to solve future problems. A prince assumes the throne solely because his father was king. An executive is selected because somebody thinks he can tackle the problems of the future. Of course family connections and nepotism continue to play a role, but when they do, it is because of a malfunctioning of the organization principle and is not an expression of its real genius.

3. The organization is *secularized*. It rejects inherited rituals that are preserved from criticism by religious taboos and makes use, instead, of technical procedures which must be constantly criticized and refined. The members of an organization submit to no blood oaths or ritual initiation. When remnants of these practices do appear today, they are obviously phony frosting on a functional cake; they are frills. They do not define the relationships within the organization the way, for example, the oath of the serf did in binding him to his feudal lord. People move from one organization to another and belong to many at the same time without violating the principle that holds them together.

4. The organization makes only a *limited claim on its members*. It is interested only in that aspect of the individual's life by which he makes a contribution to the organization's purposes. Its power is relative and not absolute. In the medieval guilds, for example, legal, economic, political, social, and religious goals were all mixed together. The authority of the leaders in a modern labor union or professional association is limited, again with obvious and anachronistic exceptions, to the activities that relate to the specific purposes of the organization.

Where the organization principle obtains, the members are assumed to be free and responsible persons with other, more definitive relationships. Only the fanatic defines his existence in terms of his membership in an organization. It serves one purpose among many and he expects it to stay in its place. In return, the organization helps the person achieve some desired

end, but does not seek to endow him with a total identity or
life meaning. The organization world confronts him with the
"terrible freedom" to choose his own associations and his own
life-style. If he chooses to abdicate that freedom to someone
else, he should not blame his misery on someone else. The
possibility for freedom-in-responsibility is there to a degree
that was impossible within the tight and sacrally ordered
culture.

Von Oppen believes the organization principle entered
Western history with the Christian Gospel. The Gospel posed
a demand for *personal* decision, if necessary at the expense of
family, religious, or ethnic relationships. The new community
of the church made a decisive break with all preceding traditional orders. It radically relativized national and racial groupings and produced a wholly new kind of integrative principle.
It was a community based on free choice and not on blood
ties or ethnic consanguinity. The first Christians shared a life
that violated previous religious and racial taboos ("There is
no longer Jew nor Greek"). They lived not to cherish a sacred
tradition but to prepare for an imminent future. Here, then,
the seeds of the organization principle were planted in the soil
of Western history.

Admittedly the tender shoot did not always prosper in the
next two thousand years. During the era of Constantine
(really only now coming to a close), the organization principle was frequently buried under "established" churches, the so-
called conversion of entire Visigothic tribes, the mistaken notion of "Western Christendom," the Reformers' acceptance of
Landeskirchen and *Volkskirchen,* and the mixture of Christianity with Americanism or the Southern way of life. During
the sixteenth and seventeenth centuries, the organization principle flourished briefly among the early Baptist, Quaker, and
Free churches. These were radical, often socially utopian free
associations whose members frequently took an active part in
political movements. Most of these people, however, were
either hounded into submission or expelled to America where
they founded their own—unfortunately often theocratically
ordered—states. Only in the past century have all the conditions been present for a flowering of the organization principle. Is it already going to seed? Christians have a special
responsibility here. In a sense they started the whole thing.
They preached about a Man who called not clans but persons,
and who called them not *out of* but *into* the world. Freedom
of association and disciplined world affirmation began with

the response to this call; the principle of organization is the twentieth-century outcome. It is hardly cricket now for Christians to back down and call the whole thing a mistake.

Of course today's colossal organizations never completely fit the description of the organization principle just outlined. Today's organizations still atrophy and lose their flexibility. They obey Parkinson's Law and multiply functionaries when their function has vanished. They cook up spurious traditions or seek to inject an *ersatz* "family spirit" through the company house organ. Most seriously, however, they extend officious tentacles into the lives of organization members at points where the organization has no legitimate business. But when the organization does any of these things, it does so in contradiction to the anonymous, functional thrust of the organization principle itself. At all of these trespass points we have every right to blow the whistle on the organization—not because it is an organization but because it is trying to be something else.

Organization is increasingly the basic integrating principle of our society. In order to live in society we have to live organizationally. Now the question is how to do so responsibly. Many believe it cannot be done. Our street-corner prattle reveals a fatalistic resignation about the possibility of authentic personal responsibility in the organization age ("You can't beat City Hall"). The cynicism comes from diverse quarters. There is a curious similarity between the beat advocates of disaffiliation and the conformist junior executives: both have decided not to fight the system. The beat chooses monasticism; the conformist prefers adjustment. Between the two there rages a symbiotic love–hate dependence. In a culture in which thrift, ambition, and hard work are psychologically bound up with deferred pleasures and sexual repression, the beats supply a convenient *alter ego* on which the junior executives can project their incompletely sublimated sexual fantasies and their resentment of the organization. The beats gleefully perform their assigned social function. They are the well-fed court jesters of modern society. But they know how long their leash is and they instinctively bark within its limits. The beat poet and the young man with attaché case agree with each other wholeheartedly on one thing: the political power struggle in America is a dirty, disgusting business. The two occasionally lay aside their dissimilar life-styles long enough to clasp hands tenderly and sing imprecatory anthems against the crooked politician.

Meanwhile the organization rolls on, deepening and extending its influence. Within, however, a titanic struggle is now going on, the outcome of which will shape the countenance of America and of the world for decades to come. It is a duel to the death between the rising new technically educated class and the old class of zealous business barons. The prize in this contest is nothing short of control of the organization itself. Bazelon describes the conflict as a "rather quiet and mostly polite revolt of the Intellectuals," the people who are trained to work with concepts and whose mental skill replaces "property" as the way to produce income. These are the people who are today in fact carrying off a revolutionary seizure of power. They are attempting to take over the organization from its present controllers, the classic, hard-hitting, inner-directed managers whose forte was administrative command rather than cerebral competence. These men liked to be called "Boss." They were tough, resilient, and lived by a fairly simple free-enterprise ideology. The intellectuals want, quite simply, to be less managed by these corporate chieftains. They want to push the managerial revolution, the "organizational principle," even further. They have no interest in "marrying" the company like an old-style martinet manager, barking into six phones at once and dying in harness. They have a different style. But one should not be deceived by their soft-sell unpretentiousness. They hold the high card in today's technically systematized organization—they know how to run it. They represent in effect the elite that is moving us from town to technopolis, but the chances that they will usher in paradise appear highly dubious. Like every revolutionary class before them, they have their own vested interests. Unlike preceding revolutionary elites, many of them seem interested in capturing the centers of power not to change things but precisely to keep things as they are. Many have simply been bought off, justifying the nastiest slams the beats can voice. Others, to revert to Marxist rhetoric once more, either have lost or never had any "class consciousness." They do not grasp what is going on in their own history or what role their own group is playing. If and when this kind of new elite gains mastery over the organization, there is no assurance whatever that they will use it more responsibly than their predecessors. Too many in the new elite either lack the willingness to use power or have no clear vision toward the realization of which power could be used.

We asked earlier about the peculiar psychological need our culture feels to stick pins in organization-man dolls. Now the answer becomes clearer. It is a residual element of tribalism, a fetish whereby the organization people purify themselves and stay in the organization without assuming responsibility for the battle now raging inside. It is a ritual by which they deny the distasteful reality, settle for a pseudo-protest, and thus abdicate the controls to others. It is a dodge.

But even if we wanted to exercise power in the organization, to what ends should such power be directed?

Here there is room for discussion, but certainly among these ends are (1) simply to produce the wherewithal for a world free of hunger, disease, and misery and (2) to extend the range of democratic decision making as widely as possible. Full production and democratic control should be the characteristics of an economic system. On both counts our system today is failing. It no longer does what it is intended to do— produce *and* distribute. Our society could produce enough to demonstrate to the world that industrial abundance does not require totalitarian politics. We are caught in the contradiction between the old free-enterprise ideology and the scientific-administrative actuality.

Our social vision must be revolutionary. The difference between us and the Communists is not that they favor a world revolution and we do not. Rather, we must espouse a different *kind* of revolution, a revolution that makes the fruits of the earth available to all people without depriving them of the benefits of political and cultural freedom. We must be *more* revolutionary than the Communists and we must carry through the revolution first in the United States if it is to convince anyone anywhere else. "It is required," as David Bazelon says, "that the most conservative nation in the world devote its great power to leading a world social revolution— beginning at home."

Our task in the age of organization is the recognition and responsible use of power. The frequent question, "How can I preserve my own individual values in a giant organization?" may be falsely put. From the biblical perspective, the first question is never "How can I save my own soul, skin, values, or personality?" Man is summoned to be concerned, first of all, for his neighbor. In the age of organization he can only do this by getting into the fray, by losing a little skin from his own nose, perhaps even a spiritual value here and there, in the tough but epochal battle for the control of the organization. But as he does leap in, perhaps at the risk of his own life, he may discover that, even in the age of organization, precisely he who loses his life gains it.

The Emancipation of Work from Religion

Secularization signifies the emancipation of man first from religious and then from metaphysical control. We have shown by comparing societies and institutions how this proceeds at different speeds on different levels of a society. In the Western world, human work presents a striking example of how we allow residual religious meanings to cling to an activity long after its authentic function has been secularized. We prove this by equating work with a job, a paid position supplied by the market. Even in technopolitan culture we still often hold to the proposition that having some kind of job is an indispensable character-building activity and perhaps even an act of religious devotion. The pay we derive from our job is a pat on the head administered by Adam Smith's invisible hand. Since that invisible hand is the closest many people get to Calvin's providential God (from whom it is directly descended), the job has a sacred value. It provides the orthodox bridge between morals and economics, the key to the kingdom of consumption. It is the admission ticket by means of which the individual gains entrance to the goods and services the society produces.

This at least is the official ideology. Exceptions are made. People who inherit great wealth or live on income from investments are excepted. The blind and the sick, those physically unable to work, are usually not permitted to starve. But in most cases, the indispensable link between production and distribution is the job, and he who has no job does not participate in the economy. The system works comparatively well in a society where the market requires enough, or nearly enough, jobs to go around. But it fails catastrophically when the number of salable jobs is fewer than the number of people who need to be linked to the distributive economy. This is why we have a crisis of work in the United States today. There is lots of work to do but not enough jobs to go around. Then why should we not modify the system to cohere with the new social reality? After all, the job system is a rather arbitrary one. The job has not played this decisive a role in all societies.

The reason we feel unable to explore other ways of linking production to consumption is the religious meaning we still attach to the job. We *can* produce enough for everyone; and we believe, or we say we do, that everyone is entitled to a decent share in the productivity of the economy. But we cannot put our convictions into practice in this instance because we still feel that only by providing a market-determined job for everyone can the ludicrous imbalance between production and distribution be reconciled. The reason we cannot take the job down from this pinnacle is that it has become a religion. For the man who has left behind the tribal cultus but has not yet reached the stage of full secularity, the job has become a spiritual devotion. Its holy mysteries infect everything it touches and the intense attitudes created make reasonable adjustments in the economy exceedingly difficult. Max Weber saw this as early as 1904, when he wrote:

> Today the spirit of religious asceticism . . . has escaped from the cage . . . and the idea of duty in one's calling prowls about in our lives like the ghost of dead religious beliefs.[5]

This persistent spirit still prowls among us today. It has not yet been exorcised, and so long as it remains, there will be enormous emotional barriers to any basic redefinition of work. In short, work is not yet completely secularized.

Our confusion of human work with a job produced by a market economy proves that our attitudes toward work have not yet been liberated from religious or metaphysical meanings, often held below the level of consciousness. These attitudes are carried over from the period of the bourgeois town. The conflict between work actualities and work attitudes is one of the clearest examples of the differential pace of secularization. We have in technopolis the technical and social basis for the emancipation of work. We could transform it from a drudgery into a delight. Yet we still cling to pious attitudes about work, predispositions inherited from a different era. But we shall eventually have to lay aside this idol too. Technopolis demands a new definition of work. Why?

The answer is the word *cybernation*. The word is a neologism that refers to the coupling of two previously discrete tendencies in technological society. The first is automation, the wholly mechanical operation of production machines; the second is cybernetics, the science of control and feedback systems, especially in electronic computers. Cybernation means the hitching of the computer to the machine. It reduces the human role to programming the task and maintaining the equipment.

The introduction of cybernation has been called the "second industrial revolution," and it has caught up to us before we have really learned to deal with the first one. It will have an emormous impact on our society. First, there will be fewer jobs in the production sector; second, the jobs remaining will demand an ever-higher level of skills; but third, we shall be able for the first time to produce enough goods and services so that no person will need to live in poverty or deprivation. UN Secretary-General U Thant has described the revolutionary implications of this new reality in these terms:

> . . . the central stupendous truth about developed economies today is that they can have—in anything but the shortest run—the kind and scale of resources they decide to have. . . . It is no longer resources that limit decisions. It is the decision that makes the resources. This is the fundamental revolutionary change—perhaps the most revolutionary man has ever known.[6]

U Thant's description indicates that the economy shares the same condition we have observed in earlier chapters of this book in the political institutions and the value system. They are all human artifices. They are the products of human decision, so they can be altered. They are not parts of some order of creation, sanctified by religious powers. The central fact is that we *can* make enough to allow everyone to share in the goods of the earth, but the system we now have for connecting individuals to the supply of goods is breaking down—and we are unable to alter the system because we have a semiconscious religious commitment to it. The job is the religion of the posttribal man in the West. We are all addicted to the overpowering habits resulting from what Max Weber called the "spirit of capitalism" and it is nearly impossible for us to shake it. But in order to try we should know how we got this way.

The modern religious sanctification of work began in the medieval monasteries. Unlike Oriental monastic orders, the Benedictines prescribed work as a spiritual discipline. Their cloister bells sounded not just to call the brothers to pray together but also to summon them to common work. The

Reformers closed the monasteries, but they did not throttle the monastic spirit. They merely loosed it into the whole society. With Luther, as Max Weber once wrote, the whole world became a monastery and every man a monk. The bells moved from the monastery to the tower of City Hall. The chimes now called not cloistered monks but worldly monks to the disciplined toil which became first the Puritan and later the secular substitute for religious devotion. Even today some people refer to the trade manual of their profession as its "bible" and speak of working at a job "religiously."

Weber believed that work in the Western Protestant world became so compulsive mainly because all ways of influencing God through traditional religious techniques had been abolished. This arose mainly through the Calvinist doctrine of predestination in which it was taught that God had determined the elect and the damned from before the foundations of the world, and consequently nothing could be done that had the remotest chance of changing the decision. In describing the dilemma in which this placed man, Weber confirms much of what we have already said about the function of biblical faith in the desacralization of the world:

> In what was for the man of the age of the Reformation the most important thing in life, his eternal salvation, he was forced to follow his path alone to meet a destiny which had been decreed for him from eternity . . . the complete elimination of salvation through the Church and the sacraments . . . was what formed the absolutely decisive difference from Catholicism. . . . The great historic process in the development of religions, the elimination of magic from the world which had begun with the old Hebrew prophets . . . came here to its logical conclusion. . . . There was not only no magical means of attaining the grace of God . . . there was no means whatever.[7]

There was no way to propitiate God. So now the energy which man had previously poured out in supplication and sacrifice had to be redirected in what Freud would call an act of massive sublimation. Religious fervor was rechanneled into energetic work in the world. Together with the invisible hand of the laissez-faire market, it provided the motor for the rise of capitalism, and the industrial revolution. Even socialism has one of its sources here, less directly. Despite so many differences, early capitalism and socialism betray marks of a common ancestor. The Marxist dialectic is the same invisible hand wearing a steel glove. The ghost of religion still prowls.

Witness the exaltation of "the worker" in both the Protestant ethic and in Marxism. When the history of our times is written many years from now, these two movements may be interpreted as parallel thrusts in a larger and more inclusive historical development, the wrenching redirection of man's attention and energy from heaven to earth. Town culture marks the transition phase and under capitalism work is identified with job.

Cybernation is not an evil. It can annihilate jobs only in a society which still relies on Smith's disembodied hand to do its planning. In societies where this task has been assumed by human hands and heads cybernation can be a deliverance rather than a curse. It becomes a curse only when a society refuses to take full responsibility for its life, when men refuse to be the stewards of their talents and vineyards. Cybernation forces societies toward adulthood or extinction. It does so in two ways. First, it increases productivity, i.e., the amount of goods and services one worker can produce. High productivity means that in order to prevent unemployment, demand must also be increased. This can easily be accomplished by adjusting interest rates, taxes, and government purchasing. But these policies demand that the dream of the economy as a mysterious, self-regulating oversoul be discarded completely.

Second, cybernation changes the *kinds* of work opportunities in a society and this produces a jarring transition problem for those whose skills become outmoded. Elevator operators and toll bridge attendants, as well as people in hundreds of other responsibilities being displaced by mechanical equipment, find little consolation in the assurances economists give them that technology does not *cause* job losses. Certain jobs *are* disappearing and will continue to do so. True, many new jobs will appear, almost all of them at higher skill levels than the ones that disappear. What we need then is a much more comprehensive system for locating the new openings, preparing people for them, and guiding people into them.

But most toll bridge dime-takers will never become computer programmers. They lack the requisite educational skills or emotional capacity to negotiate such a bewildering transition. It is especially difficult if our current crisis catches them anywhere past that peculiar period of the middle forties after which most people cannot even change the way they knot their tie, to say nothing of the whole content of their work life. In addition, as the society becomes increasingly rationalized there will be large numbers of average young people who will never be able to perform its most demanding operations. If we add to the jobless young and the displaced middle-aged another group—the victims of discrimination and poor education, especially Negroes—we discover an impressive pool of human resources now being wasted by our society. Cybernation has not "caused" this crisis. It has merely brought it to our attention so forcibly that we can no longer avoid it. How does a mature society respond?

We have already mentioned that for those who qualify, enormously extended retraining and placement programs are needed. But what are the new work opportunities for which we should be preparing people? Arthur Pearl and Frank Riessman in their book *New Careers for the Poor*[8] suggest the creation of a whole new range of positions on the subprofessional level, especially in education, health, and welfare. Their program is sensible and imaginative. It envisions, in the public schools for example, introducing a graded range of teachers' helpers—teacher aides, teacher assistants, associate teachers—who would help correct the horrendously imbalanced teacher-pupil ratio in today's classrooms, especially in cities, and also free the teacher from noninstructional chores so she can devote her real efforts to teaching. The same principle could function very easily in other service fields. The result would be the creation of paying *jobs* where we now have *work* to do but no jobs.

Finally, there will always be people in our society who because of age, taste, or temperament will not be available for retraining. Some will prefer to explore those kinds of activities the culture has not yet accepted as marketable "jobs," for example, experimenting with new forms of art and music. A few will not want to do anything at all. Many will be so emotionally attached to certain occupations, such as farming, that to remove them forcibly would cause pointless human anguish. There is no reason why an affluent society that has outgrown its obsessive religion of working-at-a-job could not make room for all of these people. It could provide at relatively modest cost, a minimum income for every adult. It could cushion the technological transition for those most painfully hit by providing some socially useful work therapy in the interim. As David Riesman once suggested, there is no reason why our society cannot subsidize those displaced from small farms by technology to grow roses until they reach retirement age.

Political leaders should now begin to plan for full employment on this basis; *employment* should mean making it possible for everyone to do something he considers worthwhile and which contributes to the society. This is an assignment far different from asking that the market be manipulated so that economically paying jobs can be obtained for everyone, whether they are worth doing or not. It involves a more direct but more realistic role for the government in assuring to all citizens the right to work. This suggests an enlargement and refinement of the political (polis) side of the technopolitan society commensurate with the enlargement of the technical side.

The most serious obstacle standing between the present definition of work and the one we need, however, is not political. It is religious. It is the halo that work has inherited from the presecular epoch. Much of the almost ineradicable religious coloration of work has been perpetuated through a misunderstanding of the Protestant doctrine of vocation. It was popularly believed that this doctrine meant that God calls certain men to be butchers, others bakers, and still others to be candlestick makers. Alan Richardson jettisons this notion in his study *The Biblical Doctrine of Work:*

> The Bible knows no instance of a man's being called to an earthly profession or trade by God. St. Paul, for example, is called to be an apostle; he is not called to be a tentmaker. . . . We cannot with propriety speak of God's calling a man to be an engineer or a doctor or a schoolmaster.[9]

Richardson believes that this mistaken notion, that God somehow "calls" people to particular jobs, thus investing them with sacral significance, comes from what he calls the "secularization of the biblical doctrine." Perhaps it would be more accurate to say that it results from an insufficient secularization of our understanding of work.

The call which comes to man from the Bible, the *vocatio,* summons him not to a job, but to joy and gratitude in whatever he is doing. It is equally relevant at work and at play—or in the "new leisure" in which work can become endowed with the quality of play. As for how to use leisure, very little direct guidance is to be derived from the Bible since the possibility of full production with minimum expenditure of energy never occurred to the biblical writers. The Bible assumes that man will have to toil with the sweat of his brow, so long as he is man. But work and even sweat need not always stunt and deform man; they can also elevate. We must see past the historically determined form of a biblical image of work to its essential depth. For the Bible, man stands before his Creator and Sustainer as the one who is expected to exercise maturity and recountability in *all* that he does.

The secularization of work will be a difficult task for a society living on the vanishing capital of a Puritan religious inheritance. Our transition to technopolis, where machines will do most of what we now classify as toil and drudgery, will be slowed down in Anglo-Saxon countries by our attitudes toward work unless those attitudes change markedly, unless we can take work much less solemnly. If we do not, cultures which have never had a Protestant Reformation or a Marxist revolution, and have not therefore developed a musclebound inflexibility about work, will certainly forge ahead in the technical era. We will become the "underdeveloped areas." Here we have much to learn from the Latin cultures, in which work has never been beatified. Indeed there is evidence that the Latins are becoming specialists on leisure. The best book on work and leisure so far was written by an Italian, Sebastian de Grazia.

Taken together, secularization and urbanization make a mighty impact on work. The technopolitan epoch separates the place of work from the place of residence. This goes on despite some efforts to "refamilialize" work. The separation, though it creates certain problems, produces an emancipation for family and for work which was not there before. Secularization also determines the way in which work itself is organized. It banishes the sacral order and produces its own characteristic system, what we have called the organization. Again, although the organization has borne the brunt of endless attacks, few of its attackers would care to live in the tightly oppressive way of ordering society and work which it replaced. Finally, we have seen that secularization liberates man for work by emptying work of the almost neurotic compulsiveness and the religious mystery in which it has been enshrouded in Western society since the monastic period and the Reformation. This dereligionization of work enables us to uncouple the customary link by which work is tied to income and therefore to the goods and services of the economy. In a cybernated age, a productive job can no longer be the passport to participation in the economy. Everyone should receive an income and therefore access to the goods and services he needs merely because he is a human being. Work, freed from captivity to the market, is freed to become something very close to what today we call leisure—doing something because one wants to. In all of these instances, rather than fighting and opposing secularization, we would do better to discern in it the action of the same One who called an earlier people out of endless toil, in a land where the taskmasters were cruel, and into a land flowing with milk and honey.

NOTES TO CHAPTER 8

1. Naturally the human factor of people too old to move from the farms must be taken into consideration. We can easily afford to keep certain people in agriculture as a kind of occupational therapy. When we have been able to break out of the restrictions which now prevent us from sending food to China and Cuba, the whole agricultural picture may change.
2. William Burroughs, *Naked Lunch* (New York: Grove Press, 1962; Paris: Olympia Press).
3. David Bazelon, *The Paper Economy* (New York: Random House, 1963).
4. Dietrich von Oppen, *Die Personale Zeitalter* (Stuttgart: Verlags gemeinschaft Burkharathaus und Kreuz-Verlag GMBH, 1960).
5. Max Weber, *The Protestant Ethic and the Spirit of Capitalism* (New York: Scribner, 1958), p. 192.
6. Quoted in Robert Theobold, "Need: A New Definition of Work," *New University Thought*, III (1963), p. 11. Theobold's larger and more inclusive statement will be found in his book *Free Men and Free Markets* (New York: C. N. Potter, 1963).
7. Max Weber, *op. cit.*, pp. 104–105.
8. Arthur Pearl and Frank Riessman, *New Careers for the Poor* (New York: The Free Press, 1965).
9. Alan Richardson, *The Biblical Doctrine of Work* (Naperville, Ill.: Alec R. Allenson, Inc., 1958; London: SCM Press), Vol. I of *Ecumenical Biblical Studies*, pp. 35, 36.

CHAPTER 9

Sex and Secularization

No aspect of human life seethes with so many unexorcised demons as does sex. No human activity is so hexed by superstition, so haunted by residual tribal lore, and so harassed by socially induced fear. Within the breast of urban-secular man, a toe-to-toe struggle still rages between his savage and his bourgeois forebears. Like everything else, the images of sex which informed tribal and town society are expiring along with the eras in which they arose. The erosion of traditional values and the disappearance of accepted modes of behavior have left contemporary man free, but somewhat rudderless. Abhoring a vacuum, the mass media have rushed in to supply a new code and a new set of behavioral prototypes. They appeal to the unexorcised demons. Nowhere is the persistence of mythical and metalogical denizens more obvious than in sex, and the shamans of sales do their best to nourish them. Nowhere is the humanization of life more frustrated. Nowhere is a clear word of exorcism more needed.

How is the humanization of sex impeded? First it is thwarted by the parading of cultural-identity images for the sexually dispossessed, to make money. These images become the tyrant gods of the secular society, undercutting its liberation from religion and transforming it into a kind of neotribal culture. Second, the authentic secularization of sex is checkmated by an anxious clinging to the sexual standards of the town, an era so recent and yet so different from ours that simply to transplant its sexual ethos into our situation is to invite hypocrisy of the worst degree.

Let us look first at the spurious sexual models conjured up for our anxious society by the sorcerers of the mass media and the advertising guild. Like all pagan deities, these come in pairs—the god and his consort. For our purposes they are best symbolized by The Playboy and Miss America, the Adonis and Aphrodite of a leisure-consumer society which still seems unready to venture into full postreligious maturity and freedom. The Playboy and Miss America represent The Boy and The Girl. They incorporate a vision of life. They function as religious phenomena and should be exorcised and exposed.

The Residue of Tribalism

Let us begin with Miss America. In the first century B.C., Lucretius wrote this description of the pageant of Cybele:

> Adorned with emblem and crown . . . she is carried in awe-inspiring state. Tight-stretched tambourines and hollow cymbals thunder all round to the stroke of open hands, hollow pipes stir with Phrygian strain. . . . She rides in procession through great cities and mutely enriches mortals with a blessing not expressed in words. They straw all her path with brass and silver, presenting her with bounteous alms, and scatter over her a snow-shower of roses.[1]

Now compare this with the annual twentieth-century Miss America pageant in Atlantic City, New Jersey. Spotlights probe the dimness like votive tapers, banks of flowers exude their varied aromas, the orchestra blends feminine strings and regal trumpets. There is a hushed moment of tortured suspense, a drumroll, then the climax—a young woman with carefully prescribed anatomical proportions and exemplary "personality" parades serenely with scepter and crown to her throne. At TV sets across the nation throats tighten and eyes moisten. "There she goes, Miss America——" sings the crooner. "There she goes, your ideal." A new queen in America's emerging cult of The Girl has been crowned.

Is it merely illusory or anachronistic to discern in the multiplying pageants of the Miss America, Miss Universe, Miss College Queen type a residuum of the cults of the pre-Christian fertility goddesses? Perhaps, but students of the history of religions have become less prone in recent years to dismiss the possibility that the cultural behavior of modern man may be significantly illuminated by studying it in the perspective of the mythologies of bygone ages. After all, did not Freud initiate a revolution in social science by utilizing the venerable myth of Oedipus to help make sense out of the strange behavior of his Viennese contemporaries? Contemporary man carries with him, like his appendix and his fingernails, vestiges of his tribal and pagan past.

In light of this fertile combination of insights from modern social science and the history of religions, it is no longer possible to see in the Miss America pageant merely an overpublicized prank foisted on us by the advertising industry. It certainly is this, but it is also much more. It represents the mass cultic celebration, complete with a rich variety of ancient ritual embellishments, of the growing place of The Girl in the collective soul of America.

This young woman—though she is no doubt totally ignorant of the fact—symbolizes something beyond herself. She symbolizes The Girl, the primal image, the one behind the many. Just as the Virgin appears in many guises—as our Lady of Lourdes or of Fatima or of Guadalupe—but is always recognizably the Virgin, so with The Girl.

The Girl is also the omnipresent icon of consumer society. Selling beer, she is folksy and jolly. Selling gems, she is chic and distant. But behind her various theophanies she remains recognizably The Girl. In Miss America's glowingly healthy smile, her openly sexual but officially virginal figure, and in the name-brand gadgets around her, she personifies the stunted aspirations and ambivalent fears of her culture. "There she goes, your ideal."

Miss America stands in a long line of queens going back to Isis, Ceres, and Aphrodite. Everything from the elaborate sexual taboos surrounding her person to the symbolic gifts at her coronation hints at her ancient ancestry. But the real proof comes when we find that the function served by The Girl in our culture is just as much a "religious" one as that served by Cybele in hers. The functions are identical—to provide a secure personal "identity" for initiates and to sanctify a particular value structure.

Let us look first at the way in which The Girl confers a kind of identity on her initiates. Simone de Beauvoir says in *The Second Sex* that "no one is *born* a woman."[2] One is merely born a female, and "*becomes* a woman" according to the models and meanings provided by the civilization. During the classical Christian centuries, it might be argued, the Virgin Mary served in part as this model. With the Reformation and especially with the Puritans, the place of Mary within the symbol system of the Protestant countries was reduced or eliminated. There are those who claim that this excision constituted an excess of zeal that greatly impoverished Western culture, an impoverishment from which it has never recovered. Some would even claim that the alleged failure of American novelists to produce a single great heroine (we have no Phaedra, no Anna Karenina) stems from this self-imposed lack of a central feminine ideal.

Without entering into this fascinating discussion, we can certainly be sure that, even within modern American Roman Catholicism, the Virgin Mary provides an identity image for few American girls. Where then do they look for the "model" Simone de Beauvoir convincingly contends they need? For most, the prototype of femininity seen in their mothers, their friends, and in the multitudinous images to which they are exposed on the mass media is what we have called The Girl.

In his significant monograph *Identity and the Life Cycle*, Erik Erikson reminds us that the child's identity is not modeled simply on the parent but on the parent's "super-ego."[3] Thus in seeking to forge her own identity the young girl is led beyond her mother to her mother's ideal image, and it is here that what Freud called "the ideologies of the superego . . . the traditions of the race and the people" become formative. It is here also that The Girl functions, conferring identity on those for whom she is—perhaps never completely consciously—the tangible incarnation of womanhood.

To describe the mechanics of this complex psychological process by which the fledgling American girl participates in the life of The Girl and thus attains a woman's identity would require a thorough description of American adolescence. There is little doubt, however, that such an analysis would reveal certain striking parallels to the "savage" practices by which initiates in the mystery cults shared in the magical life of their god.

For those inured to the process, the tortuous nightly fetish by which the young American female pulls her hair into tight bunches secured by metal clips may bear little resemblance to the incisions made on their arms by certain African tribesmen to make them resemble their totem, the tiger. But to an anthropologist comparing two ways of attempting to resemble the holy one, the only difference might appear to be that with the Africans the torture is over after initiation, while with the American it has to be repeated every night, a luxury only a culture with abundant leisure can afford.

In turning now to an examination of the second function of The Girl—supporting and portraying a value system—a comparison with the role of the Virgin in the twelfth and thirteenth centuries may be helpful. Just as the Virgin exhibited and sustained the ideals of the age that fashioned Chartres Cathedral, as Henry Adams saw, so The Girl symbolizes the values and aspirations of a consumer society. (She is crowned not in the political capital, remember, but in Atlantic City or Miami Beach, centers associated with leisure and consumption.) And she is not entirely incapable of exploitation. If men sometimes sought to buy with gold the Virgin's blessings on their questionable causes, so The Girl now dispenses her charismatic favor on watches, refrigerators, and razor blades —for a price. Though The Girl has built no cathedrals, without her the colossal edifice of mass persuasion would crumble. Her sharply stylized face and figure beckon us from every magazine and TV channel, luring us toward the beatific vision of a consumer's paradise.

The Girl is *not* the Virgin. In fact she is a kind of anti-Madonna. She reverses most of the values traditionally associated with the Virgin—poverty, humility, sacrifice. In startling contrast, particularly, to the biblical portrait of Mary in Luke 1:46–55, The Girl has nothing to do with filling the hungry with "good things," hawking instead an endless proliferation of trivia on TV spot commercials. The Girl exalts the mighty, extols the rich, and brings nothing to the hungry but added despair. So The Girl does buttress and bring into personal focus a value system, such as it is. In both social and psychological terms, The Girl, whether or not she is really a goddess, certainly acts that way.

Perhaps the most ironic element in the rise of the cult of The Girl is that Protestantism has almost completely failed to notice it, while Roman Catholics have at least given some evidence of sensing its significance. In some places, for instance, Catholics are forbidden to participate in beauty pageants, a ruling not entirely inspired by prudery. It is ironic that Protestants have traditionally been most opposed to lady cults while Catholics have managed to assimilate more than one at various points in history.

If we are correct in assuming that The Girl *functions* in many ways as a goddess, then the cult of The Girl demands careful Protestant theological criticism. Anything that functions, even in part, as a god when it is in fact not God, is an idol. When the Reformers and their Puritan offspring criticized the cult of Mary it was not because they were antifeminist. They opposed anything—man, woman, or beast (or dogma or institution)—that usurped in the slightest the prerogatives that belonged alone to God Almighty. As Max

Weber has insisted, when the prophets of Israel railed against fertility cults, they had nothing against fertility. It is not against sexuality but against a cult that protest is needed. Not, as it were, against the beauty but against the pageant.

Thus the Protestant objection to the present cult of The Girl must be based on the realization that The Girl is an *idol*. She functions as the source of value, the giver of personal identity. But the values she mediates and the identity she confers are both spurious. Like every idol she is ultimately a creation of our own hands and cannot save us. The values she represents as ultimate satisfactions—mechanical comfort, sexual success, unencumbered leisure—have no ultimacy. They lead only to endless upward mobility, competitive consumption, and anxious cynicism. The devilish social insecurities from which she promises to deliver us are, alas, still there, even after we have purified our breaths, our skins, and our armpits by applying her sacred oils. She is a merciless goddess who draws us farther and farther into the net of accelerated ordeals of obeisance. As the queen of commodities in an expanding economy, the fulfillment she promises must always remain just beyond the tips of our fingers.

Why has Protestantism kept its attention obsessively fastened on the development of Mariolatry in Catholicism and not noticed the sinister rise of this vampirelike cult of The Girl in our society? Unfortunately, it is due to the continuing incapacity of theological critics to recognize the religious significance of cultural phenomena outside the formal religious system itself. But the rise of this new cult reminds us that the work of the reformer is never done. Man's mind is indeed—as Luther said—a factory busy making idols. The Girl is a far more pervasive and destructive influence than the Virgin, and it is to her and her omnipresent altars that we should be directing our criticism.

Besides sanctifying a set of phony values, The Girl compounds her noxiousness by maiming her victims in a Procrustean bed of uniformity. This is the empty "identity" she panders. Take the Miss America pageant, for example. Are these virtually indistinguishable specimens of white, middle-class postadolescence really the best we can do? Do they not mirror the ethos of a mass-production society, in which genuine individualism somehow mars the clean, precision-tooled effect? Like their sisters, the finely calibrated Rockettes, these meticulously measured and pretested "beauties" lined up on the broadwalk bear an ominous similarity to the faceless retinues of goose-steppers and the interchangeable mass exercisers of explicitly totalitarian societies. In short, *who* says this is beauty?

The caricature becomes complete in the Miss Universe contest, when Miss Rhodesia is a blonde, Miss South Africa is white, and Oriental girls with a totally different tradition of feminine beauty are forced to display their thighs and appear in spike heels and Catalina swim suits. Miss Universe is as universal as an American adman's stereotype of what beauty should be.

The truth is that The Girl can*not* bestow the identity she promises. She forces her initiates to torture themselves with starvation diets and beauty-parlor ordeals, but still cannot deliver the satisfactions she holds out. She is young, but what happens when her followers, despite added hours in the boudoir, can no longer appear young? She is happy and smiling and loved. What happens when, despite all the potions and incantations, her disciples still feel the human pangs of rejection and loneliness? Or what about all the girls whose statistics, or "personality" (or color) do not match the authoritative "ideal"?

After all, it is God—not The Girl—who is God. He is the center and source of value. He liberates men and women from the bland uniformity of cultural deities so that they may feast on the luxurious diversity of life He has provided. The identity He confers frees men from all pseudo-identities to be themselves, to fulfill their human destinies regardless of whether their faces or figures match some predetermined abstract "ideal." As His gift, sex is freed from both fertility cults and commercial exploitation to become the thoroughly human thing He intended. And since it is one of the last items we have left that is neither prepackaged nor standardized, let us not sacrifice it too hastily on the omnivorous altar of Cybele.

The Playboy, illustrated by the monthly magazine of that name, does for the boys what Miss America does for the girls. Despite accusations to the contrary, the immense popularity of this magazine is not solely attributable to pinup girls. For sheer nudity its pictorial art cannot compete with such would-be competitors as *Dude* and *Escapade*. *Playboy* appeals to a highly mobile, increasingly affluent group of young readers, mostly between eighteen and thirty, who want much more from their drugstore reading than bosoms and thighs. They need a total image of what it means to be a man. And Mr. Hefner's *Playboy* has no hesitation in telling them.

Why should such a need arise? David Riesman has argued that the responsibility for character formation in our society has shifted from the family to the peer group and to the mass-media peer-group surrogates.[4] Things are changing so rapidly that one who is equipped by his family with inflexible, highly internalized values becomes unable to deal with the accelerated pace of change and with the varying contexts in which he is called upon to function. This is especially true in the area of consumer values toward which the "other-directed person" is increasingly oriented.

Within the confusing plethora of mass media signals and peer-group values, *Playboy* fills a special need. For the insecure young man with newly acquired free time and money who still feels uncertain about his consumer skills, *Playboy* supplies a comprehensive and authoritative guidebook to this forbidding new world to which he now has access. It tells him not only who to be; it tells him *how* to be, and even provides consolation outlets for those who secretly feel that they have not quite made it.

In supplying for the other-directed consumer of leisure both the normative identity image and the means of achieving it, *Playboy* relies on a careful integration of copy and advertising material. The comic book that appeals to a younger generation with an analogous problem skillfully intersperses illustrations of incredibly muscled men and excessively mammalian women with advertisements for body-building gimmicks and foam-rubber brassière supplements. Thus the thin-chested comic-book readers of both sexes are thoughtfully supplied with both the ends and the means for attaining a spurious brand of maturity. *Playboy* merely continues the comic-book tactic for the next age group. Since within every identity crisis, whether in teens or twenties, there is usually a sexual identity problem, *Playboy* speaks to those who desperately want to know what it means to be a man, and more specifically a *male*, in today's world.

Both the image of man and the means for its attainment exhibit a remarkable consistency in *Playboy*. The skilled consumer is cool and unruffled. He savors sports cars, liquor, high fidelity, and book-club selections with a casual, unhurried aplomb. Though he must certainly *have* and *use* the latest consumption item, he must not permit himself to get too attached to it. The style will change and he must always be ready to adjust. His persistent anxiety that he may mix a drink incorrectly, enjoy a jazz group that is passé, or wear last year's necktie style is comforted by an authoritative tone in *Playboy* beside which papal encyclicals sound irresolute.

"Don't hesitate," he is told, "this assertive, self-assured weskit is what every man of taste wants for the fall season." Lingering doubts about his masculinity are extirpated by the firm assurance that "real men demand this ruggedly masculine smoke" (cigar ad). Though "the ladies will swoon for you, no matter what they promise, don't give them a puff. This cigar is for men only." A fur-lined canvas field jacket is described as "the most masculine thing since the cave man." What to be and how to be it are both made unambiguously clear.

Since being a male necessitates some kind of relationship to females, *Playboy* fearlessly confronts this problem too, and solves it by the consistent application of the same formula. Sex becomes one of the items of leisure activity that the knowledgeable consumer of leisure handles with his characteristic skill and detachment. The girl becomes a desirable— indeed an indispensable—"Playboy accessory."

In a question-answer column entitled "The Playboy Adviser," queries about smoking equipment (how to break in a meerschaum pipe), cocktail preparation (how to mix a Yellow Fever), and whether or not to wear suspenders with a vest alternate with questions about what to do with girls who complicate the cardinal principle of casualness either by suggesting marriage or by some other impulsive gesture toward a permanent relationship. The infallible answer from the oracle never varies: sex must be contained, at all costs, within the entertainment-recreation area. Don't let her get "serious."

After all, the most famous feature of the magazine is its monthly foldout photo of a *play*mate. She is the symbol par excellence of recreational sex. When playtime is over, the playmate's function ceases, so she must be made to understand the rules of the game. As the crew-cut young man in a *Playboy* cartoon says to the rumpled and disarrayed girl he is passionately embracing, "Why speak of love at a time like this?"

The magazine's fiction purveys the same kind of severely departmentalized sex. Although the editors have recently improved the *Playboy* contents with contributions by Hemingway, Bemelmans, and even a Chekhov translation, many of the stories still rely on a repetitious and predictable formula. A successful young man, either single or somewhat less than ideally married—a figure with whom readers have no difficulty identifying—encounters a gorgeous and seductive woman who makes no demands on him except sex. She is the prose duplication of the cool-eyed but hot-blooded playmate of the foldout.

Drawing heavily on the fantasy life of all young Americans, the writers utilize for their stereotyped heroines the hero's schoolteacher, his secretary, an old girl friend, or the girl who brings her car into the garage where he works. The happy issue is always a casual but satisfying sexual experience with no entangling alliances whatever. Unlike the women he knows in real life, the *Playboy* reader's fictional girl friends know their place and ask for nothing more. They present no danger of permanent involvement. Like any good accessory, they are detachable and disposable.

Many of the advertisements reinforce the sex-accessory identification in another way—by attributing female characteristics to the items they sell. Thus a full-page ad for the MG assures us that this car is not only "the smoothest pleasure machine" on the road and that having one is a "love affair," but most important, "you drive it—it doesn't drive you." The ad ends with the equivocal question "Is it a date?"[5]

Playboy insists that its message is one of liberation. Its gospel frees us from captivity to the puritanical "hatpin brigade." It solemnly crusades for "frankness" and publishes scores of letters congratulating it for its unblushing "candor." Yet the whole phenomenon of which *Playboy* is only a part vividly illustrates the awful fact of a new kind of tyranny.

Those liberated by technology and increased prosperity to new worlds of leisure now become the anxious slaves of dictatorial taste makers. Obsequiously waiting for the latest signal on what is cool and what is awkward, they are paralyzed by the fear that they may hear pronounced on them that dread sentence occasionally intoned by "The Playboy Adviser": "You goofed!" Leisure is thus swallowed up in apprehensive competitiveness, its liberating potential transformed into a self-destructive compulsion to consume only what is *à la mode*. *Playboy* mediates the Word of the most high into one section of the consumer world, but it is a word of bondage, not of freedom.

Nor will *Playboy's* synthetic doctrine of man stand the test of scrutiny. Psychoanalysts constantly remind us how deep-seated sexuality is in the human being. But if they didn't remind us, we would soon discover it ourselves anyway. Much as the human male might like to terminate his relationship with a woman as he would snap off the stereo, or store her for special purposes like a camel's-hair jacket, it really can't be done. And anyone with a modicum of experience with women knows it can't be done. Perhaps this is the reason *Playboy's* readership drops off so sharply after the age of thirty.

Playboy really feeds on the existence of a repressed fear of involvement with women, which for various reasons is still present in many otherwise adult Americans. So *Playboy's* version of sexuality grows increasingly irrelevant as authentic sexual maturity is achieved.

The male identity crisis to which *Playboy* speaks has at its roots a deeply set fear of sex, a fear that is uncomfortably combined with fascination. *Playboy* strives to resolve this antinomy by reducing the proportions of sexuality, its power and its passion, to a packageable consumption item. Thus in *Playboy's* iconography the nude woman symbolizes total sexual accessibility but demands nothing from the observer. "You drive it—it doesn't drive you." The terror of sex, which cannot be separated from its ecstasy, is dissolved. But this futile attempt to reduce the *mysterium tremendum* of the sexual fails to solve the problem of being a man. For sexuality is the basic form of all human relationship, and therein lies its terror and its power.

Karl Barth has called this basic relational form of man's life *Mitmensch,* co-humanity.[6] This means that becoming fully human, in this case a human male, requires not having the other totally exposed to me and my purposes—while I remain uncommitted—but exposing myself to the risk of encounter with the other by reciprocal self-exposure. The story of man's refusal to be so exposed goes back to the story of Eden and is expressed by man's desire to control the other rather than to *be with* the other. It is basically the fear to be one's self, a lack of the "courage to be."

Thus any theological critique of *Playboy* that focuses on its "lewdness" will misfire completely. *Playboy* and its less successful imitators are not "sex magazines" at all. They are basically antisexual. They dilute and dissipate authentic sexuality by reducing it to an accessory, by keeping it at a safe distance.

It is precisely because these magazines are antisexual that they deserve the most searching kind of theological criticism. They foster a heretical doctrine of man, one at radical variance with the biblical view. For *Playboy's* man, others—especially women—are *for* him. They are his leisure accessories, his playthings. For the Bible, man only becomes fully man by being *for* the other.

Moralistic criticisms of *Playboy* fail because its antimoralism is one of the few places in which *Playboy* is right. But if Christians bear the name of one who was truly man because he was totally *for* the other, and if it is in him that we know who God is and what human life is for, then we must see in *Playboy* the latest and slickest espisode in man's continuing refusal to be fully human.

Freedom for mature sexuality comes to man only when he is freed from the despotic powers which crowd and cower him into fixed patterns of behavior. Both Miss America and The Playboy illustrate such powers. When they determine man's sexual life, they hold him in captivity. They prevent him from achieving maturity. They represent the constant danger of relapsing into tribal thralldom which always haunts the secular society, a threat from which the liberating, secularizing word of the Gospel repeatedly recalls it.

Remnants of Town Virtues

Equally hazardous for sexual maturity, however, is the lure of town culture, the period we have most recently left behind, at least in most respects. In the area of sexual ethics, this period speaks to us through the traditional sexual practices of our Puritan and Victorian pasts. Since the melody of this ethic lingers on today, our sexual ethics are caught in the cross fire of contradiction and confusion. To illustrate this tension, let us take the traditional ideal of premarital chastity.

I choose this not because of any belief that it is really the key issue. It does seem clear, however, that for many young adults today "to bed or not to bed" *seems* to be the Big Question, and I believe the reasons they press it so vigorously merit exploration. Three aspects of the problem require particular attention: (1) why the yes or no of premarital chastity is more critical for young adults today than in the past; (2) why the answers we usually give to this question are either not heard or provide little guidance and (3) what, if anything, we should be saying about the matter.

Let us reject at the outset any Kinseyan inference that what *is* being done should determine what *ought* to be done. But let us candidly admit that our culture has undergone drastic changes. Though our Puritan style of life has vanished almost completely, the Puritan sex ethic remains, at least on paper. We have exchanged ankle-length dresses for bikinis. We hold blanket parties instead óf bobbing for apples. But the people caught up in these epochal changes are still taught, albeit with winks and evasions, the selfsame code of total premarital abstinence that was instilled into Priscilla Alden.

We have thus fashioned for unmarried young adults a particularly unfortunate combination of emotional environments. They are constantly bombarded—through clothing styles, entertainment, advertising, and courtship mores—with perhaps the most skillfully contrived array of erotic stimulants ever amassed. Their sexual fears and fantasies are studied by motivational researchers and then ruthlessly exploited by mass-media hucksters. Elizabeth Taylor's Brobdingnagian bosom decorates billboards, and throaty songstresses hum their hoarse invitations from transistors.

Yet we pass on to our youth, unaltered, a set of behavioral taboos that, in a sex-saturated society, seem diabolicallly created to produce a high level of duplicity and desperation.

Why have we deliberately constructed such a bizarre imbalance in our moral and psychological milieu? Obviously because we want to have our cake and eat it too. We want to gorge ourselves at the table of an affluent society whose continued prosperity, we are told, necessitates a constantly expanding market. And sex sells anything. At the same time we want to cherish our national memories of Pilgrims and piety, including the sexual code of Massachusetts Bay. The inherent contradiction comes home to roost in the already tormented psyche of the unmarried young adult.

The essential contradictions of any society, as the Marxists say, are concentrated in its proletariat. In a sexually exploitative society, youth subculture becomes the psychological proletariat. It picks up the tab for our hypocrisy. Exposed to all the stimulants married people are, young people are forbidden the socially acceptable form of fulfillment. The refusal is expressed both in the laws of the realm and in the official taboos of the culture. Enforcement, however, is sporadic, and, because the signals are so confused and contradictory, adolescents suspect that it is all one vast dissimulation.

No wonder the beatnik, who rejects *both* the signals of the mass media and the sexual mores, becomes the secret hero of many young adults.

To make matters just a bit more trying, we have thoughtfully provided Jane and Joe more privacy and permissiveness in dating than ever before. This extends far beyond Harvard dormitory rooms. I wonder if Henry Ford ever realized his invention would be viewed by many not primarily as a means of transportation but as the urban society's substitute for Keats' "elfin grot."

Remember also that dating (and with it various types of petting) now reaches down to the sixth grade. Youngsters are thus exposed for a longer period and much more intensely to the mutual exploration of erogenous regions, which is the American courtship pattern. The only advice they get is "Don't go too far," and it is usually the girl who is expected to draw the line.

By the time a girl who begins petting at thirteen has reached marriageable age, she has drawn an awful lot of lines. If she is especially impressed with her religious duty to avoid sexual intercourse, she will probably have mastered, by twenty-one, all the strategems for achieving a kind of sexual climax while simultaneously preventing herself and her partner from crossing the sacrosanct line.

What this border-skirting approach does to inhibit her chances for a successful adjustment in marriage is a question now engaging the attention of psychologists and marriage counselors. One psychologist who specializes in sexual behavior remarked recently that if Americans had consciously set out to think up a system that would produce maximal marital and premarital strife for both sexes, we could scarcely have invented a sexually more sabotaging set of dating procedures than we have today. This may be an overstatement, but I suspect the inherent hypocrisy of the cultural taboo and the patterns of behavior it engenders must have considerable negative influence on marriage.

Add to this the fact that penicillin and oral contraceptives will soon remove the last built-in deterrents to premarital coitus, and the reason for the recent rumblings of discontent with traditional standards becomes clearer. Not that the young adults themselves are guiltless. They share the blame for perpetuating the same values. But they also consider themselves the victims of a kind of cultural charade. They are shown one thing, told another, and they never know when the society will wink and when it will whip them. Their suspicion that they are the fall guys in a giant collusion is expressed in their growing demand that we come clean on this matter.

Now we can turn to the question of why, amid this schizophrenic carnival of prurience and prudery, the Christian Gospel seems to offer so little positive guidance. I believe the answer to this question is that most young adults do not perceive Christian sexual ethics as "evangelical," that is, as *good news*. They are not hearing the Gospel as good news and therefore they are not hearing the Gospel at all, but something else.

The German theologian Friedrich Gogarten states that the two most serious dangers from which the Gospel must be protected are (a) its being dissolved into a myth and (b) its being hardened into a religion of Law.[7] In either case it ceases to be the Gospel. When we examine what has happened to the Gospel as it touches the area of sex, it is evident that both of these distortions have set in.

The Gospel comes to the sexual puzzlement of most young adults not as a liberating *yes*, not as God's Good News freeing them for personhood and community. It comes rather as a remnant of cultural Christendom and an assortment of confused conventions. To be heard once again as the Gospel it must be demythologized and delegalized.

Let us turn first to the task of demythologizing it from odd bits of sexual folklore with which it has been confused. I shall refer to only two of the many mythical motifs that obfuscate the Gospel in its bearing on sexual conduct. First the ideal of romantic love, which Denis de Rougement has traced to paganism and which is almost always fused with any young American's ideas about sex.[8] Second, the Western obsession with coital intercourse as normative sexuality and hence as that which defines the content of chastity and virginity. The identification is now so complete that, as Theodor W. Adorno recently pointed out, intercourse now *means* coitus.[9]

Both the romantic ideal and the identification of intercourse with coitus are cultural accretions that have been coalesced with the rule of premarital chastity. The combination has so beclouded the liberating power of the Gospel that it can scarcely be heard because of them, and the Gospel is frequently perceived to be saying almost the opposite of what is intended.

The ideal of romantic love is the most obvious mythical excrescence. It leads often to the belief, especially among girls, that certain forms of intimacy become progressively less objectionable the more you "love" the boy. The snares in this curious amalgam of Our Gal Sunday and Saint Teresa are manifold. Among adolescents of all ages, *love* has come to mean nothing more than a vague emotional glow. It's "that ol' black magic, . . . those icy fingers up and down my spine."

The belief that love is the only honest basis for sex forces countless maidens into anguished efforts to justify their sexual inconstancy by falling in and out of love with a passing parade of partners. Naturally, opportunities for self-deception are almost endless, and the outcome is often an acid cynicism about the possibility of ever really loving anyone.

Furthermore, the sex-and-romantic-love equation sets up an inevitable collision course. The conflict occurs because, although girls tend to "go the limit" only with a boy they believe they "love," many boys, as sociologist Winston Ehrmann shows in his *Premarital Dating Behavior,*[10] will stop short of intercourse with girls they "love" or "respect," though they will go as far as possible with another girl. Thus girls associate sex with romantic love far more than boys do, and emotional scars emerging from this built-in contradiction often last far into married life.

Since girls feel they must be swept into sexual experience by something "bigger than both of us," they often fail to take the precautions against pregnancy they might otherwise. Somehow it doesn't seem romantic to go out with a boy, having prepared in advance to be swept off one's feet. Consequently, many instances of intercourse are not "planned," but occur more or less spontaneously at the end of an evening of progressively heavier necking. Unwanted pregnancies, abortions, shattered family relations, and forfeited careers are the inevitable result.

One solution is to admonish everybody to avoid any physical contact that could spiral toward intercourse. But how sane or compassionate is this advice in a society where various types of petting are the only socially approved way of handling tensions exacerbated by a sexually saturated culture? Petting does sometimes lead to intercourse, but not always. Most of the time it does not. To try to abolish it while still retaining our prosperity and our aphrodisiac advertising would be even less honest than the preach-and-wink pharisaism.

Another antidote is simply to deromanticize sex. This would mean urging young people who are going to have intercourse anyway (and who, under layers of unsuccessful self-deception, know they will) to accept the full responsibility for their behavior and to take the necessary steps to avoid pregnancy.

Such a solution, although more realistic, has almost as little chance of acceptance as the first. It would necessitate dispelling the illusions of romantic love and suggesting that young people ponder soberly in the light of day what they are really doing. But it would also require our society to face up to the cant and flimflam of its sexual folkways, and this no one really wants to do. So the black magic, petting, and pregnancies will probably continue.

A more stubborn and deceptive segment of folklore that has been equated with the doctrine of premarital chastity is one that is rarely discussed openly: the curious presumption that a person who has not experienced coital intercourse remains a virgin—no matter what else he or she has done. This popular piece of legerdemain explains in part the discovery by Kinsey that, although the incidence of premarital intercourse among women has merely mounted steadily, premarital petting of all varieties has skyrocketed.

Kinsey's finding could be substantiated by the most casual observer of the American college scene. The number of students who do not pet at all is negligible. An increasing number regularly carry their necking to the point of heavy sex play and orgasm. A pert young graduate of a denominational college assured me recently that although she had necked to orgasm every weekend for two years, she had never "gone all the way." Her premarital chastity was intact.

Or was it? Only, I submit, by the most technical definition of what is meant by preserving virginity. True, some writers actually advocate such noncoital orgasm as the "safest" way for unmarried people to achieve sexual climax. However distasteful this idea may seem to some, it is extremely important to realize that the church's traditional teaching actually functions in such a fashion as to give considerable support to this view.

The ideal of premarital chastity is generally understood to mean that, although necking is somewhat questionable, the fragile gem of virginity remains intact so long as coitus is avoided. This myth has helped open the floodgate to a tidal wave of noncoital promiscuity.

Here the demythologizing process might be helped if we note Saint Paul's insistence (in I Corinthians 6:15–16) that liaisons intended to be highly casual, for example with prostitutes, nevertheless involve us in a relationship that is inevitably much deeper than we bargained for. We "become one flesh." D. S. Bailey calls this "a psychological insight . . . altogether exceptional by first-century standards."[11]

Saint Paul saw the striking fact that as human beings we both *have* and *are* bodies. This is an issue that has been explored at length by such contemporary philosophers as Gabriel Marcel and Maurice Merleau-Ponty. Paul saw that sex—unlike excretion, for example—is not simply a physiological but also a "bodily" (somatic) activity. It involves us at the deepest levels of our personal identity.

But why limit Saint Paul's insight to coital intercourse alone, or to contacts with prostitutes? The mere avoidance of coitus does not exempt anyone from becoming "one flesh" with another. All "virgins" who are promiscuous neckers should know that. Nor can the "one flesh" phenomenon be restricted to the bordello.

Saint Paul knew that no sexual relationship could be kept merely physical without ceasing to be really sexual in the fully human sense of the word. This is why the playmate-of-the-month domestication of sex as a purely recreational pursuit just doesn't work. Paul really appreciated sex more than Hugh Hefner does. He expected more from it. Sex is certainly fun, but to make it *simply* fun is to eviscerate and enfeeble it. Then it eventually ceases even to be fun.

When it is demythologized, the evangelical sexual ethic turns out to be an invitation to life together in a community of personal selves. The Gospel frees us from the need to cling to romantic self-deception and the righteousness by which we clothe our promiscuity in the costume of technical virginity. By delivering us from mythology into history, Jesus Christ allows us to see that the marvelous skein of privileges and responsibilities in which we find ourselves as human beings is something for which we are responsible. But how do we exercise this responsibility?

At this point the going becomes more difficult. Any effort to arrest the degeneration of the Gospel into some form of Law will be viewed in some quarters as antinomianism, the belief that the precepts of the Law are not binding for Christians. A Gospel ethic, however, demands more maturity and more discipline than a Law ethic. Evangelical ethics are by nature riskier. This risk must be run since the New Testament insists unequivocally that it is the Gospel and not the Law that saves. How then can we begin to "delegalize" the Gospel when sexual behavior is the question at issue?

The Gospel is addressed to persons; the Law sees acts. One weakness of the traditional ethical formulation on premarital chastity is its sweeping inclusiveness and total lack of discrimination. Reduced to a precept, the ideal of premarital chastity permits no distinction between intercourse by engaged couples, for example, and the chilling exploitation of high school girls at fraternity parties. Both are transgressions of the Law, and there is no middle ground between virginity and nonvirginity.

Consequently there emerges alongside the technical virgin her shadowy counterpart, the technically fallen woman—the girl who, because she once consented to intercourse, now feels she is permanently pastured among the goats. She has crossed the sexual Styx and there is no way back. Because she can no longer present herself to her husband in purity on the wedding night anyway, why shouldn't anything go?

Her self-condemnation arises in part because she has not heard the good news. She has perceived the traditional teaching as a *law*. Law without Gospel is arbitrary and abstract. It cannot discriminate among cases. And it has nothing helpful to say to the transgressor. Consequently, for the increasing proportion of young people who have already had sexual intercourse, the rule of permarital chastity is simply irrelevant. And since for many it appears to be the only record the church ever plays on this subject, they conclude the church has nothing to say to them.

But preaching the Gospel also entails preaching the Law— exposing the false absolutes from which one is liberated. Negatively this means making clear the distorted images of sex from which the Gospel delivers us. Positively it entails protecting sex as a fully human activity against all the principalities and powers that seek to dehumanize it. In our day these include the forces, both within and without, that pervert sex into a merchandising technique, a means of self-aggrandizement, a weapon for rebelling against parents, a recreational pursuit, a way to gain entrance into the right clique, *or*—let the reader beware—a devotional act with some sort of religious significance.

To be freed from the "bondage of the Law" means to be freed from these dehumanizing powers. It also means to be freed from those diabolical pressures toward subcultural conformity that push so many adolescents into whatever is "in" at the moment. Sexual freedom in Christ, in one concrete case, means that a harried co-ed can say *no* to a cloying Romeo without feeling she is being hopelessly square.

Evangelical ethics cease to be Law and once again become Gospel when the Word liberates people from cultural conventions and social pressures, when persons discover their sexuality as a delightful gift from God that links them in freedom and concern to their fellows. But how do we make *this* Gospel heard by young adults in today's sexually rapacious society?

Before answering this question we must admit that we have created a set of cultural conditions in which sexual responsibility is made exceedingly difficult. In our American Xanadu, exhortations to individual continence are almost as useless as urging businessmen to eschew the profit motive.

It is strange how even people who see most clearly that crime, illegitimacy, narcotics addiction, and poverty are largely structural problems still interpret the increase in premarital sexual experience as a breakdown in personal morals.

But the jig is nearly up. Our feverish effort to paper over a society propelled by drives for sex and status with a set of Victorian courtship mores is breaking down badly. We must direct our fire more toward the "feminine mystique" and the cynical misutilization of sex by the public-relations culture than toward the hapless individual offender.

This may involve some searching questions about limiting the deliberate use of sexual stimulation in selling or, even more radically, about the merit of an economic system that seems to require a constant perversion of sexuality in order to survive. Commercial exploitation of sex drives—not the call girl—is our most serious form of prostitution today.

When we do turn from the society to the individual, especially to the unmarried young adult, we must avoid giving a simple yes-or-no answer to the question of premarital chastity. Of course, this will sound like evasion, but any simple answer panders to the cheap attempt to oversimplify the issue, to reduce all the intricacies of premarital sexuality to one decision. And churchmen, by allowing the Gospel to deteriorate into folklore and fiat, have contributed to this fatal oversimplification.

I do not believe that an evangelical ethic of premarital sex can be chopped down to a flat answer to this weighted question without impoverishing and distorting it. Instead of registering an answer, the Gospel poses a question of its own (as Jesus himself frequently did with such questions). It asks how

I can best nourish the maturity of those with whom I share the torments and transports of human existence.

The Gospel liberates men from mythical taboos and rigid concepts for a purpose: so that the full and untrammeled resources of the human imagination can be exercised in responsibility for others within the patterns of public and private life. In the freedom of the Gospel, we arrive at decisions by utilizing norms that themselves must always be open to criticism and transformation and are therefore never final. Traditional Christian sexual norms are no exception. They do not stand above history. They have arisen as Christians attempted to live faithfully through constantly changing social systems. Like all human codes they stand in continuous need of revision so they will help rather than hinder God's maturation of man.

Christians believe God is at work in history bringing man to adulthood and responsibility. Within this framework the norms by which we make our decisions are fashioned and discarded in a continuing conversation with the Bible and with the culture, a conversation that is never completed. The Christian knows he is free only as a partner in this conversation and as a member of this community. This means, among other things, that his decisions about sexual conduct inevitably involve more people than he would sometimes like to involve. Sex is never simply a private matter.

To refuse to deliver a prepared answer whenever the question of premarital intercourse pops up will have a healthy influence on the continuing conversation that is Christian ethics. It moves the axis of the discussion away from the arid stereotypes by which we oversimplify intricate human issues. It gets us off dead-end arguments about virginity and chastity, forces us to think about fidelity to persons. It exposes the promiscuity of sexual pharisees and the subtle exploitation that poisons even the most immaculate Platonic relationships.

By definition, premarital refers to people who plan to marry someone someday. Premarital sexual conduct should therefore serve to strengthen the chances of sexual success and fidelity in marriage, and we must face the real question of whether avoidance of intercourse beforehand is always the best preparation.

This question includes consideration of the appropriate degree of sexual intimacy during increasingly extended engagement periods. The reason it cannot be answered once and for all is that circumstances vary from couple to couple.

Guidance must be given with specific persons rather than with general conventions in view.

Admittedly, this approach requires more resourcefulness and imagination than relying on universally applicable axioms. Principles are useful, perhaps indispensable in ethical thinking, but all too often "sticking to principles" can become just another way to avoid seeing persons. It can signify a relapse from Gospel into Law.

Perhaps one day we in America will put away childish things and become mature men and women who do not have to rely on the male and female dieties of the mass media to tell us who to be. Perhaps one day we will outgrow our ridiculous obsession with sex, of which our fixation on chastity and virginity is just the other side of the coin. Until that time, however, we should rejoice that in Jesus Christ we are freed from myth and from Law. We are placed in a community of selves, free to the extent that we live for each other, free to develop whatever styles of life will contribute to the maturation of persons in a society where persons are often overlooked as we scamper to pursue profits and piety all at once.

NOTES TO CHAPTER 9

1. This is quoted from Lucretius ii, 608f. in T. R. Glover, *The Conflict of Religions in the Early Roman Empire* (Boston: Beacon, 1960), p. 20. It was originally published in London in 1909 by Methuen & Co. Ltd.

2. Simone de Beauvoir, *The Second Sex* (New York: Knopf, 1953; London: Cape), p. 41.

3. Erik Erikson, *Identity and the Life Cycle* (New York: International University Press, 1959).

4. David Riesman, *The Lonely Crowd* (New Haven: Yale University Press, 1950; Harmondsworth, Middlesex: Penguin).

5. This whole fusing of sex and machine symbols in contemporary mass media was once brilliantly explored by Marshall McCluhan in *The Mechanical Bride* (New York: Vanguard, 1957), now out of print.

6. Karl Barth, *Church Dogmatics* (Edinburgh: T & T Clark, 1957), II/2.

7. Friedrich Gogarten, *Der Mensch zwischen Gott und Welt*, (Stuttgart: F. Vorwerk Verlag, 1956), p. 34.

8. Denis de Rougement, *Love in the Western World* (New York: Pantheon, 1956).

9. Theodor W. Adorno, *Neun Kritische Modelle* (Frankfurt: Suhrkamp Verlag, 1963), pp. 99ff.

10. Winston Ehrmann, *Premarital Dating Behavior* (New York: Holt, 1959).

11. D. S. Bailey, *Sexual Relations in Christian Thought* (New York: Harper & Row, 1959; London: Longmans, Green).

CHAPTER 10

The Church and the Secular University

The churches have never quite been reconciled to the fact that they no longer have a parental responsibility for the university. The daughter has grown up and moved out—for good. There was a time when Christians—either directly through clerical control, indirectly through cultural influence, or circuitously through infiltration—could produce some sort of Christianization of the university. Those days are either gone or fast disappearing. The university, like the culture it influences and is influenced by, has become a secular institution, a center of clashing ideas, enormous dangers, and fantastic possibilities. Its de-Christianization is not yet complete, and there is always a possibility that it will relapse into one or another orthodox world view, but the process is gaining on all fronts.

Some Christians believe it is the task of the church to wage total war against this process of secularization. This is a mistake. We have seen that secularization is a liberation and has its roots in the biblical faith itself. It is not a process which any program, ecclesiastical or otherwise, can possibly turn back. The gods and their pale children, the ciphers and symbols of metaphysics, are disappearing. The world is becoming more and more "mere world." It is being divested of its sacral and religious character. Man is becoming more and more "man" and losing the mythical meanings and cultic afterglows that marked him during the "religious" stage of history, a stage now coming to its end. Man must now assume the responsibility for his world. He can no longer shove it off on some religious power.

The university, like all the institutions of the culture, participates in the process of secularization. In fact, at certain points it even takes the lead. From its inception the university has been a kind of problem child for the church. Try as it would to use the university as an instrumentality for producing a leadership elite faithful to its philosophies and theologies, the church never succeeded very well. Arabs kept show-

ing up at the universities and even established some very good
ones of their own, and Christian and Arab scholars seemed
able to get along surprisingly well when they stopped discussing the Holy Trinity versus the one God Allah and began
dissecting animals, enumerating things, or peering through
telescopes. At the University of Paris philosophy began to
differentiate itself from theology and, under the impact of the
newly rediscovered Aristotle, Thomas Aquinas divided the
territory and assigned separate (though closely related)
realms to the theological and nontheological disciplines. The
division was decisive. It was only a matter of time until the
worldly philosophers could strike out on their own. Admittedly, they often did this by continuing to pay a kind of lip
service to theology, by muttering the scholarly equivalent of
"Paris is worth a mass" so they could get back to their books
and test tubes. Even in Oxford and Cambridge, all students
had to affirm the Apostles' Creed until the early decades of
the twentieth century. No wonder Bentham could say of
Cambridge that "the streets were paved with perjury." But the
process of secularization was under way.

In America a quaint mixture of theocracy and tolerance
characterized the universities. Those founded in the theocratic
era still display theological faculties (Harvard and Yale). So
do the private schools founded by the barons of commerce
who learned their piety and made their money in the heyday
of theocratic culture (Vanderbuilt, Chicago, Drew universities). But the land-grant colleges of what was then the West
and the burgeoning metropolitan universities of an increasingly urban country no longer sport such antiquated furniture,
and the hundreds of small denominational colleges which in
many ways are America's unique contribution to higher education are still another story. Some of them retain to this day
unrivaled reputations for the quality of their undergraduate
work, but they struggle daily with what to do about a "church
tradition" that usually seems less and less relevant to what
they have to do to exist.[1]

All types of American institutions of higher education find
themselves in the same predicament. They all need money.
And the real money today is available not mainly from
churches, which like to water a plant where piety seems to be
flourishing, but from government, and the government's attitude toward piety is a very different one. For constitutional
reasons, Uncle Sam prefers as little or at least as unsectarian a
variety of piety as possible. Another source of money is foun-

dations. They differ from one another on what role religion should play, but usually want their money to go to something experimental or at least novel. Colleges and universities also need teachers—most of whom are much happier working where the warm breath of denominational representatives is as far as possible from their necks. Schools also need students. There are of course plenty of students. But most schools want to get the best ones, and they find that the best ones are usually more interested in the laboratory and library facilities than in the decor of the chapel.

We have seen the last of elite education. The kind of society we will live in during the next twenty years will make a college diploma as important as a high school diploma was to our fathers. The cybernetic society simply requires a larger percentage of highly educated and technically adept people. Making it possible for all qualified young people to go to college is not just a handout by the welfare state. It is a desperate necessity. Untrained people cannot manage an automated society. We must accept the fact that as the percentage of students in college increases, those taking advanced degrees will increase proportionately and we will see a colossal growth in graduate education. These are the salient facts about the *actual* university as it races toward the future. But what about the church?

We have already noted that the university has always been a problem for the church. But the current cleavage between the two is wider and more impassable than ever, precisely because we now stand at the end of the epoch of the church's dominance in Western culture. The church still lives on the interest of the accumulation it laid aside during the long Constantinian era. But the capital itself is shrinking, and the whole treasure will soon be gone. Shorn of its political might by two hundred years of revolutions, deprived of its cultural influence by the Enlightenment, and finally robbed of its psychological power by the casual this-worldliness of modern urban man, the church may very soon have to go back and start from scratch. But in the meantime it limps along with a theology still not extricated from the metaphysical baggage to which it was firmly lashed during the opening centuries of the era, and with an egoistic notion of its own importance acquired during its years as the official source of the ideology of an empire.

But this is all gone, or almost gone. Western Christendom, based partly on the biblical Gospel, partly on late Greek philosophy, and partly on pagan world views, is over. It survives only in the memory of neo-Thomist theologians and cultural arcadians. The synthesis of Protestantism and the bourgeois culture which came to birth in the seventeenth and eighteenth centuries and whose death spasms we have been witnessing for the past fifty years is also over. Yet in their organization, their theology, and their ways of relating to the world, our institutional churches today are for the most part merely richer and shinier versions of their nineteenth-century parents. Their organization (residential parishes) is based on the sociological patterns of about 1885 (before automobiles, commuter trains, and industrial parks). Their Sunday-at-eleven cultus is timed to fall between the two milking hours in the agricultural society. Sermons remain one of the last forms of public discourse where it is culturally forbidden to talk back. In a mobile, scientific society rapidly moving toward what Sumner Slichter called "total industrialization," the church remains a patriarchal, agricultural, prescientific relic.

It is not that the church deplores its role as the representative of what once was. It seems rather to enjoy it. In all eras of rapid transition and cultural transformation, there is an aching need for an institution that will project the image of "things as they used to be" in all their (imagined) simplicity, security, and dependability. Hence the church in America today never tires of reminding Americans of their religious heritage. It cherishes its timeworn rituals, and never fails to celebrate an anniversary, preferably with ancestral costumes. It clings to the things that make it "ye olde kirke," because it has little to offer if people look to it for some kind of future orientation. The first Christian church was one that looked *forward* in strained and eager anticipation to the end days and the coming again of the Lord. The church of today looks *back* to the Pilgrim Fathers or to the founding of the First Church of Cedar Elms.

The anachronistic posture of the church is nowhere more obvious than in the context of the university community. The church has made three attempts to come to terms with the university problem in America, all of which have been marked by a certain recidivism. The first was the establishment of its own colleges and universities. This of course is medievalism. The whole idea of a "Christian" college or university after the breaking apart of the medieval synthesis has little meaning. The term *Christian* is not one that can be used to refer to universities any more than to observatories or laboratories. No one of the so-called Christian colleges that now dot our Midwest is able to give a very plausible theological basis for retaining the equivocal phrase *Christian college* in the catalog. Granted that there may be excellent traditional, public-relations, or sentimental reasons for calling a college Christian, there are no theological reasons. The fact that it was founded by ministers, that it has a certain number of Christians on the faculty or in the student body, that chapel is required (or not required), or that it gets part of its bills paid by a denomination—none of these factors provides any grounds for labeling an institution with a word that the Bible applies only to followers of Christ, and then very sparingly. The idea of developing "Christian universities" in America was bankrupt even before it began.

Next the churches began trying to work through nearby residential congregations to render a special ministry to people involved in university life. This was the second attempt and represents a much healthier and basically sounder impulse. But it quickly revealed its inadequacies. University people seemed to have different interests and loyalties than "townies." They were not just people who happened to be living in the same town, albeit temporarily. They really lived in *another* community, even if it was a community which geographically overlapped or coincided with the town. The slow recognition by the churches of the inadequacy of relating to the university community through parochial structures was a very important one. It marked the churches' first awareness of an elemental principle now determining twentieth-century society—that our *functional* relationships to each other in communities of common interest have become more important than our *geographic* communities. This is in fact the basic motif of what we designate urbanization. Urban man lives his life in interrelated, nonspatial groupings: work, leisure, residence, education, shopping. The church's recognition that the university was such a community was epochal. But its response to the problem, alas, was wrong.

The church tried to "follow its students." This was the third phase. It tried to transplant onto the university campus a denominational church (disguised as a "house" with Ping-Pong tables and a less ministerial minister). But it was the same old show in new costumes. People bearing the same denominational labels were expected to gather under this roof at stated intervals and to bring interested friends so long as they were not being shoplifted from the foundation houses of another denomination (the same ground rules that apply to the neighborhood church). In some cases, the student center nestled next to a traditional church building. In other cases, students were encouraged to seek out the respective local distributors of the religions bearing the labels to which they had grown accustomed. In Detroit this is called "brand loyalty." Sociologically the pattern was nearly identical with that of the home town. The student pastors of the various foundations formed the campus equivalent of ministers' councils and then councils of churches, where those endlessly repeated jokes about Baptists and Methodists could be told again and the various fellowships could be invited to one another's carpeted parlors to hear speakers of extra-special interest.

As the enterprise grew, more and more hours had to be spent in coordinating the relationships between the various foundations and in clearing schedules. As with the churches in most home towns, the complex of foundations presented a picture of lively activities and full bulletin boards. But the activities were all going on inside a special world existing *next* to the world of the university. The whole purpose of the movement to the university had been lost by the fashioning of what amounted to a "home away from home" (it was even so called on some campuses) where students with the same denominational brand mark could establish a set of relationships with each other at the expense of the relationships offered within the university itself.

Naturally, for many the fellowship of the foundation house served as a compensation. Those who didn't make the campus newspaper staff could turn the mimeo handle for the *Wesley Foundation News*. Those who could not meet the financial or genealogical standards of fraternities could find solace on a Saturday night at a Baptist doggie-roast. But the whole notion of witness and service *within* the university was often lost. Meanwhile harried foundation directors were kept busy attending two sets of conferences (those for regular ministers and those for student ministers), coordinating their work with that of the other foundations, counseling for hours on end, keeping a roof on a fifty-thousand-dollar building, and explaining to denominational officials why only 9 per cent of the Presbyterian-preference students ever participated in the program.

We are still in the third phase of this cumulative catastrophe. The only encouraging developments in recent years have been those in which denominational fragmentation has been abandoned and the effort to sweep droves of students off the campus into the foundations has been given up. The appearance of ecumenical teams and of disciplined communities of students and faculty on some campuses is encouraging. The idea of small groups that combine discipline with radical openness and the idea of engaging the university itself, on its own terms, are signs of hope. Meanwhile a word might be said in defense of two student Christian organizations on the university campus that in their own ways preserved elements of this approach during the attempt of the Guelphs and the Ghibellines to convince students to take denominational bickering seriously. I refer to two extremely different organizations, the Intervarsity Christian Fellowship and the Student YMCA–YWCA.

I make no effort to defend the indefensible theology of many IVCF people, but the strength and tenacity of this remarkable organization cannot simply be chalked up, as some people often do, to its appeal to the stupid or the closed-minded. The IVCF on many campuses sometimes provided the only place where a student Christian-movement program went on entirely without benefit of adult staff supervision. On the campus where I was an undergraduate (The University of Pennsylvania in Philadelphia), IVCF sponsored scores of student-led Bible studies, where the discussions were often hotter and more valuable than those carefully supervised by clergymen. They sponsored lectures and conferences whose content often left much to be hoped for but which attracted people because they were obviously student affairs and not foisted on them by their all-knowing elders. Furthermore, IVCF meetings and discussions were *visible*. Lacking the plush facilities of a foundation house, they often met in dormitories, student union lounges, and the like. In short, IVCF was a lay-led, highly visible, and extremely mobile organization which did not have enough money to erect separate facilities so was forced to live in the same world with everyone else.

The Student YMCA–YWCA is a very different kind of movement. It has just come through a tough decade in which epithets have been hurled at it from all sides. It has been criticized for not having the right theology, for not being "religious" enough, for allowing Jews, Turks, and heretics to hold office, and for pushing hotheads into political action before they had mastered the theological rationale for their deeds. It has been made fun of for appearing Social-Gospelish in an age of crisis theology or for allowing students to lead things even when they wreck them.

Ironically, the Student Y has not always been as good as its detractors' criticisms would make it. It has been guilty of its share of staff dominance, withdrawal into internal programs, and even ecclesiasticism. But it has generally preserved a certain healthy anticlericalism. At the very time that the church foundations were chattering with each other in an intrachurch monologue, in many campus Ys atheists, Jews, agnostics, and wavering believers were talking and working together. The Y program was indeed "worldly." It was a kind of anticipation of Dietrich Bonhoeffer's attempt to speak to the "religionless man" about God. The Y made the effort to take the university itself seriously and would not docilely submit to the galloping ecclesiasticization of the last decade.

But the crisis is not yet over. The Y may have survived the acute period of psychopathic confessionalism, but it was seriously decimated. If history finally shows that the triumphal arrival of the elaborately financed, expensively staffed, and theologically modish denominational foundation houses on the campus killed off the Ys as a viable force, it will have been one of the more disastrous chapters in the church's bumbling and ineffectual experience with the university.

In speaking of churches in the foregoing pages we have been referring to the only organizations that seem at the moment to be culturally, if not legally, permitted to call themselves churches. That means our organized denominations. These are the "churches" that have invaded the university campuses, spent millions of dollars on buildings, mimeographed billions of announcements, and sponsored numberless speakers and hayrides. But our first question about the "church" must be an utterly simple and fundamental one: What really *is* the church, and where can it be found today? We have dealt with this question in earlier chapters, describing the church as avant-garde and exorcist. At this particular point, however, it is important to remind ourselves of another important feature of the biblical view of the church: *Only faith can discern the Church of Jesus Christ.* It is not an entity that can be empirically detected and located by a bulletin board or a sociological survey. Only God knows the names of His saints. Furthermore, the Greek word for church, *ecclesia,* is a word of motion. If refers to those on the way, responding to the herald's announcement. The church is what such diverse theologians as Karl Barth, Rudolf Bultmann, and Gerhard Ebeling have called "an event." It *happens*. It occurs where the reconciling actuality of God's work in human history comes to fulfillment and is brought to human speech. The church is the pilot project of the coming era. Within it there is "no more Jew nor Greek, slave nor free. . . . ." The church is the word-event by which reconciliation across the divisive lines of race, nation, belief, sex, age, and social status occurs, and men live, if only provisionally, in the new age.

If this is what we mean by *church*, then it is clear that our use of the word in the first part of this chapter is questionable, since the church cannot simply be identified with the organizations that have preempted the name to themselves in our society. Such an identification would undercut the necessity for faith in discerning the church. The church is an object of faith, not of sight. This is not to say that the church is "invisible." It is to say rather that whenever we say something is a church, biblically speaking, we are confessing our faith. We are *not* telling someone something he can find out by consulting a phone book. The church uses buildings, budgets, and bureaucracies, but it is not to be wholly identified with them. It is a people in motion, an "eventful movement" in which barriers are being struck down and a radically new community beyond the divisiveness of inherited labels and stereotypes is emerging.

It is clear, then, that this church-event, this reconciliation in action, cannot be either restricted to or excluded from the organizations called churches. God's reconciling work *may* be going on among them. It may not be. More likely it is and it isn't. More likely it is occurring within them and also at many places outside them. I believe that the real job of those in the churches today is to discern where God's reconciliation is breaking in and to identify themselves with this action. In the university this may require stepping out of the sequestered shells in which they are imprisoned on the hinterlands of the campus and into the secular university community itself. The task of the church, referring now to the *laos theou*, the "people of God in motion" in the university might be sketched under three headings: (1) restrained reconciliation; (2) candid criticism; (3) creative disaffiliation. They correspond respectively to the priestly, the prophetic, and the ascetic traditions of church history. Let us look at each one briefly.

Reconciliation is always the primary calling of the people of God. It is a priestly responsibility, the bearing of sins and the representation of God's grace. "God was in Christ reconciling the world to himself. And we are ministers of reconciliation." The church is the partner of God in proclaiming and embodying the reconciliation that He is accomplishing. The church is never the creator of reconciliation. It is the *agent*. It demonstrates and broadcasts something that is going on independently of it, but which at the same time provides it with its *raison d'être*. The church has no purpose other than to make known to the world what God has done and is doing in history to break down the hostilities between peoples and to reconcile men to each other.

Within the specialized atmosphere of the university community, this reconciliation is most necessary at those points where the wounds of separation are most painful. This varies from campus to campus, but there are certain basic similarities. The chasms between the various departments, between the sciences and the humanities, between Greeks and independents, between teachers and administrators, between town and gown, between students of diverse racial, ethnic, or creedal backgrounds. To be ambassadors for reconciliation between these segregated realms is the privilege of the *laos theou*. Christians live precisely at the points of tensions and disagreement, of suspicion and intolerance and indifference. When they are able to serve as agents and demonstrators of reconciliation, they understand that it is God and not they themselves who accomplished it.

But it must be said right away that the reconciliation accomplished by God to which the church testifies is not one based on the acceptance of some kind of common world view. Greeks do not stop being Greeks or Jews being Jews in Christ any more than men and women stop being men and women. The Gospel offers no world view as an option along with others. It is a reconciliation accompanied by restraint. It does not reconcile people by converting them. It frees people to live with each other *despite* radically conflicting ideologies, theologies, and politics, as men with men.

Creative criticism is a task of the church which has particular relevance in the university. It is the prophetic responsibility, and Christians in the university have the job of being prophets and intellectuals at the same time. It is always the task of the intellectuals to "think otherwise." This is not just a perverse idiosyncrasy. It is an absolutely essential feature of a society. It is the task of the university as the institutionalization of the intellectual enterprise to be critical of its society.

It is likewise the task of the *laos theou* within the university to criticize both the university and the churches.

Most of us agree now that the church within the university should criticize the university not because it is not Christian or not churchly, but because it is not a university: i.e., "We must challenge the university to be the university!" But there is a real danger lurking behind this slogan. Christians have sometimes taken the university to task for failing to be the kind of university Newman or Moberly or Nash thought it ought to be. To challenge the university to "be the university" does not mean prodding it into aping *our* models of what universities ought to be.

There has been too much easy talk about the university having become a "multiversity" with no overarching and unifying motif, a "cafeteria," and so on. Certainly no one wishes to defend the often-disastrous extent to which contemporary university education has been sliced, packaged, and dished out to students who buy it by the unit. But it is also highly unlikely that we can ever again have any unifying world view under which the various departments of knowledge can be subsumed. The proliferation of world views and their progressive relativization is a hallmark of our time. It is part of what we mean by secularization. Neither Christianity, "Western civilization," nor even "Humanities" can be expected to provide what was once provided by the all-encompassing and comparatively unified world picture of the medieval university. What does this mean for our criticism of the university?[2]

It means that our criticism must *not* be on the level of comparative world views (the so-called university question, which happily seems now to have run its course). We should recognize that the unified university is no longer a possibility and we should stop hankering for it. Our criticism today should concern itself with controllable, manageable issues that concern the human destinies of those whose lives are affected by the university (and who is excluded from this?). Christians should challenge bad teaching more than they do (even if it is perpetrated by people with acceptable theologies). They should interest themselves in the problems the university has in interpreting itself to its various constituencies—alumni, fund sources, prospective students and faculty, government, the public at large. Christians should squall louder when things are made too easy or when university officials begin to take their own public-relations efforts too seriously. Especially in placement policies, in housing policies, and in the way recruitment areas are selected, Christians should make sure that particular racial and religious groups are not being slighted. If the church does have anything to say about world views, it should try to prevent the university from rummaging around for a new one, since any total world view represented by the university today would be divisive and repressive.[3]

Today's university is a political reality, with both internal and external power relationships. Christians who live for either a short or a long time within these relationships should take them seriously, exercise their critical intelligences. But they should do this with a sense of responsibility. The only thing worse than student apathy is student grumbling and protest which is not prepared to pay the price in time and initiative required to do it better.

One function of theology is the critical support and correction of the community of faith. But theology is no longer a clerical monopoly. Today it includes the kind of critical thinking anyone with education and interest can do. Whether they like it or not, those Christians who live within the University community constitute a kind of intellectual elite of the church. They are lay theologians. They fail in their responsibility if they do not express as clearly and intelligently as possible the criticisms they have of the institutional church and of the less institutionalized expressions of church life that are coming to birth on the edge of and outside the institutions.

But once again, this criticism cannot be rootless and detached. It should be uttered only when those uttering it are willing to take part in constructive formulations leading to a church which is more faithful to its purposes. The church is the church only when it is *semper reformanda,* when it is constantly being corrected and called back to its real task by the Word of God.

There was a time when the relationship between the SCM and the organized church was one of creative tension and helpful mutual criticism. This is hardly the case any more today. Occasionally students surprise us by questioning and even rejecting the pablum cooked up for them by their leaders. But not often enough. A rebirth of responsible criticism is desperately needed among Christians in the house of intellect today.

Creative disaffiliation may be the modern equivalent of asceticism, the focusing of energy on what is important at the cost of denying what is less important. I have just said that criticism must always occur within a responsible relationship, not just from the outside. It must be *engaged* criticism and not just potshots. I must add, however, that there are certain matters in which the only productive relationship must be disaffiliation. It may be that the debilitating institution-centered thinking of churches is not something that can be corrected wholly "from within." The problem with denominational organizations is not that they have splendid institutional apparatus that is simply being used in the wrong way. If this were the case, then a minor palace insurrection in denominational headquarters might win the day.

Such is not the case. The problem lies much deeper. It lies within the structure of the churches itself and not with their leadership. Even the most prophetic leadership often falters under the weight of the massive institutional determinants with which it must work. The colossal staffs, astronomical budgets, and cavernous facilities of denominationally divided Christianity absorb so much talent and time that the people of God are frequently prevented from fulfilling their real calling. Thus the churches are hindered in their attempt to see what God is doing in the world, (1) by a degree of *ingrown isolation* made unavoidable by the sheer size and complexity of the apparatus, and (2) by an institutional and social *conservatism* related to their dependence on sources of funds, a dependence which in turn makes exceedingly difficult the continuous constructive criticism of the structural elements of our society. We have noted previously that the task of Christians is to discern where God's reconciliation is breaking in and to identify themselves with it. This means locating and participating in social change. But the isolation of the denominational church hinders the perception of social change, and its conservatism hinders participation in it. Let us look briefly then at these two structural handicaps and suggest why only a kind of ascetic disaffiliation is practicable today. First, the church's isolation from the world.

It is now enormously popular in religious circles to talk about "dialogue with the world." Almost every conference of church workers must now include some exposure to art, theatre, or politics—usually carefully introduced and interpreted. The sentiment is commendable, but the reality is a caricature of dialogue with the world. What happens is that the churches try to understand and confront the world on the churches' terms and in the churches' language. But it amounts to predigested criticism. There is a kind of folk wisdom in people and in organizations which allows them to see only as much of what does not correspond to their world view as will not demand really basic alterations. Churches have an uncanny capacity to emasulate criticism simply by modifying it and and then incorporating it into the continuous but ineffectual self-flagellation that goes on in all organizations. Last year's most critical blast turns up as the study theme for next year's women's circles. Attacks on the caution, ineffectiveness, and dinosaurism of the churches can often reach a fever pitch in discussions among denominational executives—after which the executives return to more or less the same pursuits. These safe little family sessions of criticism serve the same purpose hurling an ashtray across the room would. They let off steam without really changing anything. They may allow church functionaries to remain sane, but they do *less* than nothing to alter the structure in which they are entrapped because they give the deceptive appearance that something is really happening.

The labyrinthine complexity of denominational Christianity means that disproportionate amounts of time must be devoted to coordination, clearing, and effectuating communication. Any given unit within a church bureaucracy will have structural relationships with several other units. This supplies another obstacle to communication with the world. There just isn't enough time. Anyone who has ever sat in a meeting of church functionaries trying to agree on a mutually satisfactory date for their next meeting will have noted the appalling number of coordinative relationships these people must keep up, with scheduling normally running to two or three years into the future. But how does this organizational preoccupation of denominational Christianity affect the task of Christians in the university?

Brave souls are needed to fight the battle for control of church organizations. But not everyone needs to venture into the jungle of overlapping regional, state, national, and international boards and committees. Here is where a certain asceticism must be exercised. I simply do not believe that the average student or faculty member, naïvely intent on helping his church to "move in a new direction," has any grasp whatever of the gigantic forces pushing the other way. First of all there is the religious equivalent of the managerial revolution. As a layman the well-meaning student or professor may participate in boards and conferences, but most of the work

must be done behind the scenes by the full-time functionaries.[4] This is how decisions are reached in a religious
bureaucracy and how power is really wielded. The well-intentioned layman bent on working from within will also soon
have another baffling experience. He will discover that all his
suggestions—or most of them—will be greeted with appreciation. They will be executed, however (if they are not lost sight
of), *within* the structure of the denomination and will be
fulfilled only to the extent that they do not threaten the
organization as now conceived. They will do little to change
the direction of the organization itself. The layman may be
flattered by having his voice heard, by being flown across the
country to make his contribution, by seeing his ideas duly
recorded in minutes. But he will eventually get the impression
that he is wading through a vast morass of cotton batting in
which his sharpest thrusts are merely absorbed and changes
come with agonizing slowness.

I do not believe it is always the best use of the commited
student's or staff person's time to become regional or national
committee members or officers. The careful allocation of
human resources suggests that siphoning people off the campus this way can damage the local situation. While some
people struggle within ecclesiastical structures, most should
concentrate on what is happening in the secular ones.

The *conservatism* of the churches in America also has
structural roots. This has to do with the fact that, although
most Protestant churches in the United States declaim volubly
about the priesthood of all believers and have purveyed the
latest ecumenical documents on the ministry of the laity, they
really practice neither. They have chosen not to focus their
resources and personnel on training a nonprofessional ministry, but rather to recruit and support a professional corps of
missionaries and ministers. This requires a budget that reaches
into the hundreds of millions every year. It requires the religious equivalent of ground crews—the fund raisers, administrators, typists, and so forth, who "stand behind" the missionaries. Each of these supporting functionaries understandably
has a deep-seated vested interest in maintaining the present
structure of "missions," even though the nearly unanimous
opinion of the so-called "receiving countries" is that this pattern has long since outlived its usefulness. What concerns us
here is not so much the theological distortion of "mission" but
the effect this need for colossal sums of money has on the
church's capacity to relate positively to social change.

It is difficult to say just how much money is invested by American churches in the stock and bond issues that constitute the American economic system. When all local, regional, and national agencies are included, the figure must certainly account for no inconsiderable percentage of the entire investment picture. This makes the churches directly dependent not only on the system itself but on the prosperity of the firms in which the money is funded. Their financial thralldom puts the denominations in a position where criticism of the economic system itself becomes difficult if not impossible. I am not arguing here that the churches themselves could or should totally extricate themselves from the whole fabric of the American economy. That would probably be impossible so long as Christians continue to think of themselves as huge national denominational businesses. It does mean, however, that the American church has at least as much of a vested interest in the present structure of the American economy and society as the medieval church had in feudalism or the pre-revolutionary Catholic churches of Eastern Europe had in private property. It has a vested interest strongly militating against serious social change. The American church is an "established" church. It is not free to exercise radical criticism, because it is dependent on the economy for its institutional life and because on most issues the forces of economic and social conservatism generally regard it as an ally.

Of course all that has been said about the dependence of the churches on the success of the American economy can also be said about the universities. But there is an important difference. The university speaks for the best in man, his highest attainments and the widest community of reference he has yet attained, science. It can criticize its society in the name of the worldwide community of scholars and intellectuals, or in the name of the international fraternity of science. But it has no way to bring these themselves into judgment. The churches, on the other hand, claim to speak for one who judges the churches along with everyone else, for one who stands over all cultures and all sources of worldly authority. When the Christian in the university criticizes the university he must do it from the reference point of a community which is not an expression of the culture's own accomplishments. But the churches can provide that community only if they are not subject to the vested interests of the culture, if they speak from the strength that comes from weakness and with the power that only powerlessness allows. The churches in short live under the cross if they are the church. The university is the embodiment of wisdom. But the cross is foolishness to the wise.

The need for freedom from a conservative vested interest is especially crucial for the churches today. An institution which by virtue of its organizational ideology and economic basis can neither understand nor affirm revolutionary change cannot even make the first step in the pressing task of responding to God's work in the present social revolution. There is also evidence that technology rather than ideology will be the motor of most of tomorrow's revolutions. This puts the university, whether it likes it or not, at the focal point of social change. Thus the university Christian who retreats from the campus into the enveloping inner world of the denominational church stands in deadly danger of cutting himself off from the reconciliatory action of God in the world and blinding himself to his place in the drama through which this action is taking place. Only a kind of ascetic disaffiliation, what Bonhoeffer called a "holy worldliness," will free him from the intrinsic conservatism that prevents the denominational churches from leaving their palaces behind and stepping into God's permanent revolution in history.

I have discussed the task of the church in the university in relationship to its traditional priestly, prophetic, and ascetic functions. I have tried to distinguish the "church of faith" from denominational Christianity without insisting that the two are necessarily separate and without falling into the mystical notion of an "invisible church." In this argument I have tried to stay within the main lines of the Reformation tradition in theology and ecclesiology. The importation of the denominational religious groups with their divisiveness, narcissism, and conservatism into the university community has not succeeded in producing a viable style of Christian life within the university. Worse, it has tended to drain off the Christians who are there into trivial machinations in a separate ecclesiastical make-believe world. The location of the church is an act of faith and the calling of Christians in the university today is to locate this "true church" and to participate in it.

But what are the alternative shapes of church life within the university? Perhaps the prescription of these shapes before the fact is unwise and unnecessary. When Christians have enough courage to "come out" of the present crippling structures, God Himself will provide the new ones. It is not necessary to have a street map of the Promised Land before one leaves Egypt. Nevertheless, I think God has given us some hints of the routes through the desert.

It is clear, for example, that the future witness of the church will be in the secular university and not in some reversion to the medieval pattern. It is clear that communities of Christians in the modern university should not be integrated into residential congregations, and may exist for the most part separate from them. It is clear that any work which is not radically ecumenical has no place on the university campus, or indeed anywhere else. It is clear that Christians in the university of tomorrow will live in serious openness to the university itself and to the world the university is shaping. It is also clear that the gathered stage of this church's life will occur in small, disciplined groups constituted on a functional basis. The clearest thing of all is that the future shape of the church in the university will occur only when Christians live with responsibility within it and for it, and not in and for the denominational churches that have only succeeded in weakening and fragmenting the university's life.

To say more than this would be speculation or prescription. What is the role of the church in the university? The divisiveness of denominations seeking customers and recruits has no place. The church as a reconciling community of servants determined to serve the university even when no one thanks them, praises them, or notices them *does* have a place in the community of the university. That place will be evident to those who have eyes to see.

NOTES TO CHAPTER 10

1. In his book *The Protestant Stake in Higher Education* (Washington, D.C.: Council of Protestant Colleges and Universities, 1961), Merrimon Cuninggim states a strong case for having colleges sponsored by religious denominations, but at the same time he insists that there is "no such thing as a Protestant theology of education" (p. 50).

2. See Russell Thomas, *The Search for a Common Learning 1800–1960* (New York: McGraw-Hill, 1962) for a history of attempts to fashion and administer some common framework, including an honest evaluation of the enormous difficulties involved. The book also contains a good survey of general education and humanities programs at several colleges.

3. Clark Kerr, *The Uses of the University* (Cambridge, Mass.: Harvard University Press, 1961). Kerr, as president of the University of California, knows at firsthand the breathtaking physical expansion and the political context of the modern university.

4. For an excellent investigation of the way in which power is actually wielded in a religious bureaucracy, see Paul Harrison, *Power and Authority in the Free Church Tradition* (Princeton, N.J.: Princeton University Press, 1959).

PART FOUR

GOD AND THE SECULAR MAN

CHAPTER II

To Speak in a Secular Fashion of God

On April 30, 1944, Dietrich Bonhoeffer wrote to one of his friends from his prison cell words that have both tempted and tormented theologians ever since. "We are proceeding toward a time," he wrote, "of no religion at all. . . . How do we speak of God without religion. . . . How do we speak in a secular fashion of God?"[1]

No wonder Bonhoeffer's question bothers us. It reminds us of two incontrovertible facts. The first is that the biblical faith, unlike Buddhism, for example, must *speak* of God. It cannot withdraw into silence or cryptic aphorisms. A God to whom human words cannot point is not the God of the Bible. Bonhoeffer's question also reminds us, however, that the word *God* bewilders or confuses modern secular man. His mental world and his way of using language is such that the word *God* has become more and more problematical for him. This reveals the impasse: if man cannot speak of God in the secular city, then all we have said about secularization and the biblical faith is nonsense and the whole thesis of this book is erroneous. We must deal with this painful question of Bonhoeffer satisfactorily or all that we have said so far becomes implausible.

Significantly, Bonhoeffer himself supplies a much-needed clue for where to start in seeking to answer his question. Many years before his imprisonment he wrote this paragraph in his commentary on the Second Commandment:

> "God" is not for us a common concept by which we designate that which is the highest, holiest and mightiest thinkable, but "God" is a name. It is something entirely different when the heathen say "God" as when we, to whom God himself has spoken, say "God" . . . "God" is a name. . . . The word means absolutely nothing, the name "God" is everything.[2]

Here Bonhoeffer drops an invaluable hint about how we should proceed. He reminds us that in the biblical tradition,

we do not speak "about God" at all, either "in a secular
fashion" or in any other. When we use the word *God* in the
biblical sense, we are not speaking about, but we are "naming," and that is an entirely different matter. To name is to
point, to confess, to locate something in terms of our history.
We can name something only by using the fund of memories
and meanings we carry with us as individuals and as a species.
This makes the act of naming, whether naming God or anything else, more than merely a theological or linguistic problem. Theologies and languages grow out of a sociocultural
milieu. They spring from one or another epochal *manière
d'être*. This makes the problem of "speaking in a secular
fashion about God" in part at least a sociological problem.[3]

But speaking about God in a secular fashion is not just a
sociological problem. Since we live in a period when our view
of the world is being politicized, in which, as we shall see in a
moment, the political is replacing the metaphysical as the
characteristic mode of grasping reality, "naming" today becomes in part also a political issue. It becomes a question of
where, in the push and pull of human conflict, those currents
can be detected which continue the liberating activity we witness in the Exodus and in Easter. Speaking of God in a
secular fashion is also a political issue.

But the sociological and political considerations in no sense
exhaust the depth of Bonhoeffer's riddle. Despite the efforts of
some modern theologians to sidestep it, whether God exists or
not *is* a desperately serious issue. All the palaver about the
terms *existence* and *being* and all the sophisticated in-group
bickering about nonobjectifying language cannot obscure the
fact that there remains an indissoluble question after all the
conceptualizations have been clarified. It is the question the
Spanish philosopher Miguel Unamuno rightly felt overshad-
ows all other questions man asks: Is man alone in the universe or not?

So Bonhoeffer's query has three parts. It is first of all a
sociological problem. We say problem because it can be answered at that level with relatively little difficulty. It is also a
political issue. An issue is a somewhat more demanding challenge. It requires us to take some risks and make some
choices, to take sides. It necessitates our indicating where the
same reality whom the Hebrews called Yahweh, whom the
disciples saw in Jesus, is breaking in today. But finally, Bonhoeffer presents us with what is a *theological question*. He
makes us answer for ourselves whether the God of the Bible is

real or is just a rich and imaginative way man has fashioned
to talk about himself. No amount of verbal clarification can
set this disagreement aside. In the last analysis it is not a
matter of clear thinking at all but a matter of personal decision. Luther was right: deciding on this question is a matter
which, like dying, every man must do for himself.

Speaking of God as a Sociological Problem

The reason speaking about God in the secular city is in part
a sociological problem is that all words, including the word
God, emerge from a particular sociocultural setting. No language was ever handed down from heaven. When words
change their meanings and become problematical, there is
always some social dislocation or cultural breakdown that lies
beneath the confusion. There are basically two types of such
equivocality. One is caused by historical change, the other by
social differentiation.

Equivocality through historical change means that the same
word carries different connotations in different historical periods of a given language. The English word *let*, for example,
has reversed its meaning since Shakespeare's day. When Ham-
let, lunging for his father's ghost, says "I'll slay the man that
lets me!," he means he will slay whoever tries to stop him.
Equivocality through social differentiation means that in a
complex society, the same word means different things in
different settings. It may even mean different things for the
same person, depending on where it is used. Take the work
operation. It means something very different for the surgeon,
the general, the business executive. Often equivocality through
historical change and equivocality through social differentiation combine to confound the confusion. Thus groups within
a society who retain special ties to some previous historical
stage retain ways of speaking which to the larger culture
sound like jargon. In the jargon, words will have a meaning
they do not have for the culture at large. The ebb and flow of
word meanings rides on the floods of social conflict and
change. The cultural power of certain groups and the weakness of others can often be charted by noticing which meaning of a given word predominates.

Social change alters the meaning of words. French sociologist Antoine Meillet once wrote that ". . . the essential principle of change in meaning is to be found in the existence of

social groupings in the milieu where a language is spoken—in short, in a fact of social structure."[4] Bearing this rule in mind, let us consider what has happened to the three-letter English word *God* and why it has become a virtually useless vocable today.

Historians of language indicate that the word *God* has a pre-Christian origin in the Germanic language group. During the centuries of the Christian era it was used to translate a number of different terms, including the *theos* of Greek philosophy, the *Deus* of Western metaphysics, and the *Yahweh* of the Hebrew Bible. This use of the word *God* (and its predecessors in Old and Middle English) was possible because the various cultural streams the other terms represented were more or less unified in a society where no decisive historical changes interrupted the cultural continuity. In fact, the word *God* and its modern-language equivalents served as the linguistic and conceptual linchpin by which these three traditions were fastened together in that cultural synthesis called "Christendom."

But this is just the trouble. Though it is rarely noticed by theologians, this sociocultural synthesis is now coming apart. Christendom is disappearing. We now find that the various uses of the word *God,* once conveniently fused, are now coming unstuck. Historical change and social differentiation have combined to make the word the most equivocal term in the English language. Theologians are fond of saying that the word is "empty." Its emptiness, however, is merely the symptom of a much more basic disorder, its equivocality. It is not true that no one uses the word *God* anymore. It is used all the time—by swearing sailors, impassioned preachers, and dedicated dialecticians intent on proving the nonexistence of the being or the meaninglessness of the word. The social basis for the fatal equivocality of the word *God* and its equivalents is the passing of Christendom and the emergence of a highly differentiated secular civilization.

In an important book on the problem of the existence of God in contemporary theology, Helmut Gollwitzer discusses the bewildering equivocality of the term. He shows that we use it sometimes to refer to a category of beings, as when we talk about "the Greeks and their gods." Second, we use it for the supreme being of metaphysics. Third, we use it to *name* the One who discloses Himself through the biblical witness.[5]

Though the usages have always been mixed, the first two correspond in part to the two epochs we have designated as

tribal and town. Tribal man experienced God as one of the
"gods." The Old Testament, incorporating elements of this
tribal mentality, is in no sense "monotheistic." Yahweh is the
ruler of the gods. Similarly, in the epoch of town life, the
great transition from magic through metaphysics to science,
man perceived God as a part of one unified structure including both God and man. Urban-secular man, for whom tribal
and town usages make little sense, is left with only the third
usage, and that is made difficult because the other two uses
are still in circulation, corrupting the currency. This does not
mean that the people of the tribal and town epochs did not
encounter the "true God" of the Bible. It does mean, however,
that when they did encounter Him, it was within the world
views and meaning-images of their respective eras. It is for
this reason that, if urban-secular man is to meet Him, the God
of the Bible must be carefully distinguished from the cultural
avenues of perception through which presecular man met
Him.

Gollwitzer's three usages of *God* correspond not only to
historical periods. They also correspond to disparate groups
within the present culture which still retain ties to tribal and
town patterns of perception. The tribal use survives in profanity, folklore, and maxims. It survives also wherever the
deity is perceived as the protector of one particular group.
The metaphysical deity survives in those quarters where
vestiges of the classical ontologies still hold out, where the
stream of secularization has temporarily been escaped. Paradoxically, God also survives among philosophers intent on
denying his existence. They seem to know, at least, what it is
whose existence they are denying.

Where in all this do theologians and preachers fit? Sociologically speaking, they represent the victims *both* of historical change *and* of social differentiation. Most people perceive
them as cultural antiques and may have the same fondness
for them they have for *deuxième empire* furniture. Especially
when they dress up and strut about occasionally in their vivid
ecclesiastical regalia, clergymen give people a welcome sense
of historical continuity, much like old soldiers in the dress
uniform of some forgotten war. Or clergy are perceived as
the custodians of a particular in-group lore, and as such are
usually granted an expansive deference in a culture which
has been taught to be meticulously tolerant of the beliefs of
others, however quaint. But this dual role of personification
of the past and preserver of a subcultural ethos, a role clergy-

men play quite avidly, takes its toll when they speak of God. Because of the role they have been willing to play, when they use the word *God* it is heard in a certain way. It is heard, often with deference and usually with courtesy, as a word referring to the linchpin of the era of Christendom (past) or as the totem of one of the tribal subcultures (irrelevant). The only way clergy can ever change the way in which the word they use is perceived is to refuse to play the role of antiquarian and medicine man in which the society casts them, but this is difficult, because it is what they are paid for.

This close correlation between the meaning assigned a word by its hearer and the role of the person voicing the word can be illustrated by a parable Kierkegaard once used. A traveling circus once broke into flames just after it had encamped outside a Danish village. The manager turned to the performers who were already dressed for their acts and sent the clown to call the villagers to help put out the fire, which could not only destroy the circus but might race through the dry fields and envelop the town itself. Dashing pell-mell to the village square, the painted clown shouted to everyone to come to the circus and help put out the fire. The villagers laughed and applauded this novel way of tricking them into coming to the big top. The clown wept and pleaded. He insisted that he was not putting on an act but that the town really was in mortal danger. The more he implored the more the villagers howled . . . until the fire leaped across the fields and spread to the town itself. Before the villagers knew it, their homes had been destroyed.

The sociological problem of speaking about God is that the roles of the people who try to do so places them immediately in a perceptual context where what they say can be safely ignored. Of course there remain some people who can still understand what theologians mean when they use the word *God* and other religious terms. These include not only "religious" people but also people whose occupations or family histories have given them a visitor's pass, if not a membership card, to the meaning-world in which theologians and preachers live. Such people can often be found in church laymen's organizations. Academically trained people who specialize in the humanities also qualify. As a group, all these people retain part of the cultural residue of Christendom. However indispensible the service they render in the modern world, many of them nevertheless retain a "style" that is clearly held over from a previous historical epoch. They cherish customs, rituals, and mannerisms obviously derived from that period of Western history in which metaphysical discourse made some sense. But this subculture of humanistic academia holds a place of relatively reduced importance, in the university world itself as well as in the whole of society. Its importance for purposes of the present discussion is that it constitutes the *Sitz im Leben* of the academic theologian. It provides the context in which he perceives reality, and this goes a long way in explaining why academic theologians often fail to see the issues raised by the disappearance of the metaphysical era. Academic theologians pass their days among church people and scholarly humanists, insulated by career patterns, personal schedules, and professional obligations from the emerging technical and political era. The task of learning how to speak about God without a metaphysical system seems relatively unimportant.

But it is an important issue nonetheless. C. A. van Peursen writes:

> The word "God" can no longer function as a metaphysical entity. It can no longer be used to fill the gaps in our knowledge. . . . Christianity is in danger of becoming supernatural when it remains within the realm of . . . metaphysical and substantial thinking. . . . [It] becomes only a metaphysical escape. . . . The Biblical message is something quite different from . . . a doctrine of the highest Being.[6]

If van Peursen is right, then the answer to Bonhoeffer's question is to get out of the clown suit, to alter the social context in which "speaking of God" occurs and to refuse to play out the cultural roles which trivialize whatever the speaker says. If metaphysical talk of God has been made equivocal both by historical change and by social differentiation, then it cannot be discarded until the break with Christendom is accepted and the subcultural enclave is left behind.

Speaking of God as a Political Issue

Suppose, however, those who wish to speak of the biblical God did abandon their anachronous style and did come out of the religious ghetto, in what idiom could they speak about God to technopolitan man? If mythology was the appropriate argot of the tribe, and metaphysics provided the lexicon for the age of the town, what is the peculiar parlance of the epoch of the secular city?

Some theologians say that it must be "historical language." Thus van Peursen thinks that as we lay aside the metaphysical freight we have brought to the Bible we must be ready to allow the word *God* to take on its own meaning in historical terms. The late Carl Michalson seems to have agreed when he said that the Bible does not ask the questions of being (that is, it is not metaphysical), but it asks about historical meaning and acts. He believes that the meanings the Bible has are given within the historical process itself. They are given, he says, "within history *as* history and not at the horizon of history as being."[7]

Van Peursen and Michalson are certainly right. But by saying that theology must be historical rather than metaphysical, they open the door for the same misunderstanding we dealt with in our discussion of a theology of social change. The word *historical* for most people has to do with the past. Only in a small circle of specialists does it also include the historical present. So, for the same reason we urged that we search for a theology of social change, not just a theology of history, we also believe that the idiom which must replace metaphysics is not the historical but the political. It may be objected that the term *political* has too narrow a connotation. We believe, however, that its scope of meaning is widening in our time. Politics, as J. M. B. Miller points out in his *The Nature of Politics,*[8] arises from conflict and social differentiation. It describes the way those societies which have lost a totally unified world view understand themselves. In our time it has begun to mean what it did for Aristotle, all those activities which go into making the polis what it is.

There are some theologians, however, who would object to the political genre because they advocate other ways of dealing with the death of Christendom. We will mention only two: those who would like to go back "before metaphysics," represented here by Martin Heidegger and Heinrich Ott; and those who would advocate using existentialist instead of political categories, symbolized by Rudolf Bultmann.

Heidegger is a philosopher, not a social scientist. As such, he does not say much about the sociocultural collapse that underlies the passing away of metaphysics. He does grasp something of the role of modern technology in the termination of the metaphysical era, but only in a very negative way.

Yet Heidegger knows more surely than any philosopher now writing that the era of metaphysics is dead, and as a profoundly "religious" thinker, he watches its death throes with great personal pain. He knows that it marks the end of his kind of thinking too.

But still Heidegger often sees the issues with astounding clarity. In discussing the God of philosophical theology and metaphysics, which he lumps together in the jawbreaking Teutonism *ontotheologics,* he once said:

> To this God man can neither pray nor sacrifice . . . he can neither fall on his knees in awe nor sing and dance. Accordingly, godless thinking that must give up the god of philosophy . . . is perhaps nearer to the divine God.[9]

Heinrich Ott, one of Heidegger's contemporary theological admirers, believes that his master has now given the green light for the development of an explicitly nonmetaphysical language about God.[10]

But at this point our agreement with Heidegger and his followers stops abruptly and we go in opposite directions. Both Heidegger and Ott, rather than pushing onward "beyond metaphysics," advocate what Ott has called a *Schritt zuruck* (step backward). Instead of moving toward an authentically *post*metaphysical theology, what they want is a *pre*metaphysical theology. They prefer to go back behind metaphysics to what they feel is a more primal genre of thought.

But such a course of action can only produce the final catastrophe for theology. Heidegger and Ott are entirely correct in seeing that the end of the road has come for classical metaphysics. But they are entirely wrong in believing that the escape route lies in returning to a kind of primordial mythical thinking more characteristic of tribal culture. What is needed, rather than a step backward, is a step ahead, a step into thinking theologically about the issues that confront a technical-urban society. The stance that Heideggerian thinking advocates might restore, for some people, a sense of reverence before nature and awe at the elemental pulsations of life. It could serve as a kind of *ersatz* religion. But this would be a reversion to a mental set preceding the disenchantment of nature and the desacralization of politics. Retrogressing into such attitudes would deny the God of the Creation and the Exodus. It would deny that God has made man responsible for nature and that politics is the sphere of human mastery and responsibility. If theology is to survive and to make any sense to the contemporary world, it must neither cling to a metaphysical world view nor collapse into a mythical mode. It must push into the living lexicon of the urban-secular man. Another alternative to speaking in a political fashion of God is the existentialist, but it is also a mistake. Despite its popularity with some intellectuals, existentialist theology is not an avenue into the world of urban-secular man. It is the religious branch of the larger existentialist movement. This movement, as Ernst Topitsch has shown in his essay on the sociology of existentialism, sprang from a particular social crisis in what he calls the European *Bildungsschicht,*[11] the educated middle classes who once discarded the aristocratic tradition of throne and altar and substituted their own prestigious combination of property and education. They ran Europe in the eighteenth and nineteenth centuries. Their monument can be found in the opera houses, museums, and educational institutions which still delight tourists.

But beginning in the early nineteenth century another type of person began to shoulder himself toward the center of the stage in European culture. He was the technician and scientist, the social planner and political revolutionary. It quickly became evident that in the world he was creating there was little room for the "cultivated personality" in the traditional sense. The response of the *Bildungsschicht* is not surprising. They decided that the whole world was going to the dogs. Humiliated by their own loss of prestige and by the disappearance of the secure little world in which they had exercised quiet but effective power, they concluded that a monumental decline of the whole culture had set in. They were convinced that *all* life had become meaningless, so they retreated into esthetic, spiritual, or religious detachment. It was in this heavy atmosphere of cultural *Weltschmerz* that existentialism was born.

Existentialism appeared just as the Western metaphysical tradition, whose social base was dismantled by revolution and technology, reached its end phase. It is the last child of a cultural epoch, born in its mother's senility. This is why existentalist writers seem so arcadian and antiurban. They represent an epoch marked for extinction. Consequently their thinking tends to be antitechnological, individualistic, romantic, and deeply suspicious of cities and of science.

Because the world has already moved beyond the pathos and narcissism of existentialism, such theological efforts to update the biblical message as that of Rudolf Bultmann fall far short of the mark. They fail not because they are too radical but because they are not nearly radical enough. They deliver a nineteenth-century answer to a twentieth-century dilemma. Bultmann seems incapable of believing that God could be present in the urban-secular world of today rather than in the moldering sitting rooms of the turn-of-the-century bourgeois *Bildungsschicht*. He fails to reach the man of today because he translates the Bible from mythical language into yesterday's metaphysics rather than into today's postmetaphysical lexicon.

Naturally Bultmann would deny that existentialist categories are metaphysical, but they are. The ruling figures who stand at the fountainhead of existentialist thought still breathe the air of the presecular *Bildungsschicht*. They pen weighty tomes on traditional metaphysical questions. Except for Sartre, who has written some good plays, they employ a style which speaks mainly to their scholarly peers. Their thought, though it often puts on a fiercely antimetaphysical face, turns out to be a kind of fun-house mirror of metaphysics. Everything is grotesquely reversed, but is is all recognizable nonetheless. Thus nothingness replaces being, essence and existence change seats, and man takes the place of God. The result is a kind of antitheism and antimetaphysic which fails utterly to make contact with the thought world of contemporary man. There is something immature about existentialism. Like classical theism, it longs for some ultimate explanation of reality. In this sense it is closer to traditional theism than to the starting point of urban-secular man, who does not feel this compulsion to find inclusive and overarching meaning.

Because they have been gullible enough to believe that the existentialist philosophers really spoke for modern man, theologians have found themselves in the awkward position of having first to lure people into existential vertigo as a kind of preparation for preaching. This has always been difficult, but especially so in pragmatic America, where the existentialist anxiety never really took root. It is now increasingly hard to do in Europe, where the younger generation no longer takes out its feelings of deprivation by projecting them into world views.

The theological task of transposing the biblical assertions into contemporary idiom is short-circuited both by the advocates of a "step backward" and by the existentialist theologians. Both rightly diagnose the problem in seeing that metaphysical language doesn't reach secular man. But one group reverts to mythology, the other to metaphysical antimetaphysics. One returns to the tribal campfire, the other tries to leave town culture but doesn't make the break. Both fail miserably in what van Peursen calls "reading the Bible without metaphysical presuppositions."

It is unlikely, however, that the step van Peursen calls for will originate in academic theological circles. The reason is that academic theologians, as we have said before, constitute a kind of subculture in which the residues of Christendom persist and hence metaphysical and even mythical language about God retains some meaning. So long as this condition persists, these theologians will probably not see the need to take the "step forward." They will only begin to think differently when the social context in which they theologize is altered, when they find themselves having to converse in the larger world where only a vague echo of Christendom lingers.

But our question remains. If neither "premetaphysical" nor existentialist language will reach urban-secular man, why do we believe a political theology will?

The reason is that in secular society politics does what metaphysics once did. It brings unity and meaning to human life and thought. In today's world, we unify the various scholarly and scientific specialities by focusing them on specific human issues. Intellectual teamwork does not replace the lonely grind of the disciplined mental laborer, but truth is not unified today in metaphysical systems. Rather it is functionally unified by bringing disparate specialties to bear on concrete political perplexities.[12]

Gibson Winter has described the style of theological thinking we need if we are to take a step forward instead of a step backward. He calls it "theological reflection."[13] It is coming to consciousness about the meaning of contemporary events in the light of history. It is a way of taking responsibility both for the reshaping of the past and the constitution of the future. Reflection is that act by which the church scrutinizes the issues the society confronts in light of those decisive events of the past—Exodus and Easter—in which the intent of God has been apprehended by man in faith. Thus the church looks to the hints God has dropped in the past in order to make out what He is doing today.

But clearly the focal point of such reflection, the issues

upon which it must center, are none other than the life-and-death issues of the secular metropolis. It must be reflection on how to come to political terms with the emergent technical reality which engulfs us. These are *political issues,* and the mode of theology which must replace metaphysical theology is the *political* mode. Thus one answer to Bonhoeffer's question is that the way we talk about God in a secular fashion is to talk about him politically.

But are we using the word *politics* too loosely? The word itself, as Paul Lehmann reminds us, was given its classic meaning by Aristotle. For Aristotle, politics was "the science of the polis," the activity which used all the other sciences to secure not only the good for man but the good for the whole city-state, since that is naturally higher than the good of any one man.[14] Lehmann suggests that what God is doing in the world is politics, which means making and keeping life human. Politics also describes man's role in response to God. It is "activity, and reflection on activity, which aims at and analyzes what it takes to make and keep human life human in the world."[15] Theology today must be that reflection-in-action by which the church finds out what this politician-God is up to and moves in to work along with him. In the epoch of the secular city, politics replaces metaphysics as the language of theology.

We speak of God politically whenever we give occasion to our neighbor to become the responsible, adult agent, the fully posttown and posttribal man God expects him to be today. We speak to him of God whenever we cause him to realize consciously the web of interhuman reciprocity in which he is brought into being and sustained in it as a man. We speak to him of God whenever our words cause him to shed some of the blindness and prejudice of immaturity and to accept a larger and freer role in fashioning the instrumentalities of human justice and cultural vision. We do not speak to him of God by trying to make him religious but, on the contrary, by encouraging him to come fully of age, putting away childish things.

The Swiss theologian Gerhard Ebeling, though he does not use the term *political,* means something similar when he talks about the "nonreligious." He insists that secular speaking about God must always be concrete, clear, and active or productive (*wirkendes*). It must not consist of generalities but must meet people at a point where *they* feel addressed. God comes to speech truly only as an event in which man and the world are seen for what they really are. In short, ". . . worldly talk of God is godly talk of the world."[16]

The New Testament writers constantly exhorted their readers not to be anxious about what to *say*. They were repeatedly assured that if they were obedient, if they did what they were supposed to be doing, the right words would be supplied them when the moment came. Speaking about God in a secular fashion requires first of all that we place ourselves at those points where the restoring, reconciling activity of God is occurring, where the proper relationship between man and man is appearing. This means that evangelism, the speaking about God, is political, and Phillippe Maury is right when he says that "politics is the language of evangelism."[17] We cannot know *in advance* what to say in this or that situation, what acts and words will reveal God's Word to men. Obedience and love precede the gift of tongues. The man who is doing what God intends him to do at the place He intends him to be will be supplied with the proper words. Christian evangelism, like Christian ethics, must be unreservedly contextual.

To say that speaking of God must be political means that it must engage people at particular points, not just "in general." It must be a word about their own lives—their children, their job, their hopes or disappointments. It must be a word to the bewildering crises within which our personal troubles arise —a word which builds peace in a nuclear world, which contributes to justice in an age stalked by hunger, which hastens the day of freedom in a society stifled by segregation. If the word is not a word which arises from a concrete involvement of the speaker in these realities, then it is not a Word of God at all but empty twaddle.

We speak of God to secular man by speaking about man, by talking about man as he is seen in the biblical perspective. Secular talk of God occurs only when we are away from the ghetto and out of costume, when we are participants in that political action by which He restores men to each other in mutual concern and responsibility. We speak of God in a secular fashion when we recognize man as His partner, as the one charged with the task of bestowing meaning and order in human history.

Speaking of God in a secular fashion is thus a political issue. It entails our discerning where God is working and then joining His work. Standing in a picket line is a way of speaking. By doing it a Christian speaks of God. He helps alter the word *God* by changing the society in which it has been trivialized, by moving away from the context where "God-talk" usually occurs, and by shedding the stereotyped roles in which God's name is usually intoned.

Speaking of God as a Theological Question

When all the preliminary work has been done and the ground has been cleared, the question Bonhoeffer poses is still a *theological* one. In the present theological climate it is especially important to remember this, since where theologians are not busily trying to dress God in tribal costume or enlist him in their existentialist histrionics, they may be just as avidly whittling down the fact that God does make a difference in the way men live. Their opportunity to do this arises from a new situation in theology. There have always been important similarities between biblical faith and atheism, as contrasted, for example, to belief in demons and spirits. But in our time this similarity has produced a rather novel heresy. It is a kind of atheism expressed in Christian theological terminology. This curious phenomenon is made possible by the fact that the biblical doctrine of the hiddenness of God comports so very well, at one level at least, with contemporary atheism or, better, "nontheism." The two can easily be confused unless real care is used. Thus the hidden God or *deus absconditus* of biblical theology may be mistaken for the no-god-at-all of nontheism. Though He is very different from Godot in Samuel Beckett's play, like Godot He has the similar habit of not appearing at the times and places men appoint. Because the two have often been jumbled, it is important that we distinguish them here.

Carl Michalson describes the biblical doctrine of the hiddenness of God in these terms:

> . . . it is God's way of life to be hidden. He is *ex officio* hidden. Hiddenness is intrinsic to his nature as God. . . . The doctrine of the hiddenness of God . . . is not a counsel of despair or a concession to human finitude, but a positive description of God himself which performs a merciful service. *It prevents man both from looking for God in the wrong place* and from esteeming God's role in reality with *less than ultimate seriousness.*[18]

This biblical God's hiddenness stands at the very center of the doctrine of God. It is so commanding that Pascal was echoing its intention when he said, "Every religion which does not affirm that God is hidden is not true."[19] It means that God discloses himself at those places and in those ways he chooses and not as man would want. And he always discloses himself as one who is at once different *from* man, unconditionally *for* man, and entirely unavailable for coercion and manipulation *by* man. It is his utter hiddenness which distinguishes God from the tribal deities man coaxes and expiates, and from the metaphysical deity man grandly includes in a rounded system of thought. Using God for the kingpin in an ontological system is not much different from wheedling Him into watering my corn. The hidden God of the Bible will not be utilized in either way.

But what part does Jesus of Nazareth play in this hiddenness of God? If Jesus were a theophany, an "appearance of God" in the customary religious sense, then in Jesus the hiddenness of God would be abrogated. But this is not the case. God does not "appear" in Jesus; He hides himself in the stable of human history. He hides himself in the sense that we have just mentioned, showing that He is not anything like what religions have wanted or expected from their gods. In Jesus God does not stop being hidden; rather He meets man as the unavailable "other." He does not "appear" but shows man that He acts, in His hiddenness, in human history.

No wonder the religious compulsion of man, whether in its mythological or in its metaphysical form, has never been too happy with Jesus. In Jesus, God refuses to fulfill either tribal expectations or philosophical quandaries. As Bonhoeffer says, in Jesus God is teaching man to get along without Him, to become mature, freed from infantile dependencies, fully human. Hence the act of God in Jesus offers slim pickings for those in hope of clues for the erection of some final system. God will not be used in this way. He will not perpetuate human adolescence, but insists on turning the world over to man as his responsibility.

The summons to accountability before God also precludes, however, the verbal byplay in which theologians sometimes try to convince contemporary nontheists that the differences among men today over the reality of God are merely verbal. They are not. Although to the neutral observer there may appear to be no difference between the God who absents himself, who refuses to bark at man's whistle, and the no-god-at-all; there is all the difference in the world. Given the fact that man in dialogue fashions the meanings by which history proceeds, that he is free to take responsibility for history, one

utterly crucial question remains: Is this responsibility something which man himself has conjured, or is it *given* to him?
The biblical answer, of course, is that it is given to him.
For the Bible, after mythological and metaphysical overlay
has been scraped away, God is not simply a different way of
talking about man. God is not man, and man can only be
really *"response-able"* when he *responds*. One must be responsible *for* something *before* someone. Man, in order to be
free and responsible, which means to be *man*, must answer to
that which is not man. Professor Ronald Gregor Smith sums
it up when he says that theology, in order to be theology, has
to do with what men "are not themselves"; it concerns

> what they do not and never can possess at all as part of
> their self-equipment or as material for their self-mastery,
> but with what comes to them at all times from beyond
> themselves.[20]

Such contemporary theologians as Fuchs, Ebeling, and
Braun, who are rightly concerned that God not be confused
with an object among other objects, have performed an invaluable service to theology. They are justified in emphasizing
that there can be no relationship to God which does not
include a relationship to man. But it is also true that if God is
not an object of man's knowledge or curiosity, He is also not
to be identified with some particular quality in man or in
human reciprocity, and He is not just a confused mode of
speaking about relationships between men.

There is, of course, no high court before which those who
affirm God's reality and hiddenness can press their case
against those who suspect, as Kafka did, that there is No One
There at all. But the difference is real. It is both pointless and
patronizing to try to suggest to nontheists that they are really
Christians who don't know any better, that the problem is just
semantic or conceptual. Nontheists deserve to be taken seriously, not treated as children. In fact, only when we do take
them seriously, as they understand themselves, can any real
dialogue begin, and they do have much to offer us. Because
the experience of the *deus absconditus* and that of the no-god-
at-all are so similar, because we share the common discom-
posure of those who live in a dissonant and exhilarating time,
we need the nontheists. But we need them as they are, not as
we would like them to be.

The difference between men of biblical faith and serious
nontheists is not that we do not encounter the same reality.

The difference is that we give that reality a different *name,* and in naming it differently, we differ seriously in the way we respond. Paul M. van Buren contends in his thoughtful book on the secular meaning of the Gospel[21] that our principal difficulty today in using the language of traditional religion is not bad religion but bad language. He then goes on to a discussion of the logical structure of the language of faith, in the course of which he says that modern man has difficulties with any word which refers to what he calls the "transcendent." I think at this point van Buren is wrong. The problem is not bad language. Language merely reflects reality. It is pliable and flexible. It can change. The problem *is* bad religion, as van Buren should have seen if he really wanted to suggest a "secular meaning" of the Gospel, as the title of his book implies.

But I also believe that van Buren is wrong when he states that modern, secular man does not experience the transcendent. The transcendent means that which, as Gregor Smith says, ". . . man cannot possess at all," that which is not part of the self's equipment but comes from beyond the self. No doubt urban-secular man experiences the transcendent in a radically different *way* than did his tribal and town forebears. He may find it, as Bonhoeffer once said, "in the nearest Thou at hand," but he does meet it. It is his experience of the transcendent that makes man man. Writing on "Art and Theological Meaning" in a volume of essays on Christian esthetics, Amos Wilder says:

> If we are to have any transcendence today, even Christian, it must be in and through the secular. . . . If we are to find Grace it is to be found in the world and not overhead. The sublime firmament of overhead reality that provided a spiritual home for the souls of men until the eighteenth century has collapsed.[22]

Wilder believes correctly that in this "one-story world" the transcendent is still present. Because the "overhead" world is gone, artists and poets will be more important to us than ever in dealing "at first hand with life, beyond the fences of social or religious propriety."[23]

But where else does the transcendent God meet us in the secular city? Whatever the name we give Him, however we finally respond to Him, where does He find us? Is it only through the artists?

We have already suggested that God comes to us today in

events of social change, in what theologians have often called *history,* what we call *politics.* But events of social change need not mean upheavals and revolutions. The events of everyday life are also events of social change. The smallest unit of society is two, and the relationship between two people never remains just the same. God meets us there, too. He meets us not just in the freedom revolution in America but also in a client, a customer, a patient, a co-worker.

But how? God is free and hidden. He cannot be expected to appear when we designate the place and time. This means that God is neither close nor far *as such,* but is able to be present in a situation without identifying with it, and He is always present to liberate man. This does not mean that He is there to be walked over. God frees us by supplying that framework of limitation within which alone freedom has any meaning. The freedom of man depends on the prior freedom of God, and man would be a prisoner of his own past if it were not for God who comes in that future-becoming-present where human freedom functions.

Thus we meet God at those places in life where we come up against that which is not pliable and disposable, at those hard edges where we are both stopped and challenged to move ahead. God meets us as the transcendent, at those aspects of our experience which can never be transmuted into extensions of ourselves. He meets us in the wholly other.

We have said that naming is remembering and hoping. It is a social act and is influenced by changes in social structure. In naming God, in attributing to Him a designation which relates Him to human experience, all cultures utilize symbols drawn from some aspect of social life. There are no other sources of symbols. They use political life and call God the "King"; or they utilize family relationships and call Him "Father"; or they use occupational designations and call Him the "shepherd." Thus changing family and political structures inevitably result in different symbolizations of God. To insist on calling God the "shepherd" in an industrial society may seem pious but it really marks the height of unbelief. It suggests that God will somehow slip out of existence if men alter the names they use for Him.

In the tribal society God was experienced as the One who exerted His rule over the evil spirits and lesser gods. Since tribal society is based on kinship ties, man's relationship to God was frequently symbolized with family titles. Because authority was predominantly horizontal, and tribal man's individuality was of a low order, some kind of mystical, often exotic, union with the deity was this era's characteristic relationship. It remains so even in higher religions growing out of kinship cultures such as that of India. Israelite religion had no place for this *absorptionist* type of mysticism. Family images were used, but only with considerable restraint in the Old Testament. In town culture, where a break was made with primordial kinship ties, the symbolization of the deity tended to be political. God became the chief, the ruler, the king. The most frequent relationship to God was that of the subject and the sovereign, the servant and the master.

In technopolitan culture, both horizontal kinship and vertical authority patterns are disappearing. What replaces them is a work team. A team of physicists at work on a research project or a team of land surveyors may appear to the casual observer to have the same relationship to each other as a group of tribal people mending nets. But the similarity is illusory. In the tribal setting, work groups are patterned by familial connections and locked in kinship prescriptions. The modern work team, as seen earlier, is first of all task-oriented. No doubt people receive an enormous amount of personal satisfaction from the relationships they have in the team. But this arises as a by-product; it is not the purpose of the team. Team relationships at work tend to be of a different character from family relationships. Most importantly, though people may involve themselves in the team deeply while they are at work, they have other roles and relationships which are not drawn in.

The tribal relationship is of a *pre*-I–Thou type. The deficient individuation of tribal man prevents his experiencing God as fully "other." Not only does he find God in a horizontal way, but he is always a part of God and vice versa. Man *participates* in God. In a society marked by *vertical* authority, the period of town culture and individualism, man tends to experience God in the classic I–Thou encounter. God is seen as another who has authority *over* me. The relationship is one of *confrontation*. We have suggested earlier that a new type of interhuman relationship seems to be emerging in urban society, one that is just as human as I–Thou but is qualitatively different. It occurs often in the kind of work team described above, a relationship one has in addition to I–Thou experiences in the family and with intimate friends. But it is more significant and very different from the I–It relationship. Rather than participation or confrontation, it is a relationship of *alongsideness*.

In an earlier chapter we suggested designating this peculiarly urban phenomenon the I–You relationship. It describes very well the rewarding relationship one has with a fellow team member, with whom one has worked on a research project or painted a house. It derives from work that is done together by two persons for whom the work is the key to their mutuality. This is a newly evolving mode of human relationships. It is authentically human and more or less unprecedented in previous cultures, but the important thing about this emergent I–You relationship for our purposes is that it is bound to influence our symbolization of God in one way or another. It may be that in addition to the I–Thou relationship with God, and the mystical experience which is already exceedingly rare, contemporary man could meet God as a "you."

Is this so farfetched? Recent discussions of the concept of the covenant in the Old Testament suggest it means that Yahweh was willing to stoop so low as to work in tandem with man, to work on a team, no matter how poorly the human partner was working out. Whether or not this is true, it can certainly be said that in Jesus of Nazareth God did show that He was willing to take man's side of the unfulfilled covenant, to become the junior partner in the asymmetric relationship. It is not demeaning to suggest that the notions of teamwork and partnership need to be explored much more in our conceptualization of God. He who is "high and lifted up" suggests in the life of Jesus that he is willing to put himself in the position of working within a group, of washing his fellows' feet and of needing someone to carry his cross. What seems at first sight irreverence may be closer to the heart of the self-humbling truth of God than we imagine.

The idea of an I–You partnership between God and man is strongly hinted by the language of Galatians 4 which we discussed earlier. In this passage man is viewed as a son and heir. The emphasis is on *son* as opposed to child, and on *heir* as having assumed responsibility. This implies that the strictly vertical relationship which informs a father's relationship to his minor boy is discarded for the adult partnership which obtains between a grown man and his father.

Perhaps in the secular city God calls man to meet Him first of all as a "you." This has far-reaching implications. It sug-

gests that man is not to become fascinated with God himself.
Like his relationship to his work partner, man's relationship to
God derives from the work they do together. Rather than
shutting out the world to delve into each other's depths the
way adolescent lovers do, God and man find joy together in
doing a common task. Of course this type of relationship will
not satisfy the man who is driven by a compulsive interest in
"finding" or "experiencing" God. Such people are always dis-
satisfied by the admittedly sparse revelation of Himself which
God has made. It is not the kind of revelation which encourages delving. God wants man to be interested not in Him but
in his fellow man.

There is a kind of religiousness abroad today which engages
in endless quests for a succession of holy grails. This spirit,
celebrated in Somerset Maugham's *The Razor's Edge*, has a
powerful attraction for many people today, especially those
who describe themselves as "interested in religion." But it runs
directly counter to the grain of the Bible.

Of course there is some religious questing in the Bible. The
Psalmist could say that his heart panted after God like the
hart after the water, but God's answer was never uncertain:
Yahweh was more interested in justice rolling down like
mighty waters than in religious aspiration. Paul had little patience with the religious questers after the unknown God he
ran across in Athens. "This unknown God," he said, "I de-
clare unto you." In Jesus of Nazareth, the religious quest is
ended and man is freed to serve and love his neighbor.

But how do we name the God who is not interested in our
fasting and cultic adoration but asks for acts of mercy? It is
too early to say for sure, but it may well be that our English
word *God* will have to die, corroborating in some measure
Nietzsche's apocalyptic judgment that "God is dead." By what
name shall we call the one we met both in the life of Jesus
and in our present history as the liberator and the hidden
one?

Perhaps we should not be anxious about finding a name.
Our present fit of tongue-tied verbosity, of empty and ambiguous words, will work itself out in experience, the way it
always has. "The story of the word 'God,' " says C. A. van
Peursen, "is that it has no given meaning, but acquires a
meaning in history. . . ."[24] Naming was the process by which
Israel drew more and more reality into history by relating it to
the One who had brought them up out of Egypt. First the

origin of history, then its comsummation were included in this process of "radiation" by which God was named as He was encountered in the world. God manifests Himself to us in and through secular events. The meaning of the word *God* will be altered or a new name will emerge as we encounter that presence in events which draws them into the history of which we are a part, the history of God's liberation of man. Secular talk of God is pointing and naming. As van Peursen says,

> . . . it is in a functional way that man comes into contact with the reality of God, that God acquires a meaning in history. . . . As the Church we have to respond to the world through our acts . . . transmitting the old message of a Name . . . which is taking on a new meaning in history, and especially in the functional history of our time.[25]

We cannot simply conjure up a new name. Nor can we arbitrarily discard the old one. God does reveal His name in history, through the clash of historical forces and the faithful efforts of a people to discern His presence and respond to His call. A new name will come when God is ready. A new way of conceptualizing the Other will emerge in the tension between the history which has gone before us and the events which lie ahead. It will emerge as the issues of the urban civilization are drawn into rehearsal of the past, reflection on the present, and responsibility for the future, which *is* history.

This may mean that we shall have to stop talking about "God" for a while, take a moratorium on speech until the new name emerges. Maybe the name that does emerge will not be the three-letter word *God,* but this should not dismay us. Since naming is a human activity embedded in a particular sociocultural milieu, there is no holy language as such, and the word *God* is not sacred. All languages are historical. They are born and die. Presumably God will continue to live eons after English and all other present languages have been totally forgotten. It is only word magic to believe that there is some integral connection between God and any particular linguistic vocable.

If the naming we must do in the secular city requires our dispensing with the word *God* in order not to confuse the One who reveals Himself in Jesus with the gods of mythology or the deity of philosophy, it will not be the first time this has happened in the history of biblical faith. It is common knowledge that the people of Israel went through several stages in naming Him, and they may not be through yet. At various times they used the terms *El Elyon, Elohim, El Shaddai,* and—of course—*Yahweh.* They freely borrowed these designations from neighboring peoples and discarded them with what now seems to us an amazing freedom, especially in view of the enormous power inherent in names in Hebrew culture. A remarkable evidence of this daring willingness to move to new names when the historical situation warranted it is found in Exodus 6:2–3, a part of the so-called P document:

> And God [Elohim] said to Moses, "I am the Lord [Yahweh]. I appeared to Abraham, Isaac and Jacob as God Almighty [El Shaddai], but by my name the Lord [Yahweh] I did not make myself known to them."

One could write an entire history of Israel, charting its cultural and political relationships to its neighbors, by following the conflict and development in naming, both the naming of God and the naming of children. God reveals his name to man through the abrasive experiences of social change.

After the period of the Exile, the Jews again switched their nomenclature. Disturbed by the debasement of the name *Yahweh,* which was considered too holy for everyday use, they began using the word *Adonai* which is still used in synagogues.

Perhaps for a while we shall have to do without a name for God. This may seem threatening, but there are biblical precedents for it. Moses apparently felt equally uncomfortable when he was told to go down to Egypt and lead the children of Israel to freedom. He anxiously asked for the name of the One who spoke to him from the burning bush. But the answer given to him was not very comforting. His request was simply refused. He was not given a name at all, but was told rather cryptically that if the captives were curious about who had sent him, he should simply tell them that "I will do what I will do" had sent him (Exodus 3:13–14). At one time this verse was interpreted ontologically. God was revealing Himself as "being itself." But today most Hebrew scholars agree that no metaphysical description is implied. The voice from the bush gives an answer that is intended to be terse and evasive. As Bernhard Anderson says,

> Moses had asked for information about the mystery of the divine nature [the name], but this information had been withheld. Instead God made known his demand . . . and assured him that he would know who God is by what he

brings to pass. In other words, the question "Who is God?" would be answered by events that would take place in the future.[26]

The Exodus marked for the Jews a turning point of such elemental power that a new divine name was needed to replace the titles that had grown out of their previous experience. Our transition today from the age of Christendom to the new era of urban secularity will be no less shaking. Rather than clinging stubbornly to antiquated appellations or anxiously synthesizing new ones, perhaps, like Moses, we must simply take up the work of liberating the captives, confident that we will be granted a new name by events of the future.

NOTES TO CHAPTER II

1. Dietrich Bonhoeffer, *Prisoner for God* (New York: Macmillan, 1959), p. 123.
2. Dietrich Bonhoeffer, *Gesammelte Schriften*, IV, p. 606. Author's translation.
3. For a brilliant discussion of naming by an extremely influential but little-known thinker, see Eugene Rosenstock-Heussey, *Die Sprache des Menschengeschlechts* (Heidelberg: Verlag Lambert Schneider, 1963).
4. In Talcott Parsons, *et al.* (eds.), *Theories of Personality,* (New York: The Free Press, 1961), p. 1018.
5. Helmut Gollwitzer, *Die Existenz Gottes im Bekenntnis des Glaubens* (Munich: C. Kaiser Verlag, 1963), p. 11, n. 2. English translation, London: SCM Press, 1965.
6. C. A. van Peursen, "Man and Reality, the History of Human Thought," *Student World*, No. 1 (1963), pp. 19, 20.
7. Carl Michalson, "Theology as Ontology and as History," in James Robinson and John Cobb, Jr. (eds.), *The Late Heidegger and Theology* (New York: Harper & Row, 1963), p. 147.
8. J. M. B. Miller, *The Nature of Politics* (New York: Encyclopaedia Britannica Publications, 1964).
9. Quoted by James Robinson, *op. cit.*, p. 37.
10. *Ibid.*
11. Ernst Topitsch, "Zur Soziologie des Existenzialismus. Kosmos-Existenz-Gesellschaft," *Sozialphilosophie zwischen Ideologie und Wissenschaft* (Neuwied: Hermann Luchterhand Verlag, 1961), p. 87.
12. A particularly striking example of a creative team approach to a vital subject is Roger Fisher (ed.), *International Conflict and Behavorial Science: The Craigville Papers* (New York: Basic Books, 1964).

13. Gibson Winter, *The New Creation as Metropolis* (New York: Macmillan, 1963), p. 71.

14. Quoted by Paul Lehmann in *Ethics in a Christian Context* (New York: Harper & Row, 1963; London: SCM Press), p. 167.

15. *Ibid.*, p. 85.

16. Gerhard Ebeling, *Word and Faith* (Philadelphia: Fortress Press, 1963; London: SCM Press), p. 360.

17. Phillippe Maury, *Evangelism and Politics* (Garden City, N.Y.: Doubleday, 1959; London: Lutterworth), p. 28.

18. Carl Michalson, "The Real Presence of the Hidden God," in Paul Ramsey, (ed.), *Faith and Ethics*, (New York: Harper & Row, 1957), p. 259. Emphasis added.

19. Quoted by Michalson, *ibid.*, p. 245.

20. Ronald Gregor Smith, "A Theological Perspective on the Secular," *The Christian Scholar*, XLIII (March 1960), 15.

21. Paul M. van Buren, *The Secular Meaning of the Gospel* (New York: Macmillan, 1963; London: SCM Press), p. 68.

22. Amos N. Wilder, "Art and Theological Meaning," in N. A. Scott (ed.), *The New Orpheus: Essays toward a Christian Poetic* (New York: Sheed and Ward, 1964), p. 407.

23. *Ibid.*, p. 408.

24. C. A. van Peursen, *op, cit.*, p. 21.

25. *Ibid.*

26. Bernhard W. Anderson, *Understanding the Old Testament* (Englewood Cliffs, N.J.: Prentice-Hall, 1956), p. 34.

Bibliography

BOOKS

Abel, Lionel. *Metatheatre*. New York: Hill & Wang, 1963. 146 pp.

Albrecht, Paul. *The Churches and Rapid Social Change*. Garden City, N.Y.: Doubleday & Company, Inc., 1961.

Altizer, Thomas J. J. *Mircea Eliade and the Dialectic of the Sacred*. Philadelphia: The Westminster Press, 1963. 219 pp.

Anderson, Bernhard W. *Understanding the Old Testament*. Englewood Cliffs, N.J.: Prentice-Hall, Inc., 1956. 551 pp.

———. *The Beginning of History*. London: Lutterworth Press. New York and Nashville: Abingdon Press, 1963. 96 pp.

Anderson, Nels. *The Urban Community: A World Perspective*. New York: Holt, Rinehart and Winston, Inc., 1959. 500 pp.

Auer, Alfons. "Gestaltwandel des Christlichen Weltverständnisses," *Gott in Welt, Festgabe für Karl Rahner*, Vol. 1, pp. 333–365.

Baillie, D. M. *God Was in Christ*. New York: Charles Scribner's Sons, 1955. London: Faber & Faber.

Balthaser, Hans Urs von. *A Theology of History*. New York and London: Sheed and Ward, 1963. 149 pp.

Banfield, Edward C., and Wilson, James Q. *City Politics*. Cambridge, Mass.: Harvard University Press, 1963.

Barth, Karl. *The Humanity of God*. Richmond, Va.: John Knox Press, 1960. 96 pp. London: Collins.

———. *Church Dogmatics*. Edinburgh: T & T Clark, 1956–1963.

Bendix, Reinhart. *Max Weber: An Intellectual Portrait*. Garden City, N.Y.: Doubleday & Company, Inc., 1960. 480 pp.

Berger, Peter L. *The Noise of Solemn Assemblies.* Garden City, N Y.: Doubleday & Company, Inc., 1961. 189 pp.
Bonhoeffer, Dietrich. *Ethics.* New York: The Macmillan Company, 1955. 340 pp. London: SCM Press.
————. *Letters and Papers from Prison.* New York: The Macmillan Company, 1962. 254 pp. London: SCM Press, 1953.
Brown, Norman O. *Life against Death.* New York: Random House, 1959. 366 pp.
Buber, Martin. *I and Thou.* New York: Charles Scribner's Sons, 1958. 137 pp. Edinburgh: T & T Clark.
Bultmann, Rudolf. *Theology of the New Testament.* Vol. I. New York: Charles Scribner's Sons, 1951. 366 pp. London: SCM Press.
————. *Theology of the New Testament, Volume II.* New York: Charles Scribner's Sons, 1955. 278 pp. London: SCM Press.
————. *The Presence of Eternity: History and Eschatology.* New York: Harper & Row, 1957. 171 pp. Edinburgh: Edinburgh University Press, 1957.
Burke, Kenneth. *The Rhetoric of Religion: Studies in Logology.* Boston: Beacon Press, 1961. 316 pp.
Campbell, Joseph. *The Masks of God: Primitive Mythology.* New York: The Viking Press, 1959. 504 pp.
Carpenter, Edmund, and McLuhan, Marshall, eds. *Explorations in Communication.* Boston: Beacon Press, 1960. 210 pp.
Collingwood, R. G. *The Idea of History.* Oxford: Clarendon Press, 1946. 339 pp.
Collins, James. *God in Modern Philosophy.* London: Routledge & Kegan Paul, 1960. 476 pp.
Dollard, John. *Caste and Class in a Southern Town.* Garden City, N.Y.: Doubleday & Company, Inc., 1957.
Ebeling, Gerhard von. *Theologie und Verkündigung.* Tübingen: J. C. B. Mohr-Paul Siebeck, 1962. 146 pp.
————. *Word and Faith.* Philadelphia: Fortress Press, 1963. 433 pp. London: SCM Press.
Eliade, Mircea. *Cosmos and History.* New York: Harper & Row, 1954. 176 pp.
Fetscher, Iring, ed. *Marxismusstudien.* Tübingen: J. C. B. Mohr-Paul Siebeck, 1962. 258 pp.
Fortune, Editors of. *The Exploding Metropolis.* Garden City, N.Y.: Doubleday & Company, Inc., 1958. 177 pp.

Freud, Sigmund. *Civilization and Its Discontents.* New York: Cape and Smith, 1930. London: Hogarth.
———. *Moses and Monotheism.* New York: Vintage Books, Inc., 1955. London: Hogarth.
Fustel de Coulanges, Numa Denis. *The Ancient City.* Garden City, N.Y.: Doubleday & Company, Inc., 1956. London: Mayflower Books.
Gans, Herbert J. *The Urban Villagers.* New York: The Free Press, 1962. 367 pp.
Gogarten, Friedrich. *Verhängnis und Hoffnung der Neuzeit.* Stuttgart: Friedrich Vorwerk Verlag, 1953. 229 pp.
———. *Der Mensch Zwischen Gott und Welt.* Stuttgart: Friedrich Vorwerk Verlag, 1956. 445 pp.
Gollwitzer, Helmut. *Forderungen der Freiheit.* Munich: Chr. Kaiser Verlag, 1962. 389 pp.
———. *Die Existenz Gottes im Bekenntnis des Glaubens.* Munich: Chr. Kaiser Verlag, 1963. 200 pp. English translation, London: SCM Press and Westminster Press.
Hall, Cameron. *On-the-Job Ethics.* New York: National Council of Churches, 1963. 148 pp.
Harrington, Michael. *The Other America.* Baltimore, Md.: Penguin Books, 1962. 203 pp.
Harrison, Paul. *Power and Authority in the Free Crurch Tradition.* Princeton, N.J.: Princeton University Press, 1959.
Harrison, Selig S. *India: The Most Dangerous Decades.* Princeton, N.J.: Princeton University Press, 1960. 350 pp.
Hatt, Paul K., and Reiss, Albert J., Jr., eds. *Cities and Society.* New York: The Free Press, 1957. 852 pp.
Jenkins, Daniel. *Beyond Religion.* Philadelphia: The Westminster Press, 1962. 126 pp. London: SCM Press.
Jones, W. Paul. *The Recovery of Life's Meaning.* New York: Association Press, 1963. 254 pp.
Kenrick, Bruce. *Come Out the Wilderness.* New York: Harper & Row, 1962. 220 pp. London: Collins.
Kierkegaard, Søren. *The Present Age.* New York: Harper & Row, 1962. 108 pp.
Kimball, Solon T., and McClellan, James E., Jr. *Education and the New America.* New York: Random House, 1962. 393 pp.
Kluckhohn, Clyde, and Murray, Henry A., eds. *Personality*

in Nature, Society and Culture. New York: Alfred A. Knopf, 1959. 701 pp.

Kwant, Remy C. *The Phenomenological Philosophy of Merleau-Ponty.* Pittsburgh, Pa.: Duquesne University Press, 1963. 257 pp.

Langton, Edward. *Essentials of Demonology.* London: The Epworth Press, 1949. 231 pp.

Lee, Robert, ed. *Cities and Churches.* Philadelphia: The Westminster Press, 1962. 366 pp.

Lehmann, Paul L. *Ethics in a Christian Context.* New York: Harper & Row, 1963. 384 pp. London: SCM Press.

Lewis, Arthur O., Jr. *Of Men and Machines.* New York: E. P. Dutton & Co., Inc., 1963. 349 pp.

Littell, Franklin. *From State Church to Pluralism.* Garden City, N.Y.: Doubleday & Company, Inc., 1962.

Löwith, Karl. *Meaning in History.* Chicago: University of Chicago Press, 1949.

Lynch, Kevin. *The Image of the City.* Cambridge, Mass.: Harvard University Press and The M.I.T. Press, 1960. 194 pp.

McKelvey, Blake. *The Urbanization of America.* New Brunswick, N.J.: Rutgers University Press, 1963. 370 pp.

Malinowski, Bronislaw. *Magic, Science and Religion and Other Essays.* Garden City, N.Y.: Doubleday & Company, Inc., 1954. 274 pp.

Marcel, Gabriel. *The Mystery of Being.* Chicago: Henry Regnery Company, 1960. 270 pp.

Margull, Hans J. *Hope in Action.* Philadelphia: Muhlenberg Press, 1962. 298 pp.

Marty, Martin E., ed. *The Place of Bonhoeffer.* New York: Association Press, 1962. 224 pp. London: SCM Press.

————. *Second Chance for American Protestants.* New York: Harper & Row, 1963. 175 pp.

Marx, Karl. *The Economic and Philosophic Manuscripts of 1844.* New York: International Publishers, 1964. 255 pp.

Mazlish, Bruce. *Psychoanalysis and History.* Englewood Cliffs, N.J.: Prentice-Hall, Inc., 1963. 183 pp.

Mehl, Roger. *The Condition of the Christian Philosopher.* London: James Clarke, 1963. 211 pp.

Merleau-Ponty, Maurice. *Eloge de la Philosophie.* Paris: Gallimard, 1948.

———. *Sens et non-sens.* Paris: Nagel, 1948.

———. *Phenomenology of Perception.* New York: The Humanities Press, 1962. 466 pp.

Michonneau, Abbé. *Revolution in a City Parish.* Westminster: Newman Press, 1963.

Mumford, Lewis. *The City in History.* New York: Harcourt, Brace & World, Inc., 1961. 657 pp. London: Secker and Warburg.

Munby, D. L. *The Idea of a Secular Society.* New York: Oxford University Press, 1963. 91 pp.

Niebuhr, H. Richard. *Radical Monotheism and Western Culture.* New York: Harper & Row, 1943. 144 pp. London: Faber & Faber.

———. *The Meaning of Revelation.* New York: The Macmillan Company, 1960. 196 pp.

———. *The Responsible Self.* New York: Harper & Row, 1963. 183 pp.

Oppen, Dietrich von. *Das Personale Zeitalter.* Stuttgart: Verlagsgemeinschaft Burchkhardthaus und Kreuz-Verlag GMBH, 1960. 239 pp.

Pannenberg, Wolfhart. *Offenbarung als Geschichte.* Göttingen: Vandenhoeck & Ruprecht, 1961. 130 pp.

———. *Was Ist der Mensch?* Göttingen: Vanderhoeck & Ruprecht, 1962. 111 pp.

Parsons, Talcott, Shils, Edward, Naegele, Kaspar D., and Pitts, Jesse R., eds. *Theories of Society.* New York: The Free Press, 1961. 1479 pp.

Pearl, Arthur, and Riessman, Frank. *New Careers for the Poor.* New York: The Free Press, 1965.

Perrin, Norman. *The Kingdom of God in the Teachings of Jesus Christ.* Philadelphia: The Westminster Press, 1963. London: SCM Press.

Rad, Gerhard von. *Genesis: A Commentary.* Philadelphia: The Westminster Press, 1961. 434 pp. London: SCM Press.

Radcliffe-Brown, A. F. *Structure and Function in Primitive Society.* New York: The Free Press, 1952. London: Cohen & West.

Radin, Paul, ed. *Primitive Religion.* New York: Dover Publications, Inc., 1957. 322 pp.

Ramsey, Paul. *Faith and Ethics.* New York: Harper & Row, 1957, 306 pp.

Ratschow, C. H. "Säkularismus," *Religion in Geschichte and Gegenwart,* 3rd ed., pp. 1288–1296.

242   *Bibliography*

Redfield, Robert. *The Primitive World and Its Transformations.* Ithaca, N.Y.: Great Seal Books, 1953. 185 pp.

Ristow, Helmut, and Burgert, Helmuth. *Evangelium und mündige Welt.* Berlin: Evangelische Verlagsanstalt, 1962. 192 pp.

Robinson, James M. *The Problem of History in Mark.* Naperville, Ill.: Alec R. Allenson, Inc., 1957. 95 pp. London: SCM Press.

————. *New Frontiers in Theology.* Vol. II. New York: Harper & Row, 1964. 243 pp.

————, and Cobb, John B., Jr., eds. *New Frontiers in Theology.* New York: Harper & Row, 1963. 212 pp.

Schmidt, Hans. *Verheissung und Schrecken der Freiheit.* Stuttgart: Kreuz-Verlag, 1964.

Schutz, Paul. *Charisma Hoffnung: Von der Zukunft der Welt.* Hamburg: Furche-Verlag, 1962. 122 pp.

Scott, Nathan A., Jr., ed. *The New Orpheus: Essays toward a Christian Poetic.* New York: Sheed and Ward, 1964. 431 pp.

Seznac, Jean. *The Survival of the Pagan Gods.* New York: Harper & Row, 1953. 376 pp.

Smith, Ronald Gregor. *The New Man.* New York: Harper & Row, 1956. 120 pp. London: SCM Press.

Storck, Hans. *Kirche im Neuland der Industrie.* Berlin: Kaethe Vogt Verlag, 1959. 189 pp.

Stover, Carl F. *The Technological Order.* Detroit: Wayne State University Press, 1963. 280 pp.

Symanowski, Horst. *The Christian Witness in an Industrial Society.* Philadelphia: The Westminster Press, 1964. 160 pp.

Tawney, R. H. *Religion and the Rise of Capitalism.* New York: Harcourt, Brace and World, Inc., 1926. 280 pp.

Theobold, Robert. *Free Men and Free Markets.* New York: C. N. Potter, 1963.

Thomas, M. M., and McCaughey, J. D. *The Christian in the World Struggle.* Geneva: World Student Christian Federation, 1952. 165 pp.

Tillich, Paul. *Systematic Theology.* Vol. I. Chicago: The University of Chicago Press, 1951. 300 pp. London: Nisbet & Co.

————. *The Courage to Be.* New Haven: Yale University Press, 1952. 197 pp. London: Fontana Books.

Topitsch, Ernst. *Sozialphilosophie zwischen Ideologie und*

Wissenschaft. Neuwied: Hermann Luchterhand Verlag, 1961. 302 pp.

Vahanian, Gabriel. *The Death of God.* New York: George Braziller, 1961. 253 pp.

———. *Wait Without Idols.* New York: George Braziller, 1964. 256 pp.

Van Buren, Paul M. *The Secular Meaning of the Gospel.* New York: The Macmillan Company, 1963. 205 pp. London: SCM Press.

de Vries, Egbert. *Man in Rapid Social Change.* Garden City, N.Y.: Doubleday & Company, Inc., 1961. London: SCM Press.

Voegelin, Eric. *Order and History.* Vol. I: "Israel and Revelation." Baton Rouge, La.: Louisiana State University Press, 1956. 533 pp.

Vidich, Arthur J., and Bensman, Joseph. *Small Town in Mass Society.* Garden City, N.Y.: Anchor Books, 1958.

Warner, Sam B., Jr. *Streetcar Suburbs.* Cambridge, Mass.: Harvard University Press and The M.I.T. Press, 1962. 208 pp.

Warner, W. Lloyd. *A Black Civilization.* New York: Harper & Row, 1958.

Webber, George. *The Congregation in Mission.* New York and Nashville: Abingdon Press, 1964. 208 pp.

Weber, Hans-Ruedi. *The Militant Ministry.* Philadelphia: Fortress Press, 1963. 108 pp.

Weber, Max. *The Sociology of Religion.* Boston: Beacon Press, 1922. 304 pp.

———. *Ancient Judaism.* New York: The Free Press, 1952. London: Allen & Unwin.

———. *The City.* New York: Collier Books, 1958. 256 pp. London: Heinemann.

———. *The Protestant Ethic and the Spirit of Capitalism.* New York: Charles Scribner's Sons, 1958. 292 pp. London: Allen & Unwin.

Wendland, Heinz-Dietrich. *Die Kirche in Der Modernen Gesellschaft.* Hamburg: Im Furche-Verlag, 1956. 285 pp.

White, Hugh C., Jr., ed. *Christians in a Technological Era.* New York: Seabury Press, 1964. 143 pp.

White, Morton and Lucia. *The Intellectual Versus the City.* Cambridge, Mass.: Harvard University Press and The M.I.T. Press, 1962. 270 pp.

Wild, John. *Human Freedom and Social Order.* Durham, N.C.: Duke University Press, 1959. 250 pp.

Wilder, Amos Niven. *Eschatology and Ethics in the Teaching of Jesus.* New York: Harper & Row, 1950. 223 pp. London: SCM Press.

————. *Modern Poetry and the Christian Tradition.* New York: Charles Scribner's Sons, 1952. 287 pp.

Williams, Colin W. *Where in the World?* New York: National Council of Churches, 1963. 116 pp.

Williams, George H., and Mergal, Angel M., eds. *Spiritual and Anabaptist Writers.* Philadelphia: The Westminster Press, 1957. 421 pp.

Wilmore, Gayraud S. *The Secular Relevance of the Church.* Philadelphia: The Westminster Press, 1962. 89 pp.

Winter, Gibson. *The New Creation as Metropolis.* New York: The Macmillan Company, 1963. 152 pp.

JOURNALS, PAMPHLETS, PERIODICALS

The Christian Scholar, XLIII/1, March 1960; Ronald Gregor Smith, "A Theological Perspective of the Secular," p. 11.

Daedalus, Journal of the American Academy of Arts and Sciences, Winter 1961; entire issue on "The Future Metropolis."

Student World, No. 1 (Geneva: World Student Christian Federation), 1963; entire issue on "Secularization."

Trutz Rendtorff, "Säkularisierung als Theologisches Problem," *Neue Zeitschrift für Systematische Theologie* (1962), pp. 318–339.

INDEX

Ad hoc congregations, 140
Adams, Henry, 171
Adorno, Karl, 131
Adorno, Theodor W., 181
Africa
 youth and Christianity in,
 91–92
Alinsky, Saul D., 123
Ancient City, The (Fustel de
 Coulanges), 8
Anderson, Bernhard, 234
Andorra (Frisch), 132
Anonymity, 33–34
 Buber and, 38
 choice, exercise of, 35
 as deliverance from Law,
 40–43
 freedom and, 35
 I-Thou relationships and,
 38–40, 42–43
 "immunization" against
 personal encounters and,
 36
 intellectual ancestry of, 34–35
 organic vs. functional
 relationships and, 37–38
 positive aspects of, 34–35
 private and public
 relationships, 36–40
 selectivity of relationships,
 36
 Tönnies on, 37
 urban neighborliness and, 42
Anticlericalism, 2
Antigone (Sophocles), 8–9, 11
Aristotle, 65, 191, 218, 223
Ark of the Covenant, 48–49

"Art of Theological Meaning"
 (Wilder), 228
Augustine (saint), 23, 24, 60

Bailey, D. S., 184
Bakunin, Mikhail, 61
Banfield, Edward C., 83, 115, 116,
 117
Barth, Karl, 71–72, 125, 177, 197
 two periods of theology of,
 71–72
Bayle, Pierre, 25
Bazelon, David, 151, 156, 157
Beauvoir, Simone de, 169–70
Beckett, Samuel, 225
Bensman, Joseph, 4
Bentham, Jeremy, 191
Biblical Doctrine of Work, The
 (Richardson), 164
Biblical source of secularization,
 15–32
 deconsecration of values and,
 26–31
 desacralization of politics and,
 22–26
 disenchantment of nature and,
 19–21
 Hebrew faith and, 16–17
 three pivotal elements, 15
Bildungsschicht, 220
Billy Budd (Melville), 44
Black Muslims, 2
Blue Hill Community Church,
 139
Bonhoeffer, Dietrich, xi, 2, 3, 24,
 53, 71, 197, 211, 226, 228
 on Second Commandment, 211